Dispatches
Michael Herr

Vintage Books
A Division of Penguin Random House LLC
New York

For my mother and father

First Vintage Books Edition, August 1991

Copyright © 1968, 1969, 1970, 1977, by Michael Herr

All rights reserved. Published in the United States of by Vintage Books, a division of Penguin Random House LLC, New York, and simultaneously in Canada by Random House of Canada, a division of Penguin Random House Canada Limited, Toronto. Originally published in hardcover by Alfred A. Knopf, Inc., New York, in 1977.

Portions of this book were originally published in *New American Review #7, Esquire* and *Rolling Stone.*

Library of Congress Cataloging-in-Publication Data
Herr, Michael.
    Dispatches / Michael Herr.
      p. cm.
    Reprint. Originally published: New York : Knopf, 1977.
    1. Vietnamese Conflict, 1961-1975–Personal narratives, American.
  2. Herr, Michael.   I. Title.
  [DS559.5.H47 1991]
  959.704'38–dc20   90-50771
                     CIP

Vintage Books Trade Paperback ISBN: 978-0-679-73525-0
eBook ISBN: 978-0-307-81416-6

Manufactured in the United States of America
45 44

Michael Herr's
Dispatches

"The best book to have been written about the Vietnam War."
—The New York Times Book Review

"Having read *Dispatches*, it is difficult to convey the impact of total experience as all the facades of patriotism, heroism and the whole colossal fraud of American intervention fall away to the bare bones of fear, war and death."
—William S. Burroughs

"Tough, profane, relentless . . . elegant."
—Newsweek

"A classic!"
—David Halberstam

"Herr . . . hurls one into his experience, insists an uninitiated reader be comforted with no politics, no certain morality, no clear outline of history."
—The New York Review of Books

"Stunning."
—The New York Times

"Some stories must be told—not because they will delight and instruct but because they happened."
—Time

"Splendid . . . He brings alive the terror of combat in a way that rivals *All Quiet on the Western Front*."
—Tom Wolfe

Michael Herr's
Dispatches

Michael Herr is the author of *Dispatches, The Big Room,* and *Walter Winchell,* and coauthor of the screenplays for *Apocalypse Now* and *Full Metal Jacket.* He died in 2016.

Contents

Dispatches

Breathing In

There was a map of Vietnam on the wall of my apartment in Saigon and some nights, coming back late to the city, I'd lie out on my bed and look at it, too tired to do anything more than just get my boots off. That map was a marvel, especially now that it wasn't real anymore. For one thing, it was very old. It had been left there years before by another tenant, probably a Frenchman, since the map had been made in Paris. The paper had buckled in its frame after years in the wet Saigon heat, laying a kind of veil over the countries it depicted. Vietnam was divided into its older territories of Tonkin, Annam and Cochin China, and to the west past Laos and Cambodge sat Siam, a kingdom. That's old, I'd tell visitors, that's a really old map.

If dead ground could come back and haunt you the way dead people do, they'd have been able to mark my map CURRENT and burn the ones they'd been using since '64, but count on it, nothing like that was going to happen. It was late '67 now, even the most detailed maps didn't reveal much anymore; reading them was like trying to read the faces of the Vietnamese, and that was like trying to read the wind. We knew that the uses of most information were flexible, different pieces of ground told different stories to different people. We also knew that for years now there had been no country here but the war.

The Mission was always telling us about VC units being engaged and wiped out and then reappearing a month later in full strength, there was nothing very spooky about that, but when we went up against his terrain we usually took it defini-

tively, and even if we didn't keep it you could always see that we'd at least been there. At the end of my first week in-country I met an information officer in the headquarters of the 25th Division at Cu Chi who showed me on his map and then from his chopper what they'd done to the Ho Bo Woods, the vanished Ho Bo Woods, taken off by giant Rome plows and chemicals and long, slow fire, wasting hundreds of acres of cultivated plantation and wild forest alike, "denying the enemy valuable resources and cover."

It had been part of his job for nearly a year now to tell people about that operation; correspondents, touring con-gressmen, movie stars, corporation presidents, staff officers from half the armies in the world, and he still couldn't get over it. It seemed to be keeping him young, his enthusiasm made you feel that even the letters he wrote home to his wife were full of it, it really showed what you could do if you had the know-how and the hardware. And if in the months fol-lowing that operation incidences of enemy activity in the larger area of War Zone C had increased "significantly," and American losses had doubled and then doubled again, none of it was happening in any damn Ho Bo Woods, you'd better believe it. . . .

I

Going out at night the medics gave you pills, Dexedrine breath like dead snakes kept too long in a jar. I never saw the need for them myself, a little contact or anything that even sounded like contact would give me more speed than I could bear. Whenever I heard something outside of our clenched little circle I'd practically flip, hoping to God that I wasn't the only one who'd noticed it. A couple of rounds fired off in the dark a kilometer away and the Elephant would be there kneeling on my chest, sending me down into my boots for a breath. Once I thought I saw a light moving in the jungle and I caught myself just under a whisper saying, "I'm not ready for this, I'm not ready for this." That's when I decided to drop it and do something else with my nights. And I wasn't going out like the night ambushers did, or the Lurps, long-range recon patrollers who did it night after night for weeks and months, creeping up on VC base camps or around moving columns of North Vietnamese. I was living too close to my bones as it was, all I had to do was accept it. Anyway, I'd save the pills for later, for Saigon and the awful depressions I always had there.

I knew one 4th Division Lurp who took his pills by the fistful, downs from the left pocket of his tiger suit and ups from the right, one to cut the trail for him and the other to send him down it. He told me that they cooled things out just right for him, that he could see that old jungle at night like he was looking at it through a starlight scope. "They sure give you the range," he said.

This was his third tour. In 1965 he'd been the only survivor in a platoon of the Cav wiped out going into the Ia Drang Valley. In '66 he'd come back with the Special Forces and one morning after an ambush he'd hidden under the bodies of his team while the VC walked all around them with knives, making sure. They stripped the bodies of their gear, the berets too, and finally went away, laughing. After that, there was nothing left for him in the war except the Lurps.

"I just can't hack it back in the World," he said. He told me that after he'd come back home the last time he would sit in his room all day, and sometimes he'd stick a hunting rifle out the window, leading people and cars as they passed his house until the only feeling he was aware of was all up in the tip of that one finger. "It used to put my folks real uptight," he said. But he put people uptight here too, even here.

"No man, I'm sorry, he's just too crazy for me," one of the men in his team said. "All's you got to do is look in his eyes, that's the whole fucking story right there."

"Yeah, but you better do it quick," someone else said. "I mean, you don't want to let him catch you at it."

But he always seemed to be watching for it, I think he slept with his eyes open, and I was afraid of him anyway. All I ever managed was one quick look in, and that was like looking at the floor of an ocean. He wore a gold earring and a headband torn from a piece of camouflage parachute material, and since nobody was about to tell him to get his hair cut it fell below his shoulders, covering a thick purple scar. Even at division he never went anywhere without at least a .45 and a knife, and he thought I was a freak because I wouldn't carry a weapon.

"Didn't you ever meet a reporter before?" I asked him.

"Tits on a bull," he said. "Nothing personal."

But what a story he told me, as one-pointed and resonant as any war story I ever heard, it took me a year to understand it:

"Patrol went up the mountain. One man came back. He died before he could tell us what happened."

I waited for the rest, but it seemed not to be that kind of story; when I asked him what had happened he just looked like he felt sorry for me, fucked if he'd waste time telling stories to anyone dumb as I was.

His face was all painted up for night walking now like a bad hallucination, not like the painted faces I'd seen in San Francisco only a few weeks before, the other extreme of the same theater. In the coming hours he'd stand as faceless and quiet in the jungle as a fallen tree, and God help his opposite numbers unless they had at least half a squad along, he was a good killer, one of our best. The rest of his team were gathered outside the tent, set a little apart from the other division units, with its own Lurp-designated latrine and its own exclusive freeze-dry rations, three-star war food, the same chop they sold at Abercrombie & Fitch. The regular division troops would almost shy off the path when they passed the area on their way to and from the mess tent. No matter how toughened up they became in the war, they still looked innocent compared to the Lurps. When the team had grouped they walked in a file down the hill to the lz across the strip to the perimeter and into the treeline.

I never spoke to him again, but I saw him. When they came back in the next morning he had a prisoner with him, blindfolded and with his elbows bound sharply behind him. The Lurp area would definitely be off limits during the interrogation, and anyway, I was already down at the strip waiting for a helicopter to come and take me out of there.

"Hey what're you guys, with the USO? Aw, we thought you was with the USO 'cause your hair's so long." Page took the kid's picture, I got the words down and Flynn laughed and told him we were the Rolling Stones. The three of us traveled around together for about a month that summer. At one lz the brigade chopper came in with a real foxtail hanging off the aerial, when the commander walked by us he almost took an infarction.

"Don't you men salute officers?"

"We're not men," Page said. "We're correspondents."

When the commander heard that, he wanted to throw a spontaneous operation for us, crank up his whole brigade and get some people killed. We had to get out on the next chopper to keep him from going ahead with it, amazing what some of them would do for a little ink. Page liked to augment his field gear with freak paraphernalia, scarves and beads, plus he was English, guys would stare at him like he'd just come down off a wall on Mars. Sean Flynn could look more incredibly beautiful than even his father, Errol, had thirty years before as Captain Blood, but sometimes he looked more like Artaud coming out of some heavy heart-of-darkness trip, overloaded on the information, the input! The input! He'd give off a bad sweat and sit for hours, combing his mustache through with the saw blade of his Swiss Army knife. We packed grass and tape: Have You Seen Your Mother Baby Standing in the Shadows, Best of the Animals, Strange Days, Purple Haze, Archie Bell and the Drells, "C'mon now everybody, do the Tighten Up. . . ." Once in a while we'd catch a chopper straight into one of the lower hells, but it was a quiet time in the war, mostly it was lz's and camps, grunts hanging around, faces, stories.

"Best way's to just keep moving," one of them told us. "Just keep moving, stay in motion, you know what I'm saying?"

We knew. He was a moving-target-survivor subscriber, a true child of the war, because except for the rare times when you were pinned or stranded the system was geared to keep you mobile, if that was what you thought you wanted. As a technique for staying alive it seemed to make as much sense as anything, given naturally that you were there to begin with and wanted to see it close; it started out sound and straight but it formed a cone as it progressed, because the more you moved the more you saw, the more you saw the more besides death and mutilation you risked, and the more you risked of that the more you would have to let go of one day as a "survivor." Some of us moved around the war like crazy people until we couldn't see which way the run was even taking us anymore, only the war all over its surface with occasional, unexpected penetration. As long as we could have choppers like taxis it took real exhaustion or depression near shock or a dozen pipes of opium to keep us even apparently quiet, we'd still be running around inside our skins like something was after us, ha ha, La Vida Loca.

In the months after I got back the hundreds of helicopters I'd flown in began to draw together until they'd formed a collective meta-chopper, and in my mind it was the sexiest thing going; saver-destroyer, provider-waster, right hand–left hand, nimble, fluent, canny and human; hot steel, grease, jungle-saturated canvas webbing, sweat cooling and warming up again, cassette rock and roll in one ear and door-gun fire in the other, fuel, heat, vitality and death, death itself, hardly an intruder. Men on the crews would say that once you'd carried a dead person he would always be there, riding with you. Like all combat people they were incredibly superstitious and invariably self-dramatic, but it was (I knew) unbearably true that close exposure to the dead sensitized you to the force of their presence and made for long reverberations; long. Some people were so delicate that one look was enough to wipe them away, but even bone-dumb grunts seemed to feel that something weird and extra was happening to them.

Helicopters and people jumping out of helicopters, people so in love they'd run to get on even when there wasn't any pressure. Choppers rising straight out of small cleared jungle spaces, wobbling down onto city rooftops, cartons of rations and ammunition thrown off, dead and wounded loaded on. Sometimes they were so plentiful and loose that you could touch down at five or six places in a day, look around, hear the talk, catch the next one out. There were installations as big as cities with 30,000 citizens, once we dropped in to feed supply to one man. God knows what kind of Lord Jim phoenix numbers he was doing in there, all he said to me was, "You didn't see a thing, right Chief? You weren't even here." There were posh fat air-conditioned camps like comfortable middle-class scenes with the violence tacit, "far away";

camps named for commanders' wives, LZ Thelma, LZ Betty Lou; number-named hilltops in trouble where I didn't want to stay; trail, paddy, swamp, deep hairy bush, scrub, swale, village, even city, where the ground couldn't drink up what the action spilled, it made you careful where you walked.

Sometimes the chopper you were riding in would top a hill and all the ground in front of you as far as the next hill would be charred and pitted and still smoking, and something between your chest and your stomach would turn over. Frail gray smoke where they'd burned off the rice fields around a free-strike zone, brilliant white smoke from phosphorus ("Willy Peter/Make you a buh liever"), deep black smoke from 'palm, they said that if you stood at the base of a column of napalm smoke it would suck the air right out of your lungs. Once we fanned over a little ville that had just been airstruck and the words of a song by Wingy Manone that I'd heard when I was a few years old snapped into my head, "Stop the War, These Cats Is Killing Themselves." Then we dropped, hovered, settled down into purple lz smoke, dozens of children broke from their hootches to run in toward the focus of our landing, the pilot laughing and saying, "Vietnam, man. Bomb 'em and feed 'em, bomb 'em and feed 'em."

Flying over jungle was almost pure pleasure, doing it on foot was nearly all pain. I never belonged in there. Maybe it really was what its people had always called it, Beyond; at the very least it was serious, I gave up things to it I probably never got back. ("Aw, jungle's okay. If you know her you can live in her real good, if you don't she'll take you down in an hour. Under.") Once in some thick jungle corner with some grunts standing around, a correspondent said, "Gee, you must really see some beautiful sunsets in here," and they almost pissed themselves laughing. But you could fly up and into hot tropic sunsets that would change the way you thought about light forever. You could also fly out of places that were so grim they turned to black and white in your head five minutes after you'd gone.

That could be the coldest one in the world, standing at the edge of a clearing watching the chopper you'd just come in on taking off again, leaving you there to think about what it was going to be for you now: if this was a bad place, the wrong place, maybe even the last place, and whether you'd made a terrible mistake this time.

There was a camp at Soc Trang where a man at the lz said, "If you come looking for a story this is your lucky day, we got Condition Red here," and before the sound of the chopper had faded out, I knew I had it too.

"That's affirmative," the camp commander said, "we are *definitely* expecting rain. Glad to see you." He was a young captain, he was laughing and taping a bunch of sixteen clips together bottom to bottom for faster reloading, "grease." Everyone there was busy at it, cracking crates, squirreling away grenades, checking mortar pieces, piling rounds, clicking banana clips into automatic weapons that I'd never even seen before. They were wired into their listening posts out around the camp, into each other, into themselves, and when it got dark it got worse. The moon came up nasty and full, a fat moist piece of decadent fruit. It was soft and saffron-misted when you looked up at it, but its light over the sandbags and into the jungle was harsh and bright. We were all rubbing Army-issue nightfighter cosmetic under our eyes to cut the glare and the terrible things it made you see. (Around midnight, just for something to do, I crossed to the other perimeter and looked at the road running engineer-straight toward Route 4 like a yellow frozen ribbon out of sight and I saw it move, the whole road.) There were a few sharp arguments about who the light really favored, attackers or defenders, men were sitting around with Cinemascope eyes and jaws stuck out like they could shoot bullets, moving and antsing and shifting around inside their fatigues. "No sense us getting too relaxed, Charlie don't relax, just when you get good and comfortable is when he comes over and takes a giant shit on you." That was the level until morning, I smoked a pack an hour all night long, and nothing happened. Ten minutes after daybreak I was down at the lz asking about choppers.

A few days later Sean Flynn and I went up to a big firebase in the American TAOR that took it all the way over to another extreme, National Guard weekend. The colonel in command was so drunk that day that he could barely get his words out, and when he did, it was to say things like, "We aim to make good and goddammit sure that if *those guys* try *anything cute* they won't catch us with our pants down." The main mission there was to fire H&I, but one man told us that their record was the worst in the whole Corps, probably the whole country, they'd harassed and interdicted a lot of sleeping civilians and Korean Marines, even a couple of American patrols, but hardly any Viet Cong. (The colonel kept calling it "artillerary." The first time he said it Flynn and I looked away from each other, the second time we blew beer through our noses, but the colonel fell in laughing right away and more than covered us.) No sandbags, exposed shells, dirty pieces, guys going around giving us that look, "We're cool, how come you're not?" At the strip Sean was talking to the operator about it and the man got angry. "Oh *yeah?* Well fuck *you*, how tight do you think you want it? There ain't been any veecees around here in three months."

"So far so good," Sean said. "Hear anything on that chopper yet?"

But sometimes everything stopped, nothing flew, you

couldn't even find out why. I got stuck for a chopper once in some lost patrol outpost in the Delta where the sergeant chain-ate candy bars and played country-and-western tapes twenty hours a day until I heard it in my sleep, some sleep, *Up on Wolverton Mountain* and *Lonesome as the bats and the bears in Miller's Cave* and *I fell into a burning ring of fire,* surrounded by strungout rednecks who weren't getting much sleep either because they couldn't trust one of their 400 mercenary troopers or their own hand-picked perimeter guards or anybody else except maybe Baby Ruth and Johnny Cash, they'd been waiting for it so long now they were afraid they wouldn't know it when they finally got it, *and it burns burns burns.* . . . Finally on the fourth day a helicopter came in to deliver meat and movies to the camp and I went out on it, so happy to get back to Saigon that I didn't crash for two days.

Airmobility, dig it, you weren't going anywhere. It made you feel safe, it made you feel Omni, but it was only a stunt, technology. Mobility was just mobility, it saved lives or took them all the time (saved mine I don't know how many times, maybe dozens, maybe none), what you really needed was a flexibility far greater than anything the technology could provide, some generous, spontaneous gift for accepting surprises, and I didn't have it. I got to hate surprises, control freak at the crossroads, if you were one of those people who always thought they had to know what was coming next, the war could cream you. It was the same with your ongoing attempts at getting used to the jungle or the blow-you-out climate or the saturating strangeness of the place which didn't lessen with exposure so often as it fattened and darkened in accumulating alienation. It was great if you could adapt, you had to try, but it wasn't the same as making a discipline, going into your own reserves and developing a real war metabolism, slow yourself down when your heart tried to punch its way through your chest, get swift when everything went to stop and all you could feel of your whole life was the entropy whipping through it. Unlovable terms.

The ground was always in play, always being swept. Under the ground was his, above it was ours. We had the air, we could get up in it but not disappear in *to* it, we could run but we couldn't hide, and he could do each so well that sometimes it looked like he was doing them both at once, while our finder just went limp. All the same, one place or another it was always going on, rock around the clock, we had the days and he had the nights. You could be in the most protected space in Vietnam and still know that your safety was provisional, that early death, blindness, loss of legs, arms or balls, major and lasting disfigurement—the whole rotten deal—could come in on the freakyfluky as easily as in the so-called expected ways, you heard so many of those stories it was a wonder anyone was left alive to die in firefights and mortar-rocket attacks. After a few weeks, when the nickel had jarred loose and dropped and I saw that everyone around me was carrying a gun, I also saw that any one of them could go off at any time, putting you where it wouldn't matter whether it had been an accident or not. The roads were mined, the trails booby-trapped, satchel charges and grenades blew up jeeps and movie theaters, the VC got work inside all the camps as shoeshine boys and laundresses and honey-dippers, they'd starch your fatigues and burn your shit and then go home and mortar your area. Saigon and Cholon and Danang held such hostile vibes that you felt you were being dry-sniped every time someone looked at you, and choppers fell out of the sky like fat poisoned birds a hundred times a day. After a while I couldn't get on one without thinking that I must be out of my fucking mind.

Fear and motion, fear and standstill, no preferred cut there, no way even to be clear about which was really worse, the wait or the delivery. Combat spared far more men than it wasted, but everyone suffered the time between contact, especially when they were going out every day looking for it; bad going on foot, terrible in trucks and APC's, awful in helicopters, the worst, traveling so fast toward something so frightening. I can remember times when I went half dead with my fear of the motion, the speed and direction already fixed and pointed one way. It was painful enough just flying "safe" hops between firebases and lz's; if you were ever on a helicopter that had been hit by ground fire your deep, perpetual chopper anxiety was guaranteed. At least actual contact when it was happening would draw long raggedy strands of energy out of you, it was juicy, fast and refining, and traveling toward it was hollow, dry, cold and steady, it never let you alone. All you could do was look around at the other people on board and see if they were as scared and numbed out as you were. If it looked like they weren't you thought they were insane, if it looked like they were it made you feel a lot worse.

I went through that thing a number of times and only got a fast return on my fear once, a too classic hot landing with the heat coming from the trees about 300 yards away, sweeping machine-gun fire that sent men head down into swampy water, running on their hands and knees toward the grass where it wasn't blown flat by the rotor blades, not much to be running for but better than nothing. The helicopter pulled up before we'd all gotten out, leaving the last few men to jump twenty feet down between the guns across the paddy and the gun on the chopper door. When we'd all reached the cover of the wall and the captain had made a check, we were amazed to see that no one had even been hurt, except for one man who'd sprained both his ankles jumping. Afterward, I remembered that I'd been down in the muck worrying about leeches. I guess you could say that I was refusing to accept the situation.

"Boy, you sure get offered some shitty choices," a Marine once said to me, and I couldn't help but feel that what he really meant was that you didn't get offered any at all. Specifically, he was just talking about a couple of C-ration cans, "dinner," but considering his young life you couldn't blame him for thinking that if he knew one thing for sure, it was that there was no one anywhere who cared less about what *he* wanted. There wasn't anybody he wanted to thank for his food, but he was grateful that he was still alive to eat it, that the motherfucker hadn't scarfed him up first. He hadn't been anything but tired and scared for six months and he'd lost a lot, mostly people, and seen far too much, but he was breathing in and breathing out, some kind of choice all by itself.

He had one of those faces, I saw that face at least a thousand times at a hundred bases and camps, all the youth sucked out of the eyes, the color drawn from the skin, cold white lips, you knew he wouldn't wait for any of it to come back. Life had made him old, he'd live it out old. All those faces, sometimes it was like looking into faces at a rock concert, locked in, the event had them; or like students who were very heavily advanced, serious beyond what you'd call their years if you didn't know for yourself what the minutes and hours of those years were made up of. Not just like all the ones you saw who looked like they couldn't drag their asses through another day of it. (How do you feel when a nineteen-year-old kid tells you from the bottom of his heart that he's gotten too old for this kind of shit?) Not like the faces of the dead or wounded either, they could look more released than overtaken. These were the faces of boys whose whole lives seemed to have backed up on them, they'd be a few feet away but they'd be looking back at you over a distance you knew you'd never really cross. We'd talk, sometimes fly together, guys going out on R&R, guys escorting bodies, guys who'd flipped over into extremes of peace or violence. Once I flew with a kid who was going home, he looked back down once at the ground where he'd spent the year and spilled his whole load of tears. Sometimes you even flew with the dead.

Once I jumped on a chopper that was full of them. The kid in the op shack had said that there would be a body on board, but he'd been given some wrong information. "How bad do you want to get to Danang?" he'd asked me, and I'd said, "Bad."

When I saw what was happening I didn't want to get on, but they'd made a divert and a special landing for me, I had to go with the chopper I'd drawn, I was afraid of looking squeamish. (I remember, too, thinking that a chopper full of dead men was far less likely to get shot down than one full of living.) They weren't even in bags. They'd been on a truck near one of the firebases in the DMZ that was firing support for Khe Sanh, and the truck had hit a Command-detonated mine, then they'd been rocketed. The Marines were always running out of things, even food, ammo and medicine, it wasn't so strange that they'd run out of bags too. The men had been wrapped around in ponchos, some of them carelessly fastened with plastic straps, and loaded on board. There was a small space cleared for me between one of them and the door gunner, who looked pale and so tremendously furious that I thought he was angry with me and I couldn't look at him for a while. When we went up the wind blew through the ship and made the ponchos shake and tremble until the one next to me blew back in a fast brutal flap, uncovering the face. They hadn't even closed his eyes for him.

The gunner started hollering as loud as he could, "Fix it! Fix it!," maybe he thought the eyes were looking at him, but there wasn't anything I could do. My hand went there a couple of times and I couldn't, and then I did. I pulled the poncho tight, lifted his head carefully and tucked the poncho under it, and then I couldn't believe that I'd done it. All during the ride the gunner kept trying to smile, and when we landed at Dong Ha he thanked me and ran off to get a detail. The pilots jumped down and walked away without looking back once, like they'd never seen that chopper before in their lives. I flew the rest of the way to Danang in a general's plane.

II

You know how it is, you want to look and you don't want to look. I can remember the strange feelings I had when I was a kid looking at war photographs in *Life,* the ones that showed dead people or a lot of dead people lying close together in a field or a street, often touching, seeming to hold each other. Even when the picture was sharp and cleanly defined, something wasn't clear at all, something repressed that monitored the images and withheld their essential information. It may have legitimized my fascination, letting me look for as long as I wanted; I didn't have a language for it then, but I remember now the shame I felt, like looking at first porn, all the porn in the world. I could have looked until my lamps went out and I still wouldn't have accepted the connection between a detached leg and the rest of a body, or the poses and positions that always happened (one day I'd hear it called "response-to-impact"), bodies wrenched too fast and violently into unbelievable contortion. Or the total impersonality of group death, making them lie anywhere and any way it left them, hanging over barbed wire or thrown promiscuously on top of other dead, or up into the trees like terminal acrobats, *Look what I can do.*

Supposedly, you weren't going to have that kind of obscuration when you finally started seeing them on real ground in front of you, but you tended to manufacture it anyway because of how often and how badly you needed protection from what you were seeing, had actually come 30,000 miles to see. Once I looked at them strung from the perimeter to the treeline, most of them clumped together nearest the wire, then in smaller numbers but tighter groups midway, fanning out into lots of scattered points nearer the treeline, with one all by himself half into the bush and half out. "Close but no cigar," the captain said, and then a few of his men went out there and kicked them all in the head, thirty-seven of them. Then I heard an M-16 on full automatic starting to go through clips, a second to fire, three to plug in a fresh clip, and I saw a man out there, doing it. Every round was like a tiny concentration of high-velocity wind, making the bodies wince and shiver. When he finished he walked by us on the way back to his hootch, and I knew I hadn't seen anything until I saw his face. It was flushed and mottled and twisted like he had his face skin on inside out, a patch of green that was too dark, a streak of red running into bruise purple, a lot of sick gray white in between, he looked like he'd had a heart attack out there. His eyes were rolled up half into his head, his mouth was sprung open and his tongue was out, but he was smiling. Really a dude who'd shot his wad. The captain wasn't too pleased about my having seen that.

There wasn't a day when someone didn't ask me what I was doing there. Sometimes an especially smart grunt or another correspondent would even ask me what I was *really* doing there, as though I could say anything honest about it except "Blah blah blah cover the war" or "Blah blah blah write a book." Maybe we accepted each other's stories about why we were there at face value: the grunts who "had" to be there, the spooks and civilians whose corporate faith had led them there, the correspondents whose curiosity or ambition drew them over. But somewhere all the mythic tracks intersected, from the lowest John Wayne wetdream to the most aggravated soldier-poet fantasy, and where they did I believe that everyone knew everything about everyone else, every one of us there a true volunteer. Not that you didn't hear some overripe bullshit about it: Hearts and Minds, Peoples of the Republic, tumbling dominoes, maintaining the equilibrium of the Dingdong by containing the ever encroaching Doodah; you could also hear the other, some young soldier speaking in all bloody innocence, saying, "All that's just a *load,* man. We're here to kill gooks. Period." Which wasn't at all true of me. I was there to watch.

Talk about impersonating an identity, about locking into a role, about irony: I went to cover the war and the war covered me; an old story, unless of course you've never heard it. I went there behind the crude but serious belief that you had to be able to look at anything, serious because I acted on it and went, crude because I didn't know, it took the war to teach it, that you were as responsible for everything you saw as you were for everything you did. The problem was that you didn't always know what you were seeing until later, maybe years later, that a lot of it never made it in at all, it just stayed stored there in your eyes. Time and information, rock and roll, life itself, the information isn't frozen, you are.

Sometimes I didn't know if an action took a second or an hour or if I dreamed it or what. In war more than in other life you don't really know what you're doing most of the time, you're just behaving, and afterward you can make up any kind of bullshit you want to about it, say you felt good or bad, loved it or hated it, did this or that, the right thing or the wrong thing; still, what happened happened.

Coming back, telling stories, I'd say, "Oh man I was scared," and, "Oh God I thought it was all over," a long time before I knew how scared I was really supposed to be, or how clear and closed and beyond my control "all over" could become. I wasn't dumb but I sure was raw, certain connections are hard to make when you come from a place where they go around with war in their heads all the time.

"If you get hit," a medic told me, "we can chopper you back to base-camp hospital in like twenty minutes."

"If you get hit real bad," a corpsman said, "they'll get your case to Japan in twelve hours."

"If you get killed," a spec 4 from Graves promised, "we'll have you home in a week."

TIME IS ON MY SIDE, already written there across the first helmet I ever wore there. And underneath it, in smaller lettering that read more like a whispered prayer than an assertion, *No lie, GI.* The rear-hatch gunner on a Chinook threw it to me that first morning at the Kontum airstrip, a few hours after the Dak To fighting had ended, screaming at me through the rotor wind, "You *keep* that, we got *plenty, good luck!*" and then flying off. I was so glad to have the equipment that I didn't stop to think where it had to have come from. The sweatband inside was seasoned up black and greasy, it was more alive now than the man who'd worn it, when I got rid of it ten minutes later I didn't just leave it on the ground, I snuck away from it furtive and ashamed, afraid that someone would see it and call after me, "Hey numbnuts, you forgot something. . . ."

That morning when I tried to go out they sent me down the line from a colonel to a major to a captain to a sergeant, who took one look, called me Freshmeat, and told me to go find some other outfit to get myself killed with. I didn't know what was going on, I was so nervous I started to laugh. I told him that nothing was going to happen to me and he gave my shoulder a tender, menacing pat and said, "This ain't the fucking movies over here, you know." I laughed again and said that I knew, but he knew that I didn't.

Day one, if anything could have penetrated that first innocence I might have taken the next plane out. Out absolutely. It was like a walk through a colony of stroke victims, a thousand men on a cold rainy airfield after too much of something I'd never really know, "a way you'll never be," dirt and blood and torn fatigues, eyes that poured out a steady charge of wasted horror. I'd just missed the biggest battle of the war so far, I was telling myself that I was sorry, but it was right there all around me and I didn't even know it. I couldn't look at anyone for more than a second, I didn't want to be caught listening, some war correspondent, I didn't know what to say or do, I didn't like it already. When the rain stopped and the ponchos came off there was a smell that I thought was going to make me sick: rot, sump, tannery, open grave, dump-fire—awful, you'd walk into pockets of Old Spice that made it even worse. I wanted badly to find some place to sit alone and smoke a cigarette, to find a face that would cover my face the way my poncho covered my new fatigues. I'd worn them once before, yesterday morning in Saigon, bringing them out of the black market and back to the hotel, dressing up in front of the mirror, making faces and moves I'd never make again. And loving it. Now, nearby on the ground, there was a man sleeping with a poncho over his head and a radio in his arms, I heard Sam the Sham singing, "Lil' Red Riding Hood, I don't think little big girls should, Go walking in these spooky old woods alone. . . ."

I turned to walk some other way and there was a man

standing in front of me. He didn't exactly block me, but he didn't move either. He tottered a little and blinked, he looked at me and through me, no one had ever looked at me like that before. I felt a cold fat drop of sweat start down the middle of my back like a spider, it seemed to take an hour to finish its run. The man lit a cigarette and then sort of slobbered it out, I couldn't imagine what I was seeing. He tried again with a fresh cigarette. I gave him the light for that one, there was a flicker of focus, acknowledgment, but after a few puffs it went out too, and he let it drop to the ground. "I couldn't spit for a week up there," he said, "and now I can't fucking stop."

When the 173rd held services for their dead from Dak To the boots of the dead men were arranged in formation on the ground. It was an old paratrooper tradition, but knowing that didn't reduce it or make it any less spooky, a company's worth of jump boots standing empty in the dust taking benediction, while the real substance of the ceremony was being bagged and tagged and shipped back home through what they called the KIA Travel Bureau. A lot of the people there that day accepted the boots as solemn symbols and went into deep prayer. Others stood around watching with grudging respect, others photographed it and some just thought it was a lot of bitter bullshit. All they saw out there was one more set of spare parts, and they wouldn't have looked around for holy ghosts if some of those boots filled up again and walked.

Dak To itself had only been the command point for a combat without focus that tore a thirty-mile arc over the hills running northeast to southwest of the small base and airfield there from early November through Thanksgiving 1967, fighting that grew in size and fame while it grew more vicious and out of control. In October the small Dak To Special

Forces compound had taken some mortar and rocket fire, patrols went out, patrols collided, companies splintered the action and spread it across the hills in a sequence of small, isolated firefights that afterward were described as strategy; battalions were sucked into it, then divisions, then reinforced divisions. Anyway, we knew for sure that we had a reinforced division in it, the 4th plus, and we said that they had one in it too, although a lot of people believed that a couple of light flexible regiments could have done what the NVA did up and down those hills for three weeks, leaving us to claim that we'd driven him up 1338, up 943, up 875 and 876, while the opposing claims remained mostly unspoken and probably unnecessary. And then instead of really ending, the battle vanished. The North Vietnamese collected up their gear and most of their dead and "disappeared" during the night, leaving a few bodies behind for our troops to kick and count.

"Just like goin' in against the Japs," one kid called it; the heaviest fighting in Vietnam since the Ia Drang Valley two years before, and one of the only times after Ia Drang when ground fire was so intense that the medevacs couldn't land through it. Wounded backed up for hours and sometimes days, and a lot of men died who might have been saved. Resupply couldn't make it in either, and the early worry about running out of ammunition grew into a panic and beyond, it became real. At the worst, a battalion of Airborne assaulting 875 got caught in an ambush sprung from behind, where no NVA had been reported, and its three companies were pinned and cut off in the raking fire of that trap for two days. Afterward, when a correspondent asked one of the survivors what had happened he was told, "What the fuck do you think happened? We got shot to pieces." The correspondent started to write that down and the paratrooper said, "Make that 'little

pieces.' *We were still shaking the trees for dog tags when we pulled back out of there."*

Even after the North had gone away, logistics and transport remained a problem. A big battle had to be dismantled piece by piece and man by man. It was raining hard every day now, the small strip at Dak To became overloaded and unworkable, and a lot of troops were shuttled down to the larger strip at Kontum. Some even ended up as far out of their way as Pleiku, fifty miles to the south, for sorting and transport back to their units around II Corps. The living, the wounded and the dead flew together in crowded Chinooks, and it was nothing for guys to walk on top of the half-covered corpses packed in the aisles to get to a seat, or to make jokes among themselves about how funny they all looked, the dumb dead fuckers.

There were men sitting in loose groups all around the strip at Kontum, hundreds of them arranged by unit waiting to be picked up again and flown out. Except for a small sandbagged ops shack and a medical tent, there was no shelter anywhere from the rain. Some of the men had rigged up mostly useless tents with their ponchos, a lot lay out sleeping in the rain with helmets or packs for pillows, most just sat or stood around waiting. Their faces were hidden deep inside the cover of their poncho hoods, white eye movement and silence, walking among them made you feel like you were being watched from hundreds of isolated caves. Every twenty minutes or so a helicopter would land, men would come out or be carried out, others would get on and the chopper would rear up on the strip and fly away, some toward Pleiku and the hospital, others back to the Dak To area and the mop-up operations there. The rotors of the Chinooks cut twin spaces out of the rain, forcing the spray in slanting jets for fifty yards around. Just knowing what was in those choppers gave the spray a bad taste, strong and briny. You didn't want to leave it on your face long enough to dry.

Back from the strip a fat, middle-aged man was screaming at some troops who were pissing on the ground. His poncho was pulled back away from the front of his helmet enough to show captain's bars, but nobody even turned around to look at him. He groped under his poncho and came up with a .45, pointed it into the rain and fired off a shot that made an empty faraway pop, like it had gone off under wet sand. The men finished, buttoned up and walked away laughing, leaving the captain alone shouting orders to police up the filth; thousands of empty and half-eaten ration cans, soggy clots of Stars and Stripes, *an M-16 that someone had just left lying there and, worse, evidence of a carelessness unimaginable to the captain, it stank even in the cold rain, but it would police itself in an hour or two if the rain kept up.*

The ground action had been over for nearly twenty-four hours now, but it was still going on in compulsive replay among the men who'd been there:

"A dead buddy is some tough shit, but bringing your own ass out alive can sure help you to get over it."

"We had this lieutenant, honest to Christ he was about the biggest dipshit fool of all time, all time. We called him Lieutenant Gladly 'cause he was always going like, 'Men . . . Men, I won't never ask you to do nothing I wouldn't do myself gladly,' what an asshole. We was on 1338 and he goes to me, 'Take a little run up to the ridge and report to me,' and I goes like, 'Never happen, Sir.' So he does, he goes up there himself and damned if the fucker didn't get zapped. He said we was gonna have a real serious talk when he come back, too. Sorry 'bout that."

"Kid here [not really here, "here" just a figure of speech] gets blown away ten feet in back of us. I swear to God, I

*thought I was looking at ten different guys when I turned
around. . . ."*

"*You guys are so full of shit it's coming out of your fucking ears!*" *one man was saying.* PRAY FOR WAR *was written
on the side of his helmet, and he was talking mostly to a man
whose helmet name was* SWINGING DICK. "*You were pissing
up everything but your fucking toenails, Scudo, don't you tell
me you weren't scared man, don't you fucking dare, 'cause I
was right fucking there man, and I was scared shit! I was
scared every fucking minute, and I'm no different from any
body else!*"

"*Well big deal, candy ass,*" *Swinging Dick said.* "*You
were scared.*"

"*Damn straight! Damn straight! You're damn fucking
straight I was scared! You're about the dumbest motherfucker I ever met, Scudo, but you're not that dumb. The*
Marines *aren't even that dumb man, I don't care, all that
bullshit they've got in the Marine Corps about how Marines
aren't ever afraid, oh wow, I'll fucking bet. . . . I'll bet the
Marines are* just as scared!"

*He started to get up but his knees gave under him. He
made a quick grasping spasm out of control, like a misfire in
the nervous system, and when he fell back he brought a stack
of M-16's with him. They made a sharp clatter and everyone
jerked and twitched out of the way, looking at each other as
though they couldn't remember for a minute whether they
needed to find cover or not.*

"*Hey baby, hey, watch where you're goin' there,*" *a paratrooper said, but he was laughing, they were all laughing,
and Pray For War was laughing harder than any of them, so
hard that it filled suddenly with air and cracked over into
high giggles. When he lifted his face again it was all tracked
with tears.*

"You gonna stand there, asshole?" he said to Swinging Dick. "Or are you gonna help me up on my fucking feet?" Swinging Dick reached down and grabbed his wrists, locking them and pulling him up slowly until their faces were a couple of inches apart. For a second it looked like they were going to kiss.

"Looking good," Pray For War said. "Mmmm, Scudo, you are really looking good, man. It don't look to me like you were scared at all up there. You only look like about ten thousand miles of bad road."

What they say is totally true, it's funny the things you remember. Like a black paratrooper with the 101st who glided by and said, "I been *scaled* man, I'm *smooth* now," and went on, into my past and I hope his future, leaving me to wonder not what he meant (that was easy), but where he'd been to get his language. On a cold wet day in Hue our jeep turned into the soccer stadium where hundreds of North Vietnamese bodies had been collected, I saw them, but they don't have the force in my memory that a dog and a duck have who died together in a small terrorist explosion in Saigon. Once I ran into a soldier standing by himself in the middle of a small jungle clearing where I'd wandered off to take a leak. We said hello, but he seemed very uptight about my being there. He told me that the guys were all sick of sitting around waiting and that he'd come out to see if he could draw a little fire. What a look we gave each other. I backed out of there fast, I didn't want to bother him while he was working.

This is already a long time ago, I can remember the feelings but I can't still have them. A common prayer for the overattached: You'll let it go sooner or later, why not do it now? Memory print, voices and faces, stories like filament through a piece of time, so attached to the experience that nothing moved and nothing went away.

"First letter I got from my old man was all about how proud he was that I'm here and how we have this *duty* to, you know, *I* don't fucking know, whatever . . . and it really made me feel great. Shit, my father hardly said good morning to me before. Well, I been here eight months now, and when I get home I'm gonna have all I can do to keep from killing that cocksucker. . . ."

Everywhere you went people said, "Well, I hope you get a story," and everywhere you went you did.

"Oh, it ain't so bad. My last tour was better though, not so much mickeymouse, Command gettin' in your way so you can't even do your job. Shit, last three patrols I was on we had fucking *orders* not to return fire going through the villages, that's what a fucked-up war it's gettin' to be anymore. My *last* tour we'd go through and that was it, we'd rip out the hedges and burn the hootches and blow all the wells and kill every chicken, pig and cow in the whole fucking ville. I mean, if we can't shoot these people, what the fuck are we doing here?"

Some journalists talked about no-story operations, but I never went on one. Even when an operation never got off the ground, there was always the strip. Those were the same journalists who would ask us what the fuck we ever found to talk to grunts about, who said they never heard a grunt talk about anything except cars, football and chone. But they all had a story, and in the war they were driven to tell it.

"We was getting killed and the Dinks was panicking, and when the choppers come in to get us out, there wasn't enough room for everybody. The Dinks was screaming and carrying on, grabbing hold of the treads and grabbing hold of our legs till we couldn't get the choppers up. So we just said smack it, let these people get their own fucking choppers, and we started shooting them. And even then they kept on coming, oh man it was wild. I mean they could sure as shit believe that Charlie was shooting them, but they couldn't believe that we was doing it too. . . ."

That was a story from the A Shau Valley years before my time there, an old story with the hair still growing on it. Sometimes the stories were so fresh that the teller was in shock, sometimes they were long and complex, sometimes the whole thing was contained in a few words on a helmet or a wall, and sometimes they were hardly stories at all but sounds and gestures packed with so much urgency that they became more dramatic than a novel, men talking in short violent bursts as though they were afraid they might not get to finish, or saying it almost out of a dream, innocent, offhand and mighty direct, "Oh you know, it was just a firefight, we killed some of them and they killed some of us." A lot of what you heard, you heard all the time, men on tape, deceitful and counterarticulate, and some of it was low enough, guys whose range seemed to stop at "Git some, git some, harharhar!" But once in a while you'd hear something fresh, and a couple of times you'd even hear something high, like the corpsman at Khe Sanh who said, "If it ain't the fucking incoming it's the fucking outgoing. Only difference is who gets the fucking grease, and that ain't no fucking difference at all."

The mix was so amazing; incipient saints and realized homicidals, unconscious lyric poets and mean dumb motherfuckers with their brains all down in their necks; and even though by the time I left I knew where all the stories came from and where they were going, I was never bored, never even unsurprised. Obviously, what they really wanted to tell you was how tired they were and how sick of it, how moved they'd been and how afraid. But maybe that was me, by then my posture was shot: "reporter." ("Must be pretty hard to stay detached," a man on the plane to San Francisco said, and I said, "Impossible.") After a year I felt so plugged in to all the stories and the images and the fear that even the dead started telling me stories, you'd hear them out of a remote but accessible space where there were no ideas, no emotions, no facts, no proper language, only clean information. However many times it happened, whether I'd known them or not, no matter what I'd felt about them or the way they'd died, their story was always there and it was always the same: it went, "Put yourself in my place."

One afternoon I mistook a bloody nose for a headwound, and I didn't have to wonder anymore how I'd behave if I ever got hit. We were walking out on a sweep north of Tay Ninh City, toward the Cambodian border, and a mortar round came in about thirty yards away. I had no sense of those distances then, even after six or seven weeks in Vietnam I still thought of that kind of information as a journalists' detail that could be picked up later, not something a survivor might have to know. When we fell down on the ground the kid in front of me put his boot into my face. I didn't feel the boot, it got lost in the tremendous concussion I made hitting the ground, but I felt a sharp pain in a line over my eyes. The kid turned around and started going into something insane right away, "Aw I'm sorry, shit I'm sorry, oh no man I'm *sorry*." Some hot stinking metal had been put into my mouth, I thought I tasted brains there sizzling on the end of my tongue, and the kid was fumbling for his canteen and looking really scared, pale, near tears, his voice shaking, "Shit I'm just a fucking oaf, I'm a fucking clod, you're okay, you're really okay," and somewhere in there I got the feeling that it was him, somehow he'd just killed me. I don't think I said anything, but I made a sound that I can remember now, a shrill blubbering pitched to carry more terror than I'd ever known existed, like the sounds they've recorded off of plants being burned, like an old woman going under for the last time. My hands went flying everywhere all over my head, I had to find it and touch it. There seemed to be no blood coming from the top, none from the forehead, none running out of my eyes, my *eyes!* In a moment of half-relief the pain became specific, I thought that just my nose had been blown off, or in, or apart, and the kid was still going into it for himself, "Oh man, I'm really fucking sorry."

Twenty yards in front of us men were running around totally out of their minds. One man was dead (they told me later it was only because he'd been walking forward with his flak jacket open, another real detail to get down and never fuck with again), one was on his hands and knees vomiting some evil pink substance, and one, quite near us, was propped up against a tree facing away from the direction of the round, making himself look at the incredible thing that had just happened to his leg, screwed around about once at some point below his knee like a goofy scarecrow leg. He looked away and then back again, looking at it for a few seconds longer each time, then he settled in for about a minute, shaking his head and smiling, until his face became serious and he passed out.

By then I'd found my nose and realized what had happened, all that had happened, not even broken, my glasses weren't even broken. I took the kid's canteen and soaked my sweat scarf, washing the blood off where it had caked on my lip and chin. He had stopped apologizing, and there was no pity in his face anymore. When I handed his canteen back to him, he was laughing at me.

I never told that story to anyone, and I never went back to that outfit again either.

III

In Saigon I always went to sleep stoned so I almost always lost my dreams, probably just as well, sock in deep and dim under that information and get whatever rest you could, wake up tapped of all images but the ones remembered from the day or the week before, with only the taste of a bad dream in your mouth like you'd been chewing on a roll of dirty old pennies in your sleep. I'd watched grunts asleep putting out the REM's like a firefight in the dark, I'm sure it was the same with me. They'd say (I'd ask) that they didn't remember their dreams either when they were in the zone, but on R&R or in the hospital their dreaming would be constant, open, violent and clear, like a man in the Pleiku hospital on the night I was there. It was three in the morning, scary and upsetting like hearing a language for the first time and somehow understanding every word, the voice loud and small at the same time, insistent, calling, *"Who? Who?* Who's in the next room?" There was a single shaded light over the desk at the end of the ward where I sat with the orderly. I could only see the first few beds, it felt like there were a thousand of them running out into the darkness, but actually there were only twenty in each row. After the man had repeated it a few times there was a change like the break in a fever, he sounded like a pleading little boy. I could see cigarettes being lighted at the far end of the ward, mumbles and groans, wounded men returning to consciousness, pain, but the man who'd been dreaming slept through it. . . . As for my own dreams, the ones I lost there would make it through later, I should have known, some things will just naturally follow until they take. The night would come when they'd be vivid and unremitting, that night the beginning of a long string, I'd remember then and wake up half believing that I'd never really been in any of those places.

Saigon *cafarde,* a bitch, nothing for it but some smoke and a little lie-down, waking in the late afternoon on damp pillows, feeling the emptiness of the bed behind you as you walked to the windows looking down at Tu Do. Or just lying there tracking the rotations of the ceiling fan, reaching for the fat roach that sat on my Zippo in a yellow disk of grass tar. There were mornings when I'd do it before my feet even hit the floor. Dear Mom, stoned again.

In the Highlands, where the Montagnards would trade you a pound of legendary grass for a carton of Salems, I got stoned with some infantry from the 4th. One of them had worked for months on his pipe, beautifully carved and painted with flowers and peace symbols. There was a reedy little man in the circle who grinned all the time but hardly spoke. He pulled a thick plastic bag out of his pack and handed it over to me. It was full of what looked like large pieces of dried fruit. I was stoned and hungry, I almost put my hand in there, but it had a bad weight to it. The other men were giving each other looks, some amused, some embarrassed and even angry. Someone had told me once, there were a lot more ears than heads in Vietnam; just information. When I handed it back he was still grinning, but he looked sadder than a monkey.

In Saigon and Danang we'd get stoned together and keep the common pool stocked and tended. It was bottomless and alive with Lurps, seals, recondos, Green-Beret bushmasters, redundant mutilators, heavy rapers, eye-shooters, widow-makers, nametakers, classic essential American types; point men, *isolatos* and outriders like they were programmed in their genes to do it, the first taste made them crazy for it, just like they knew it would. You thought you were separate and protected, you could travel the war for a hundred years, a swim in that pool could still be worth a piece of your balance.

We'd all heard about the man in the Highlands who was "building his own gook," parts were the least of his troubles. In Chu Lai some Marines pointed a man out to me and swore to God they'd seen him bayonet a wounded NVA and then lick the bayonet clean. There was a famous story, some reporters asked a door gunner, "How can you shoot women and children?" and he'd answered, "It's easy, you just don't lead 'em so much." Well, they said you needed a sense of humor, there you go, even the VC had one. Once after an ambush that killed a lot of Americans, they covered the field with copies of a photograph that showed one more young, dead American, with the punch line mimeographed on the back, "Your X-rays have just come back from the lab and we think we know what your problem is."

"I was sitting in a Chinook and this guy across from me had his sixteen loaded and it was pointing like ha-ha at my heart. I made signs for him to kind of put it up and he started laughing. He said something to the guys next to him and they started laughing too. . . ."

"He probably said, 'Asshole here wants me to put my gun up,'" Dana said.

"Yeah, well, you know . . . sometimes I think one of them's going to just do it, clear his weapon like bbbdddrrrpp, ya ha! I got a reporter!"

"There's a colonel in the Seventh Marines who said he'd

give a three-day pass to any one of his men who killed a correspondent for him," Flynn said. "A week if they get Dana."

"Well that's just bullshit," Dana said. "They fucking think I'm God."

"Yeah, it's true," Sean said. "It's true, you little fucker, you're just like they are."

Dana Stone had just come down from Danang for more equipment, he'd fed all his cameras to the war again, they were either in the shop or totaled. Flynn had come back the night before from six weeks with the Special Forces in III Corps, he hadn't said a word about what had gone on up there. "Spaced": he was sitting on the floor by the air-conditioner with his back against the wall trying to watch the sweat running down from his hairline.

We were all in a room at the Continental Hotel that belonged to Keith Kay, the CBS cameraman. It was early May and there was a lot of heavy combat all around the city, a big offensive, friends came in from there and went out again all week long. Across the way, on the latticed porches of the Continental annex, we could see the Indians shuffle back and forth in their underwear, bushed from another hard day of buying and selling money. (Their mosque, near L'Amiral Restaurant, was called the Bank of India. When the Saigon police, the White Mice, raided it they found two million in cold green.) There were trucks and jeeps and a thousand bikes moving in the street, and a little girl with a withered leg darting back and forth on wooden crutches faster than a dragonfly to sell her cigarettes. She had a face like a child dakini, so beautiful that people who needed to keep their edge blunt could hardly bear to look at her. Her competition were street boys, "Changee money," "Boom-boom picture," "Dinkydao cigarette," hustle and connection ran like a current down Tu Do, from the cathedral to the river. Rounding

Le Loi there was a large group of correspondents coming back from the briefing, standard diurnal informational freak-o-rama, Five O'Clock Follies, Jive at Five, war stories; at the corner they broke formation and went to their offices to file, we watched them, the wasted clocking the wasted.

A new correspondent came into the room to say hello, just arrived from New York, and he started asking Dana a lot of questions right away, sort of bullshit questions about the killing radius of various mortars and the penetration capability of rockets, the ranges of AK's and 16's, what shells did when they hit treetops, paddy and hard ground. He was in his late thirties and he was dressed in one of those jungle-hell leisure suits that the tailors on Tu Do were getting rich cranking out, with enough flaps and slots and cargo pockets to carry supply for a squad. Dana would answer one question and the man would ask two more, but that made sense since the man had never been out and Dana hardly ever came in. Oral transmission, those who knew and those who didn't, new people were always coming in with their own basic load of questions, energetic and hungry; someone had done it for you, it was a kind of blessing if you were in a position to answer some questions, if only to say that the questions couldn't be answered. This man's questions were something else, they seemed to be taking on hysteria as they went along.

"Is it exhilarating? Boy, I'll bet it's exhilarating."

"Aw you wouldn't believe it," Dana said.

Tim Page came in. He'd been out at the Y Bridge all day taking pictures of the fighting there and he'd gotten some CS in his eyes. He was rubbing them and weeping and bitching.

"Oh you're English," the new man said. "I was just there. What's CS?"

"It's a gas gas gas," Page said. "Gaaaaaa. Arrrrgggh!" and he did a soft version of raking his nails down his face, he

used his fingertips but it left red marks anyway. "Blind Lemon Page," Flynn said, and laughed while Page took the record that was playing on the turntable off without asking anybody and put on Jimi Hendrix: long tense organic guitar line that made him shiver like frantic electric ecstasy was shooting up from the carpet through his spine straight to the old pleasure center in his cream-cheese brain, shaking his head so that his hair waved all around him, Have You Ever Been Experienced?

"What does it look like when a man gets hit in the balls?" the new man said, as though that was the question he'd really meant to ask all along, and it came as close as you could get to a breach of taste in that room; palpable embarrassment all around, Flynn moved his eyes like he was following a butter-fly up out of sight, Page got sniffy and offended, but he was amused, too. Dana just sat there putting out the still rays, taking snaps with his eyes. "Oh I dunno," he said. "It all just goes sort of gooey."

We all started to laugh, everyone except Dana, because he'd seen that, he was just telling the man. I didn't hear what the man started to ask next, but Dana stopped him and said, "Only thing I can tell you that might actually do you some good is to go back up to your room and practice hitting the floor for a while."

Beautiful for once and only once, just past dawn flying to-ward the center of the city in a Loach, view from a bubble floating at 800 feet. In that space, at that hour, you could see what people had seen forty years before, Paris of the East, Pearl of the Orient, long open avenues lined and bowered over by trees running into spacious parks, precisioned scale, all under the soft shell from a million breakfast fires, cam-phor smoke rising and diffusing, covering Saigon and the shining veins of the river with a warmth like the return of better times. Just a projection, that was the thing about choppers, you had to come down sometime, down to the moment, the street, if you found a pearl down there you got to keep it.

By 7:30 it was beyond berserk with bikes, the air was like L.A. on short plumbing, the subtle city war inside the war had renewed itself for another day, relatively light on actual violence but intense with bad feeling: despair, impacted rage, impotent gnawing resentment; thousands of Vietnamese in the service of a pyramid that wouldn't stand for five years, plugging the feed tube into their own hearts, grasping and gorging; young Americans in from the boonies on TDY, charged with hatred and grounded in fear of the Vietnamese; thousands of Americans sitting in their offices crying in bored chorus, "You can't get these people to do a fucking thing, you can't get these people to do a fucking thing." And all the others, theirs and ours, who just didn't want to play, it sickened them. That December the GVN Department of Labor had announced that the refugee problem had been solved, that "all refugees [had] been assimilated into the economy," but mostly they seemed to have assimilated themselves into the city's roughest corners, alleyways, mud slides, under parked cars. Cardboard boxes that had carried air-conditioners and refrigerators housed up to ten children, most Americans and plenty of Vietnamese would cross the street to avoid trash heaps that fed whole families. And this was still months before Tet, "refugees up the gazops," a flood. I'd heard that the GVN Department of Labor had nine American advisors for every Vietnamese.

In Broddards and La Pagode and the pizzeria around the corner, the Cowboys and Vietnamese "students" would hang out all day, screaming obscure arguments at each other, cadging off Americans, stealing tips from the tables, reading

Pléiade editions of Proust, Malraux, Camus. One of them talked to me a few times but we couldn't really communicate, all I understood was his obsessive comparison between Rome and Washington, and that he seemed to believe that Poe had been a French writer. In the late afternoon the Cowboys would leave the cafés and milk bars and ride down hard on Lam Son Square to pick the Allies. They could snap a Rolex off your wrist like a hawk hitting a field mouse; wallets, pens, cameras, eyeglasses, anything; if the war had gone on any longer they'd have found a way to whip the boots off your feet. They'd hardly leave their saddles and they never looked back. There was a soldier down from the 1st Division who was taking snapshots of his friends with some bar girls in front of the Vietnamese National Assembly. He'd gotten his shot focused and centered but before he pushed the button his camera was a block away, leaving him in the bike's backwash with a fresh pink welt on his throat where the cord had been torn and helpless amazement on his face, "Well I'll be dipped in shit!"; as a little boy raced across the square, zipped a piece of cardboard up the soldier's shirtfront and took off around the corner with his Paper Mate. The White Mice stood around giggling, but there were a lot of us watching from the Continental terrace, a kind of gasp went up from the tables, and later when he came up for a beer he said, "I'm goin' back to the war, man, this fucking Saigon is too much for me." There was a large group of civilian engineers there, the same men you'd see in the restaurants throwing food at each other, and one of them, a fat old boy, said, "You ever catch one of them li'l nigs just pinch 'em. Pinch 'em hard. Boy, they hate that."

Five to seven were bleary low hours in Saigon, the city's energy ebbing at dusk, until it got dark and movement was replaced with apprehension. Saigon at night was still Vietnam at night, night was the war's truest medium; night was when it got really interesting in the villages, the TV crews couldn't film at night, the Phoenix was a night bird, it flew in and out of Saigon all the time.

Maybe you had to be pathological to find glamour in Saigon, maybe you just had to settle for very little, but Saigon had it for me, and danger activated it. The days of big, persistent terror in Saigon were over, but everyone felt that they could come back again any time, heavy like 1963–5, when they hit the old Brinks BOQ on Christmas Eve, when they blew up the My Canh floating restaurant, waited for it to be rebuilt and moved to another spot on the river, and then blew it up again, when they bombed the first U.S. embassy and changed the war forever from the intimate inside out. There were four known VC sapper battalions in the Saigon–Cholon area, dread sappers, guerrilla superstars, they didn't even have to do anything to put the fear out. Empty ambulances sat parked at all hours in front of the new embassy. Guards ran mirrors and "devices" under all vehicles entering all installations, BOQ's were fronted with sandbags, checkpoints and wire, high-gauge grilles filled our windows, but they still got through once in a while, random terror but real, even the supposedly terror-free safe spots worked out between the Corsican mob and the VC offered plenty of anxiety. Saigon just before Tet; guess, guess again.

Those nights there was a serious tiger lady going around on a Honda shooting American officers on the street with a .45. I think she'd killed over a dozen in three months; the Saigon papers described her as "beautiful," but I don't know how anybody knew that. The commander of one of the Saigon MP battalions said he thought it was a man dressed in an *ao dai* because a .45 was "an awful lot of gun for a itty bitty Vietnamese woman."

Saigon, the center, where every action in the bushes hundreds of miles away fed back into town on a karmic wire strung so tight that if you touched it in the early morning it would sing all day and all night. Nothing so horrible ever happened upcountry that it was beyond language fix and press relations, a squeeze fit into the computers would make the heaviest numbers jump up and dance. You'd either meet an optimism that no violence could unconvince or a cynicism that would eat itself empty every day and then turn, hungry and malignant, on whatever it could for a bite, friendly or hostile, it didn't matter. Those men called dead Vietnamese "believers," a lost American platoon was "a black eye," they talked as though killing a man was nothing more than depriving him of his vigor.

It seemed the least of the war's contradictions that to lose your worst sense of American shame you had to leave the Dial Soapers in Saigon and a hundred headquarters who spoke goodworks and killed nobody themselves, and go out to the grungy men in the jungle who talked bloody murder and killed people all the time. It was true that the grunts stripped belts and packs and weapons from their enemies; Saigon wasn't a flat market, these goods filtered down and in with the other spoils: Rolexes, cameras, snakeskin shoes from Taiwan, air-brush portraits of nude Vietnamese women with breasts like varnished beach balls, huge wooden carvings that they set on their desks to give you the finger when you walked into their offices. In Saigon it never mattered what they told you, even less when they actually seemed to believe it. Maps, charts, figures, projections, fly fantasies, names of places, of operations, of commanders, of weapons; memories, guesses, second guesses, experiences (new, old, real, imagined, stolen); histories, attitudes—you could let it go, let it all go. If you wanted some war news in Saigon you had to hear it in stories brought from the field by friends, see it in the lost watchful eyes of the Saigonese, or do it like Trash-man, reading the cracks in the sidewalk.

Sitting in Saigon was like sitting inside the folded petals of a poisonous flower, the poison history, fucked in its root no matter how far back you wanted to run your trace. Saigon was the only place left with a continuity that someone as far outside as I was could recognize. Hue and Danang were like remote closed societies, mute and intractable. Villages, even large ones, were fragile, a village could disappear in an after-noon, and the countryside was either blasted over cold and dead or already back in Charles' hands. Saigon remained, the repository and the arena, it breathed history, expelled it like toxin, Shit Piss and Corruption. Paved swamp, hot mushy winds that never cleaned anything away, heavy thermal seal over diesel fuel, mildew, garbage, excrement, atmosphere. A five-block walk in that could take it out of you, you'd get back to the hotel with your head feeling like one of those chocolate apples, tap it sharply in the right spot and it falls apart in sections. Saigon, November 1967: "The animals are sick with love." Not much chance anymore for history to go on unselfconsciously.

You'd stand nailed there in your tracks sometimes, no bearings and none in sight, thinking, *Where the fuck am I?*, fallen into some unnatural East-West interface, a California corridor cut and bought and burned deep into Asia, and once we'd done it we couldn't remember what for. It was axiomatic that it was about ideological space, we were there to bring them the choice, bringing it to them like Sherman bringing the Jubilee through Georgia, clean through it, wall to wall with pacified indigenous and scorched earth. (In the Vietnamese sawmills they had to change the blades every five minutes, some of our lumber had gotten into some of theirs.)

There was such a dense concentration of American energy
there, American and essentially adolescent, if that energy
could have been channeled into anything more than noise,
waste and pain it would have lighted up Indochina for a
thousand years.

The Mission and the motion: military arms and civilian
arms, more combatant between themselves than together
against the Cong. Gun arms, knife arms, pencil arms, head-
and-stomach arms, hearts-and-minds arms, flying arms,
creeping-peeping arms, information arms as tricky as the
arms of Plastic Man. At the bottom was the shitface grunt, at
the top a Command trinity: a blue-eyed, hero-faced general,
a geriatrics-emergency ambassador and a hale, heartless CIA
performer. (Robert "Blowtorch" Komer, chief of COORDS,
spook anagram for Other War, pacification, another word
for war. If William Blake had "reported" to him that he'd
seen angels in the trees, Komer would have tried to talk him
out of it. Failing there, he'd have ordered defoliation.) All
through the middle were the Vietnam War and the Vietnamese, not always exactly innocent bystanders, probably no
accident that we'd found each other. If milk snakes could
kill, you might compare the Mission and its arms to a big
intertwined ball of baby milk snakes. Mostly they were that
innocent, and about that conscious. And a lot, one way or
the other, had some satisfaction. They believed that God was
going to thank them for it.

Innocent; for the noncombatants stationed in Saigon or
one of the giant bases, the war wasn't much more real than if
they'd been getting it on TV back at Leonard Wood or
Andrews. There was the common failure of feeling and
imagination compounded by punishing boredom, an alienation beyond tolerance and a terrible, ongoing anxiety that it
might one day, any day, come closer than it had so far. And
operating inside of that fear was the half-hidden, half-

vaunted jealousy of every grunt who ever went out there and killed himself a gook, furtive vicarious bloodthirsting behind 10,000 desks, a fantasy life rich with lurid war-comics adventure, a smudge of closet throatsticker on every morning report, requisition slip, pay voucher, medical profile, information handout and sermon in the entire system.

Prayers in the Delta, prayers in the Highlands, prayers in the Marine bunkers of the "frontier" facing the DMZ, and for every prayer there was a counter-prayer—it was hard to see who had the edge. In Dalat the emperor's mother sprinkled rice in her hair so the birds could fly around her and feed while she said her morning prayers. In wood-paneled, air-conditioned chapels in Saigon, MACV padres would fire one up to sweet muscular Jesus, blessing ammo dumps and 105's and officers' clubs. The best-armed patrols in history went out after services to feed smoke to people whose priests could let themselves burn down to consecrated ash on street corners. Deep in the alleys you could hear small Buddhist chimes ringing for peace, *hoa bien;* smell incense in the middle of the thickest Asian street funk; see groups of ARVN with their families waiting for transport huddled around a burning prayer strip. Sermonettes came over Armed Forces radio every couple of hours, once I heard a chaplain from the 9th Division starting up, "Oh Gawd, help us learn to live with Thee in a more dynamic way in these perilous times, that we may better serve Thee in the struggle against Thine enemies. . . ." Holy war, long-nose jihad like a face-off between one god who would hold the coonskin to the wall while we nailed it up, and another whose detachment would see the blood run out of ten generations, if that was how long it took for the wheel to go around.

And around. While the last falling-off contacts were still

going on and the last casualties being dusted off, Command added Dak To to our victory list, a reflexive move supported by the Saigon press corps but never once or for a minute by reporters who'd seen it going on from meters or even inches away, and this latest media defection added more bitterness to an already rotten mix, leaving the commanding general of the 4th to wonder out loud and in my hearing whether we were or weren't all Americans in this thing together. I said I thought we were. For sure we were.

"... *Wow I love it in the movies when they say like,* '*Okay Jim, where do you want it?*' "

"*Right! Right! Yeah, beautiful, I don't want it at all! Haw, shit . . . where do you fucking want it?*"

Mythopathic moment; *Fort Apache,* where Henry Fonda as the new colonel says to John Wayne, the old hand, "We saw some Apache as we neared the Fort," and John Wayne says, "If you saw them, sir, they weren't Apache." But this colonel is obsessed, brave like a maniac, not very bright, a West Point aristo wounded in his career and his pride, posted out to some Arizona shithole with only marginal consolation: he's a professional and this is a war, the only war we've got. So he gives the John Wayne information a pass and he and half his command get wiped out. More a war movie than a Western, Nam paradigm, Vietnam, not a movie, no jive cartoon either where the characters get smacked around and electrocuted and dropped from heights, flattened out and frizzed black and broken like a dish, then up again and whole and back in the game, "Nobody dies," as someone said in another war movie.

In the first week of December 1967 I turned on the radio and heard this over AFVN: "The Pentagon announced today that, compared to Korea, the Vietnam War will be an economy war, provided that it does not exceed the Korean War in length, which means that it will have to end *sometime* in 1968."

By the time that Westmoreland came home that fall to cheerlead and request-beg another quarter of a million men, with his light-at-the-end-of-the-tunnel collateral, there were people leaning so far out to hear good news that a lot of them slipped over the edge and said that they could see it too. (Outside of Tay Ninh City a man whose work kept him "up to fucking here" in tunnels, lobbing grenades into them, shooting his gun into them, popping CS smoke into them, crawling down into them himself to bring the bad guys out dead or alive, he almost smiled when he heard that one and said, "What does that asshole know about tunnels?")

A few months earlier there had been an attempt Higher to crank up the Home For Christmas rumor, but it wouldn't take, the troop consensus was too strong, it went, "Never happen." If a commander told you he thought he had it pretty well under control it was like talking to a pessimist. Most would say that they either had it wrapped up or wound down; "He's all pissed out, Charlie's all pissed out, booger's shot his whole wad," one of them promised me, while in Saigon it would be restructured for briefings, "He no longer maintains in our view capability to mount, execute or sustain a serious offensive action," and a reporter behind me, from *The New York Times* no less, laughed and said, "Mount this, Colonel." But in the boonies, where they were deprived of all information except what they'd gathered for themselves on either side of the treeline, they'd look around like someone was watching and say, "I dunno, Charlie's up to something. Slick, slick, that fucker's *so* slick. Watch!"

The summer before, thousands of Marines had gone humping across northern I Corps in multi-division sweeps, "Taking the D out of DMZ," but the North never really broke out into the open for it, hard to believe that anyone ever thought that they would. Mostly it was an invasion of a thousand operation-miles of high summer dry season stroke weather, six-canteen patrols that came back either contactless or chewed over by ambushes and quick, deft mortar-rocket attacks, some from other Marine outfits. By September they were "containing" at Con Thien, sitting there while the NVA killed them with artillery. In II Corps a month of random contact near the Laotian border had sharpened into the big war around Dak To. III Corps, outside of Saigon, was most confusing of all, the VC were running what was described in a month-end, sit/rep handout as "a series of half-hearted, unambitious ground attacks" from Tay Ninh through Loc Ninh to Bu Dop, border skirmishes that some reporters saw as purposely limited rather than half-hearted, patterned and extremely well coordinated, like someone was making practice runs for a major offensive. IV Corps was what it had always been, obscure isolated Delta war, authentic guerrilla action where betrayal was as much an increment as bullets. People close to Special Forces had heard upsetting stories about the A Camps down there, falling apart from inside, mercenary mutinies and triple cross, until only a few were still effective.

That fall, all that the Mission talked about was control: arms control, information control, resources control, psycho-political control, population control, control of the almost supernatural inflation, control of terrain through the Strategy of the Periphery. But when the talk had passed, the only thing left standing up that looked true was your sense of how out of control things really were. Year after year, season after season, wet and dry, using up options faster than rounds on a machine-gun belt, we called it right and right-eous, viable and even almost won, and it still only went on the way it went on. When all the projections of intent and strategy twist and turn back on you, tracking team blood, "sorry" just won't cover it. There's nothing so embarrassing as when things go wrong in a war.

You couldn't find two people who agreed about when it began, how could you say when it began going off? Mission intellectuals like 1954 as the reference date; if you saw as far back as War II and the Japanese occupation you were practically a historical visionary. "Realists" said that it began for us in 1961, and the common run of Mission flack insisted on 1965, post-Tonkin Resolution, as though all the killing that had gone before wasn't really war. Anyway, you couldn't use standard methods to date the doom; might as well say that Vietnam was where the Trail of Tears was headed all along, the turnaround point where it would touch and come back to form a containing perimeter; might just as well lay it on the proto-Gringos who found the New England woods too raw and empty for their peace and filled them up with their own imported devils. Maybe it was already over for us in Indochina when Alden Pyle's body washed up under the bridge at Dakao, his lungs all full of mud; maybe it caved in with Dien Bien Phu. But the first happened in a novel, and while the second happened on the ground it happened to the French, and Washington gave it no more substance than if Graham Greene had made it up too. Straight history, auto-revised history, history without handles, for all the books and articles and white papers, all the talk and the miles of film, something wasn't answered, it wasn't even asked. We were backgrounded, deep, but when the background started sliding forward not a single life was saved by the information. The thing had transmitted too much energy, it heated up too hot, hiding low under the fact-figure crossfire there was a secret history, and not a lot of people felt like running in there to bring it out.

One day in 1963 Henry Cabot Lodge was walking around the Saigon Zoo with some reporters, and a tiger pissed on him through the bars of its cage. Lodge made a joke, something like, "He who wears the pee of the tiger is assured of success in the coming year." Maybe nothing's so unfunny as an omen read wrong.

Some people think 1963's a long time ago; when a dead American in the jungle was an event, a grim thrilling novelty. It was spookwar then, adventure; not exactly soldiers, not even advisors yet, but Irregulars, working in remote places under little direct authority, acting out their fantasies with more freedom than most men ever know. Years later, leftovers from that time would describe it, they'd bring in names like Gordon, Burton and Lawrence, elevated crazies of older adventures who'd burst from their tents and bungalows to rub up hard against the natives, hot on the sex-and-death trail, "lost to headquarters." There had been Ivy League spooks who'd gone bumbling and mucking around in jeeps and beat-up Citroëns, Swedish K's across their knees, literally picnicking along the Cambodian border, buying Chinese-made shirts and sandals and umbrellas. There'd been ethnologue spooks who loved with their brains and forced that passion on the locals, whom they'd imitate, squatting in black pajamas, jabbering in Vietnamese. There had been one man who "owned" Long An Province, a Duke of Nha Trang, hundreds of others whose authority was absolute in hamlets or hamlet complexes where they ran their ops until the wind changed and their ops got run back on them. There were spook deities, like Lou Conein, "Black Luigi," who (they said) ran it down the middle with the VC, the GVN, the Mission and the Corsican Maf; and Edward

Landsdale himself, still there in '67, his villa a Saigon landmark where he poured tea and whiskey for second-genera-
tion spooks who adored him, even now that his batteries
were dead. There were executive spooks who'd turn up at
airstrips and jungle clearings sweating like a wheel of cheese
in their white suits and neckties; bureau spooks who sat on
dead asses in Dalat and Qui Nhon, or out jerking off in some
New Life Village; Air America spooks who could take guns
or junk or any kind of death at all and make it fly; Special
Forces spooks running around in a fury of skill to ice Victor
Charlie.

History's heavy attrition, tic and toc with teeth, the
smarter ones saw it winding down for them on the day that
Lodge first arrived in Saigon and commandeered the villa of
the current CIA chief, a moment of history that seemed even
sweeter when you knew that the villa had once been headquarters of the Deuxième Bureau. Officially, the complexion
of the problem had changed (too many people were getting
killed, for one thing), and the romance of spooking started
to fall away like dead meat from a bone. As sure as heat
rises, their time was over. The war passed along, this time
into the hard hands of firepower freaks out to eat the country
whole, and with no fine touches either, leaving the spooks on
the beach.

They never became as dangerous as they'd wanted to be,
they never knew how dangerous they really were. Their adventure became our war, then a war bogged down in time, so
much time so badly accounted for that it finally became en-
trenched as an institution because there had never been room
made for it to go anywhere else. The Irregulars either got out
or became regular in a hurry. By 1967 all you saw was the
impaired spook reflex, prim adventurers living too long on
the bloodless fringes of the action, heartbroken and memory-
ruptured, working alone together toward a classified uni-

verse. They seemed like the saddest casualties of the Sixties, all the promise of good service on the New Frontier either gone or surviving like the vaguest salvages of a dream, still in love with their dead leader, blown away in his prime and theirs; left now with the lonely gift they had of trusting no one, the crust of ice always forming over the eye, the jargon stream thinning and trickling out: *Frontier sealing, census grievance, black operations* (pretty good, for jargon), *revolutionary development, armed propaganda.* I asked a spook what that one meant and he just smiled. Surveillance, collecting and reporting, was like a carnival bear now, broken and dumb, an Intelligence beast, our own. And by late 1967, while it went humping and stalking all over Vietnam the Tet Offensive was already so much incoming.

IV

There were times during the night when all the jungle sounds would stop at once. There was no dwindling down or fading away, it was all gone in a single instant as though some signal had been transmitted out to the life: bats, birds, snakes, monkeys, insects, picking up on a frequency that a thousand years in the jungle might condition you to receive, but leaving you as it was to wonder what you weren't hearing now, straining for any sound, one piece of information. I had heard it before in other jungles, the Amazon and the Philippines, but those jungles were "secure," there wasn't much chance that hundreds of Viet Cong were coming and going, moving and waiting, living out there just to do you harm. The thought of that one could turn any sudden silence into a space that you'd fill with everything you thought was quiet in you, it could even put you on the approach to clairaudience. You thought you heard impossible things: damp roots breathing, fruit sweating, fervid bug action, the heartbeat of tiny animals.

You could sustain that sensitivity for a long time, either until the babbling and chittering and shrieking of the jungle had started up again, or until something familiar brought you out of it, a helicopter flying around above your canopy or the strangely reassuring sound next to you of one going into the chamber. Once we heard a really frightening thing blaring down from a Psyops soundship broadcasting the sound of a baby crying. You wouldn't have wanted to hear that during daylight, let alone at night when the volume and distortion came down through two or three layers of cover and froze us all in place for a moment. And there wasn't much release in the pitched hysteria of the message that followed, hyper-Vietnamese like an icepick in the ear, something like, "Friendly Baby, GVN Baby, Don't Let This Happen to *Your* Baby, Resist the Viet Cong Today!"

Sometimes you'd get so tired that you'd forget where you were and sleep the way you hadn't slept since you were a child. I know that a lot of people there never got up from that kind of sleep; some called them lucky (Never knew what hit him), some called them fucked (If he'd been on the stick . . .), but that was worse than academic, everyone's death got talked about, it was a way of constantly touching and turning the odds, and real sleep was at a premium. (I met a ranger-recondo who could go to sleep just like that, say, "Guess I'll get some," close his eyes and be there, day or night, sitting or lying down, sleeping through some things but not others; a loud radio or a 105 firing outside the tent wouldn't wake him, but a rustle in the bushes fifty feet away would, or a stopped generator.) Mostly what you had was on the agitated side of half-sleep, you thought you were sleeping but you were really just waiting. Night sweats, harsh func-tionings of consciousness, drifting in and out of your head, pinned to a canvas cot somewhere, looking up at a strange ceiling or out through a tent flap at the glimmering night sky of a combat zone. Or dozing and waking under mosquito netting in a mess of slick sweat, gagging for air that wasn't 99 percent moisture, one clean breath to dry-sluice your anxiety and the backwater smell of your own body. But all you got and all there was were misty clots of air that corroded your appetite and burned your eyes and made your cigarettes taste like swollen insects rolled up and smoked alive, crackling and wet. There were spots in the jungle where you had to have a cigarette going all the time, whether you smoked or not, just to keep the mosquitoes from swarming into your mouth. War under water, swamp fever and instant involuntary weight control, malarias that could burn you out and cave you in, put you into twenty-three hours of sleep a day without giving you a minute of rest, leaving you there to listen to the trance music that they said came in with terminal brain funk. ("Take your pills, baby," a medic in Can Tho told me. "Big orange ones every week, little white ones every day, and don't miss a day whatever you do. They got strains over here that could waste a heavy-set fella like you in a week.") Sometimes you couldn't live with the terms any longer and headed for air-conditioners in Danang and Saigon. And sometimes the only reason you didn't panic was that you didn't have the energy.

Every day people were dying there because of some small detail that they couldn't be bothered to observe. Imagine being too tired to snap a flak jacket closed, too tired to clean your rifle, too tired to guard a light, too tired to deal with the half-inch margins of safety that moving through the war often demanded, just too tired to give a fuck and then dying behind that exhaustion. There were times when the whole war itself seemed tapped of its vitality: epic enervation, the machine running half-assed and depressed, fueled on the watery residue of last year's war-making energy. Entire divisions would function in a bad dream state, acting out a weird set of moves without any connection to their source. Once I talked for maybe five minutes with a sergeant who had just brought his squad in from a long patrol before I realized that the dopey-dummy film over his eyes and the fly abstraction of his words were coming from deep sleep. He was standing there at the bar of the NCO club with his eyes open and a beer in his hand, responding to some dream conversation far inside his head. It really gave me the creeps—this was the second day of the Tet Offensive, our installation was more or less surrounded, the only secure road out of there was littered with dead Vietnamese, information was scarce and I was pretty touchy and tired myself—and for a second I imagined that I was talking to a dead man. When I told him about it later he just laughed and said, "Shit, that's nothing. I do that all the time."

One night I woke up and heard the sounds of a firefight going on kilometers away, a "skirmish" outside our perimeter, muffled by distance to sound like the noises we made playing guns as children, KSSSHH KSSSHH; we knew it was more authentic than BANG BANG, it enriched the game and this game was the same, only way out of hand at last, too rich for all but a few serious players. The rules now were tight and absolute, no arguing over who missed who and who was really dead; *No fair* was no good, *Why me?* the saddest question in the world.

Well, good luck, the Vietnam verbal tic, even Ocean Eyes, the third-tour Lurp, had remembered to at least say it to me that night before he went on the job. It came out dry and distant, I knew he didn't care one way or the other, maybe I admired his detachment. It was as though people couldn't stop themselves from saying it, even when they actually meant to express the opposite wish, like, "Die, motherfucker." Usually it was only an uninhabited passage of dead language, sometimes it came out five times in a sentence, like punctuation, often it was spoken flat side up to telegraph the belief that there wasn't any way out; tough shit, *sin loi,* smack it, good luck. Sometimes, though, it was said with such feeling and tenderness that it could crack your mask, that much love where there was so much war. Me too, every day, compulsively, good luck: to friends in the press corps going out on operations, to grunts I'd meet at firebases and airstrips, to the wounded, the dead and all the Vietnamese I ever saw getting fucked over by us and each other, less often but most passionately to myself, and though I meant it every time I said it, it was meaningless. It was like telling someone going out in a storm not to get any on him, it was the same as saying, "Gee, I hope you don't get killed or wounded or see anything that drives you insane." You could make all the ritual moves, carry your lucky piece, wear your magic jungle hat, kiss your thumb knuckle smooth as stones under running water, the Inscrutable Immutable was still out there, and you kept on or not at its pitiless discretion. All you could say that wasn't fundamentally lame was something like, "He who bites it this day is safe from the next," and that was exactly what nobody wanted to hear.

After enough time passed and memory receded and settled, the name itself became a prayer, coded like all prayer to go past the extremes of petition and gratitude: Vietnam Vietnam Vietnam, say again, until the word lost all its old loads of pain, pleasure, horror, guilt, nostalgia. Then and there, everyone was just trying to get through it, existential crunch, no atheists in foxholes like you wouldn't believe. Even bitter refracted faith was better than none at all, like the black

Marine I'd heard about during heavy shelling at Con Thien who said, "Don't worry, baby, God'll think of something."

Flip religion, it was so far out, you couldn't blame anybody for believing anything. Guys dressed up in Batman fetishes, I saw a whole squad like that, it gave them a kind of dumb esprit. Guys stuck the ace of spades in their helmet bands, they picked relics off of an enemy they'd killed, a little transfer of power; they carried around five-pound Bibles from home, crosses, St. Christophers, mezuzahs, locks of hair, girlfriends' underwear, snaps of their families, their wives, their dogs, their cows, their cars, pictures of John Kennedy, Lyndon Johnson, Martin Luther King, Huey Newton, the Pope, Che Guevara, the Beatles, Jimi Hendrix, wiggier than cargo cultists. One man was carrying an oatmeal cookie through his tour, wrapped up in foil and plastic and three pair of socks. He took a lot of shit about it ("When you go to sleep we're gonna eat your fucking cookie"), but his wife had baked it and mailed it to him, he wasn't kidding.

On operations you'd see men clustering around the charmed grunt that many outfits created who would take himself and whoever stayed close enough through a field of safety, at least until he rotated home or got blown away, and then the outfit would hand the charm to someone else. If a bullet creased your head or you'd stepped on a dud mine or a grenade rolled between your feet and just lay there, you were magic enough. If you had any kind of extra-sense capacity, if you could smell VC or their danger the way hunting guides smelled the coming weather, if you had special night vision, or great ears, you were magic too; anything bad that happened to you could leave the men in your outfit pretty depressed. I met a man in the Cav who'd been "fucking the duck" one afternoon, sound asleep in a huge tent with thirty cots inside, all empty but his, when some mortar rounds came in, tore the tent down to canvas slaw and put frags through every single cot but his, he was still high out of his mind from it, speedy, sure and lucky. The Soldier's Prayer came in two versions: Standard, printed on a plastic-coated card by the Defense Department, and Standard Revised, impossible to convey because it got translated outside of language, into chaos—screams, begging, promises, threats, sobs, repetitions of holy names until their throats were cracked and dry, until some men had bitten through their collar points and rifle straps and even their dog-tag chains.

Varieties of religious experience, good news and bad news; a lot of men found their compassion in the war, some found it and couldn't live with it, war-washed shutdown of feeling, like who gives a fuck. People retreated into positions of hard irony, cynicism, despair, some saw the action and declared for it, only heavy killing could make them feel so alive. And some just went insane, followed the black-light arrow around the bend and took possession of the madness that had been waiting there in trust for them for eighteen or twenty-five or fifty years. Every time there was combat you had a license to go maniac, everyone snapped over the line at least once there and nobody noticed, they hardly noticed if you forgot to snap back again.

One afternoon at Khe Sanh a Marine opened the door of a latrine and was killed by a grenade that had been rigged on the door. The Command tried to blame it on a North Vietnamese infiltrator, but the grunts knew what had happened: "Like a gook is really gonna tunnel all the way in here to booby-trap a shithouse, right? Some guy just flipped out is all." And it became another one of those stories that moved across the DMZ, making people laugh and shake their heads and look knowingly at each other, but shocking no one. They'd talk about physical wounds in one way and psychic wounds in another, each man in a squad would tell you how

crazy everyone else in the squad was, everyone knew grunts
who'd gone crazy in the middle of a firefight, gone crazy on
patrol, gone crazy back at camp, gone crazy on R&R, gone
crazy during their first month home. Going crazy was built
into the tour, the best you could hope for was that it didn't
happen around you, the kind of crazy that made men empty
clips into strangers or fix grenades on latrine doors. That was
really crazy; anything less was almost standard, as standard
as the vague prolonged stares and involuntary smiles, common as ponchos or 16's or any other piece of war issue. If
you wanted someone to know you'd gone insane you really
had to sound off like you had a pair, "Scream a lot, and all
the time."

Some people just wanted to blow it all to hell, animal vege-
table and mineral. They wanted a Vietnam they could fit into
their car ashtrays; the joke went, "What you do is, you load
all the Friendlies onto ships and take them out to the South
China Sea. Then you bomb the country flat. Then you sink
the ships." A lot of people knew that the country could never
be won, only destroyed, and they locked into that with
breathtaking concentration, no quarter, laying down the
seeds of the disease, roundeye fever, until it reached plague
proportions, taking one from every family, a family from
every hamlet, a hamlet from every province, until a million
had died from it and millions more were left uncentered and
lost in their flight from it.

Up on the roof of the Rex BOQ in Saigon I walked into a
scene more bellicose than a firefight, at least 500 officers
nailed to the bar in a hail of chits, shiny irradiant faces
talking war, men drinking like they were going to the front,
and maybe a few of them really were. The rest were already
there, Saigon duty; coming through a year of that without

becoming totally blown out indicated as much heart as you'd need to take a machine-gun position with your hands, you sure couldn't take one with your mouth. We'd watched a movie (*Nevada Smith*, Steve McQueen working through a hard-revenge scenario, riding away at the end burned clean but somehow empty and old too, like he'd lost his margin for regeneration through violence); now there was a live act, Tito and His Playgirls, "Up up and awayeeyay in my beaudifoo balloooon," one of those Filipino combos that even the USO wouldn't touch, hollow beat, morbid rock and roll like steamed grease in the muggy air.

Roof of the Rex, ground zero, men who looked like they'd been suckled by wolves, they could die right there and their jaws would work for another half-hour. This is where they asked you, "Are you a Dove or a Hawk?" and "Would you rather fight them here or in Pasadena?" *Maybe we could beat them in Pasadena,* I'd think, but I wouldn't say it, especially not here where they knew that I knew that they really weren't fighting anybody anywhere anyway, it made them pretty touchy. That night I listened while a colonel explained the war in terms of protein. We were a nation of high-protein, meat-eating hunters, while the other guy just ate rice and a few grungy fish heads. We were going to club him to death with our meat; what could you say except, "Colonel, you're insane"? It was like turning up in the middle of some black looneytune where the Duck had all the lines. I only jumped in once, spontaneous as shock, during Tet when I heard a doctor bragging that he'd refused to allow wounded Vietnamese into his ward. "But Jesus Christ," I said, "didn't you take the Hippocratic Oath?" but he was ready for me. "Yeah," he said, "I took it in America." Doomsday celebs, technomaniac projectionists; chemicals, gases, lasers, sonic-electric ballbreakers that were still on the boards; and for back-up, deep in all their hearts, there were always the

Nukes, they loved to remind you that we had some, "right here in-country." Once I met a colonel who had a plan to shorten the war by dropping piranha into the paddies of the North. He was talking fish but his dreamy eyes were full of mega-death.

"Come on," the captain said, "we'll take you out to play Cowboys and Indians." We walked out from Song Be in a long line, maybe a hundred men; rifles, heavy automatics, mortars, portable one-shot rocket-launchers, radios, medics; breaking into some kind of sweep formation, five files with small teams of specialists in each file. A gunship flew close hover-cover until we came to some low hills, then two more ships came along and peppered the hills until we'd passed safely through them. It was a beautiful operation. We played all morning until someone on the point got something—a "scout," they thought, and then they didn't know. They couldn't even tell for sure whether he was from a friendly tribe or not, no markings on his arrows because his quiver was empty, like his pockets and his hands. The captain thought about it during the walk back, but when we got to camp he put it in his report, "One VC killed"; good for the unit, he said, not bad for the captain either.

Search and Destroy, more a gestalt than a tactic, brought up alive and steaming from the Command psyche. Not just a walk and a firefight, in action it should have been named the other way around, pick through the pieces and see if you could work together a count, the sponsor wasn't buying any dead civilians. The VC had an ostensibly similar tactic called Find and Kill. Either way, it was us looking for him looking for us looking for him, war on a Cracker Jack box, repeated to diminishing returns.

A lot of people used to say that it got fucked up when they

made it as easy for us to shoot as not to shoot. In I and II Corps it was "loose policy" for gunships to fire if the subjects froze down there, in the Delta it was to shoot if they ran or "evaded," either way a heavy dilemma, which would you do? "Air sports," one gunship pilot called it, and went on to describe it with fervor, "Nothing finer, you're up there at two thousand, you're God, just open up the flexies and watch it pee, nail those slime to the paddy wall, nothing finer, double back and get the caribou."

"Back home I used to fill my own cartridges for hunting," a platoon leader told me. "Me and my father and my brothers used to make a hundred a year between us maybe. I swear to God, I never saw anything like this."

Who had? Nothing like it ever when we caught a bunch of them out in the open and close together, we really ripped it then, volatile piss-off, crazed expenditure, Godzilla never drew that kind of fire. We even had a small language for our fire: "discreet burst," "probe," "prime selection," "constructive load," but I never saw it as various, just compulsive eruption, the Mad Minute for an hour. Charles really wrote the book on fire control, putting one round into the heart of things where fifty of ours might go and still not hit anything. Sometimes we put out so much fire you couldn't tell whether any of it was coming back or not. When it was, it filled your ears and your head until you thought you were hearing it with your stomach. An English correspondent I knew made a cassette of one of the heavy ones, he said he used it to seduce American girls.

Sometimes you felt too thin and didn't want to get into anything at all and it would land on you like your next-to-last breath. Sometimes your chops for action and your terror would reach a different balance and you'd go looking for it everywhere, and nothing would happen, except a fire ant would fly up your nose or you'd grow a crotch rot or you'd

lie awake all night waiting for morning so you could get up
and wait on your feet. Whichever way it went, you were
covering the war, your choice of story told it all and in Vietnam an infatuation like that with violence wouldn't go unre-
quited for very long, it would come and put its wild mouth
all over you.

"Quakin' and Shakin'," they called it, great balls of fire,
Contact. Then it was you and the ground: kiss it, eat it, fuck
it, plow it with your whole body, get as close to it as you can
without being in it yet or of it, guess who's flying around
about an inch above your head? Pucker and submit, it's the
ground. Under Fire would take you out of your head and
your body too, the space you'd seen a second ago between
subject and object wasn't there anymore, it banged shut in a
fast wash of adrenaline. Amazing, unbelievable, guys who'd
played a lot of hard sports said they'd never felt anything like
it, the sudden drop and rocket rush of the hit, the reserves of
adrenaline you could make available to yourself, pumping it
up and putting it out until you were lost floating in it, not
afraid, almost open to clear orgasmic death-by-drowning in
it, actually relaxed. Unless of course you'd shit your pants or
were screaming or praying or giving anything at all to the
hundred-channel panic that blew word salad all around you
and sometimes clean through you. Maybe you couldn't love
the war and hate it inside the same instant, but sometimes
those feelings alternated so rapidly that they spun together in
a strobic wheel rolling all the way up until you were literally
High On War, like it said on all the helmet covers. Coming
off a jag like that could really make a mess out of you.

In early December I came back from my first operation
with the Marines. I'd lain scrunched up for hours in a flimsy
bunker that was falling apart even faster than I was, listening
to it going on, the moaning and whining and the dull repetitions of whump whump whump and dit dit dit, listening to a

boy who'd somehow broken his thumb sobbing and gagging, thinking, "Oh my *God,* this fucking thing is on a *loop!*" until the heavy shooting stopped but not the thing: at the lz waiting for choppers to Phu Bai one last shell came in, landing in the middle of a pile of full body bags, making a mess that no one wanted to clean up, "a real shit detail." It was after midnight when I finally got back to Saigon, riding in from Tan Son Nhut in an open jeep with some sniper-obsessed MP's, and there was a small package of mail waiting for me at the hotel. I put my fatigues out in the hall room and closed the door on them, I may have even locked it. I had the I Corps DT's, livers, spleens, brains, a blue-black swollen thumb moved around and flashed to me, they were playing over the walls of the shower where I spent a half-hour, they were on the bedsheets, but I wasn't afraid of them, I was laughing at them, what could they do to me? I filled a water glass with Armagnac and rolled a joint, and then I started to read my mail. In one of the letters there was news that a friend of mine had killed himself in New York. When I turned off the lights and got into bed I lay there trying to remember what he had looked like. He had done it with pills, but no matter what I tried to imagine, all I saw was blood and bone fragment, not my dead friend. After a while I broke through for a second and saw him, but by that time all I could do with it was file him in with the rest and go to sleep.

Between what contact did to you and how tired you got, between the farout things you saw or heard and what you personally lost out of all that got blown away, the war made a place for you that was all yours. Finding it was like listening to esoteric music, you didn't hear it in any essential way through all the repetitions until your own breath had entered it and become another instrument, and by then it wasn't just music anymore, it was experience. Life-as-movie, war-as-(war) movie, war-as-life; a complete process if you got to complete it, a distinct path to travel, but dark and hard, not any easier if you knew that you'd put your own foot on it yourself, deliberately and—most roughly speaking—consciously. Some people took a few steps along it and turned back, wised up, with and without regrets. Many walked on and just got blown off it. A lot went farther than they probably should have and then lay down, falling into a bad sleep of pain and rage, waiting for release, for peace, any kind of peace that wasn't just the absence of war. And some kept going until they reached the place where an inversion of the expected order happened, a fabulous warp where you took the journey first and then you made your departure.

Once your body was safe your problems weren't exactly over. There was the terrible possibility that a search for information there could become so exhausting that the exhaustion itself became the information. Overload was such a real danger, not as obvious as shrapnel or blunt like a 2,000-foot drop, maybe it couldn't kill you or smash you, but it could bend your aerial for you and land you on your hip. Levels of information were levels of dread, once it's out it won't go back in, you can't just blink it away or run the film backward out of consciousness. How many of those levels did you really want to hump yourself through, which plateau would you reach before you shorted out and started sending the messages back unopened?

Cover the war, what a gig to frame for yourself, going out after one kind of information and getting another, totally other, to lock your eyes open, drop your blood temperature down under the 0, dry your mouth out so a full swig of water disappeared in there before you could swallow, turn your breath fouler than corpse gas. There were times when your fear would take directions so wild that you had to stop and watch the spin. Forget the Cong, the *trees* would kill you, the elephant grass grew up homicidal, the ground you were walking over possessed malignant intelligence, your whole environment was a bath. Even so, considering where you were and what was happening to so many people, it was a privilege just to be able to feel afraid.

So you learned about fear, it was hard to know what you really learned about courage. How many times did somebody have to run in front of a machine gun before it became an act of cowardice? What about those acts that didn't require courage to perform, but made you a coward if you didn't? It was hard to know at the moment, easy to make a mistake when it came, like the mistake of thinking that all you needed to perform a witness act were your eyes. A lot of what people called courage was only undifferentiated energy cut loose by the intensity of the moment, mind loss that sent the actor on an incredible run; if he survived it he had the chance later to decide whether he'd really been brave or just overcome with life, even ecstasy. A lot of people found the guts to just call it all off and refuse to ever go out anymore, they turned and submitted to the penalty end of the system or they just split. A lot of reporters, too, I had friends in the press corps who went out once or twice and then never again. Sometimes I thought that they were the sanest, most serious people of all, although to be honest I never said so until my time there was almost over.

"We had this gook and we was gonna skin him" (a grunt told me), "I mean he was already dead and everything, and the lieutenant comes over and says, 'Hey asshole, there's a reporter in the TOC, you want him to come out and see that? I mean, use your fucking heads, there's a time and place for everything. . . ."

"Too bad you wasn't with us last week" (another grunt told me, coming off a no-contact operation), "we killed so many gooks it wasn't even funny."

Was it possible that they were there and not haunted? No, not possible, not a chance, I know I wasn't the only one. Where are they now? (Where am I now?) I stood as close to them as I could without actually being one of them, and then I stood as far back as I could without leaving the planet. Disgust doesn't begin to describe what they made me feel, they threw people out of helicopters, tied people up and put the dogs on them. Brutality was just a word in my mouth before that. But disgust was only one color in the whole mandala, gentleness and pity were other colors, there wasn't a color left out. I think that those people who used to say that they only wept for the Vietnamese never really wept for anyone at all if they couldn't squeeze out at least one for these men and boys when they died or had their lives cracked open for them.

But of course we were intimate, I'll tell you how intimate: they were my guns, and I let them do it. I never let them dig my holes or carry my gear, there were always grunts who offered, but I let them do that for me while I watched, maybe for them, maybe not. We covered each other, an exchange of services that worked all right until one night when I slid over to the wrong end of the story, propped up behind some sandbags at an airstrip in Can Tho with a .30-caliber automatic in my hands, firing cover for a four-man reaction team trying to get back in. One last war story.

The first night of the Tet Offensive we were in the Special Forces C Camp for the Delta, surrounded, as far as we knew, and with nothing but bad news filtering in: from Hue, from

Danang, from Qui Nhon, from Khe Sanh, from Ban Me Thuot, from Saigon itself, "lost" as we understood it at the moment, they had the embassy, they had Cholon, Tan Son Nhut was burning, we were in the Alamo, no place else, and I wasn't a reporter, I was a shooter.

In the morning there were about a dozen dead Vietnamese across the field there where we'd been firing. We sent a truck over to load them on and get them away. It all happened so fast, as they say, as everyone who has ever been through it has always said; we were sitting around smoking grass and listening to what we thought were Tet fireworks coming from the town, and then coming closer until we weren't stoned anymore, until the whole night had passed and I was looking at the empty clips around my feet behind the berm, telling myself that there would never be any way to know for sure. I couldn't remember ever feeling so tired, so changed, so happy.

Thousands of people died in Vietnam that night, the twelve across the field, a hundred more along the road between the camp and the Can Tho hospital compound where I worked all the next day, not a reporter or a shooter but a medic, unskilled and scared. When we got back to the camp that night I threw away the fatigues I'd been wearing. And for the next six years I saw them all, the ones I'd really seen and the ones I'd imagined, theirs and ours, friends I'd loved and strangers, motionless figures in a dance, the old dance. Years of thinking this or that about what happens to you when you pursue a fantasy until it becomes experience, and then afterward you can't handle the experience. Until I felt that I was just a dancer too.

From outside we say that crazy people think they hear voices, but of course inside they really hear them. (Who's crazy? What's insane?) One night, like a piece of shrapnel that takes years to work its way out, I dreamed and saw a field that was crowded with dead. I was crossing it with a friend, more than a friend, a guide, and he was making me get down and look at them. They were powdered with dust, bloodied like it had been painted on with a wide brush, some were blown out of their pants, just like they looked that day being thrown onto the truck at Can Tho, and I said, "But I've already seen them." My friend didn't say anything, he just pointed, and I leaned down again and this time I looked into their faces. New York City, 1975, when I got up the next morning I was laughing.

Hell Sucks

During the first weeks of the Tet Offensive the curfew began early in the afternoon and was strictly enforced. By 2:30 each day Saigon looked like the final reel of *On the Beach,* a desolate city whose long avenues held nothing but refuse, windblown papers, small distinct piles of human excrement and the dead flowers and spent firecracker casings of the Lunar New Year. Alive, Saigon had been depressing enough, but during the Offensive it became so stark that, in an odd way, it was invigorating. The trees along the main streets looked like they'd been struck by lightning, and it became unusually, uncomfortably cold, one more piece of freak luck in a place where nothing was in its season. With so much filth growing in so many streets and alleys, an epidemic of plague was feared, and if there was ever a place that suggested plague, demanded it, it was Saigon in the Emergency. American civilians, engineers and construction workers who were making it here like they'd never made it at home began forming into large armed bands, carrying .45's and grease guns and Swedish K's, and no mob of hysterical vigilantes ever promised more bad news. You'd see them at ten in the morning on the terrace of the Continental waiting for the bar to open, barely able to light their own cigarettes until it did. The crowds on Tu Do Street looked like Ensor proces- sioners, and there was a corruption in the air that had noth- ing to do with government workers on the take. After seven in the evening, when the curfew included Americans and became total, nothing but White Mice patrols and MP jeeps moved in the streets, except for a few young children who raced up and down over the rubbish, running newspaper kites up into the chilling wind.

We took a huge collective nervous breakdown, it was the compression and heat of heavy contact generated out until every American in Vietnam got a taste. Vietnam was a dark room full of deadly objects, the VC were everywhere all at once like spider cancer, and instead of losing the war in little pieces over years we lost it fast in under a week. After that, we were like the character in pop grunt mythology, dead but too dumb to lie down. Our worst dread of yellow peril became realized; we saw them now dying by the thousands all over the country, yet they didn't seem depleted, let alone exhausted, as the Mission was claiming by the fourth day. We took space back quickly, expensively, with total panic and close to maximum brutality. Our machine was devastating. And versatile. It could do everything but stop. As one American major said, in a successful attempt at attaining history, "We had to destroy Ben Tre in order to save it." That's how most of the country came back under what we called control, and how it remained essentially occupied by the Viet Cong and the North until the day years later when there were none of us left there.

The Mission Council joined hands and passed together through the Looking Glass. Our general's chariot was on fire, he was taking on smoke and telling us such incredible stories of triumph and victory that a few high-level Americans had to ask him to just cool it and let them do the talking. A British correspondent compared the Mission posture to the captain of the *Titanic* announcing, "There's no cause for alarm, we're only stopping briefly to take on a little ice."

By the time I got back to Saigon on the fourth day a lot of information from around the country had settled, and it was bad, even after you picked out the threads of rumor: like the one about the "Caucasians," obviously Americans, fighting for the VC, or the one about thousands of NVA executions in Hue and the "shallow graves" in the flats outside the city, both of which proved true. Almost as much as the grunts and the Vietnamese, Tet was pushing correspondents closer to the wall than they'd ever wanted to go. I realized later that, however childish I might remain, actual youth had been pressed out of me in just the three days that it took me to cross the sixty miles between Can Tho and Saigon. In Saigon, I saw friends flipping out almost completely; a few left, some took to their beds for days with the exhaustion of deep depression. I went the other way, hyper and agitated, until I was only doing three hours of sleep a night. A friend on the *Times* said he didn't mind his nightmares so much as the waking impulse to file on them. An old-timer who'd covered war since the Thirties heard us pissing and moaning about how *terrible* it was and he snorted, "Ha, I love you guys. You guys are beautiful. What the fuck did you think it was?" We thought it was already past the cut-off point where every war is just like every other war; if we knew how rough it was going to get, we might have felt better. After a few days the air routes opened again, and we went up to Hue.

Going in, there were sixty of us packed into a deuce-and-a-half, one of eight trucks moving in convoy from Phu Bai, bringing in over 300 replacements for the casualties taken in the earliest fighting south of the Perfume River. There had been a harsh, dark storm going on for days, and it turned the convoy route into a mudbed. It was terribly cold in the trucks, and the road was covered with leaves that had either been blown off the trees by the storm or torn away by our artillery, which had been heavy all along the road. Many of the houses had been completely collapsed, and not one had been left without pitting from shell fragments. Hundreds of refugees held to the side of the road as we passed, many of them wounded. The kids would laugh and shout, the old would look on with that silent tolerance for misery that made so many Americans uneasy, which was usually misread as indifference. But the younger men and women would often look at us with unmistakable contempt, pulling their cheering children back from the trucks.

We sat there trying to keep it up for each other, grinning at the bad weather and the discomfort, sharing the first fear, glad that we weren't riding point or closing the rear. They had been hitting our trucks regularly, and a lot of the convoys had been turned back. The houses that we passed so slowly made good cover for snipers, and one B-40 rocket could have made casualties out of a whole truckload of us. All the grunts were whistling, and no two were whistling the same tune, it sounded like a locker room before a game that nobody wanted to play. Or almost nobody. There was a black Marine called Philly Dog who'd been a gang lord in Philadelphia and who was looking forward to some street fighting after six months in the jungle, he could show the kickers what he could do with some city ground. (In Hue he turned out to be incredibly valuable. I saw him pouring out about a hundred rounds of .30-caliber fire into a breach in the wall, laughing, "You got to bring some to get some"; he seemed to be about the only man in Delta Company who hadn't been hurt yet.) And there was a Marine correspondent, Sergeant Dale Dye, who sat with a tall yellow flower sticking out of his helmet cover, a really outstanding target. He was rolling his eyes around and saying, "Oh yes, oh yes, Charlie's got his shit together here, this will be *bad*," and smiling happily. It was the same smile I saw a week later when a sniper's bullet tore up a wall two inches above his head, odd cause for amusement in anyone but a grunt. Everyone else in the truck had that wild haunted going-West look that said it was perfectly correct to be here where the fighting would be the worst, where you wouldn't have half of what you needed, where it was colder than Nam ever got. On their helmets and flak jackets they'd written the names of old operations, of girlfriends, their war names (FAR FROM FEARLESS, MICKEY'S MONKEY, AVENGER V, SHORT TIME SAFETY MOE), their fantasies (BORN TO LOSE, BORN TO RAISE HELL, BORN TO KILL, BORN TO DIE), their ongoing information (HELL SUCKS, TIME IS ON MY SIDE, JUST YOU AND ME GOD—RIGHT?). One kid called to me, "Hey man! You want a story, man? Here man, write this: I'm up there on 881, this was May, I'm just up there walkin' the ridgeline like a movie star and this Zip jumps up smack into me, lays his AK-47 fucking right *into* me, only he's so *amazed* at my *cool* I got my whole clip off 'fore he knew how to thank me for it. Grease one." After twenty kilometers of this, in spite of the black roiling sky ahead, we could see smoke coming up from the far side of the river, from the Citadel of Hue.

The bridge was down that spanned the canal dividing the village of An Cuu and the southern sector of Hue, blown the night before by the Viet Cong, and the forward area beyond the far bank wasn't thought to be secure, so we bivouacked in the village for the night. It had been completely deserted, and we set ourselves up in empty hootches, laying our poncho liners out over broken glass and shattered brick. At dusk, while we all stretched out along the canal bank eating dinner, two Marine gunships came down on us and began strafing us, sending burning tracers up along the canal, and we ran for cover, more surprised than scared. "Way to go, motherfucker, way to pinpoint the fuckin' enemy," one of the grunts said, and he set up his M-60 machine gun in case they came back. "I don't guess we got to take *that* shit," he said. Patrols were sent out, guards posted, and we went into the hootches to sleep. For some reason, we weren't even mortared that night.

In the morning we crossed the canal on a two-by-four and started walking in until we came across the first of the hundreds of civilian dead that we were to see in the next weeks: an old man arched over his straw hat and a little girl who'd been hit while riding her bicycle, lying there with her arm up like a reproach. They'd been lying out like that for a week, for the first time we were grateful for the cold.

Along the Perfume River's south bank there is a long, graceful park that separates Hue's most pleasant avenue, Le Loi, from the riverfront. People will talk about how they'd sit out there in the sun and watch the sampans moving down the river, or watch the girls bicycling up Le Loi, past the villas of officials and the French-architected University buildings. Many of those villas had been destroyed and much of the University permanently damaged. In the middle of the street a couple of ambulances from the German Mission had been blown up, and the Cercle Sportif was covered with bullet holes and shrapnel. The rain had brought up the green, it stretched out cased in thick white fog. In the park itself, four fat green dead lay sprawled around a tall, ornate cage, inside of which sat a small, shivering monkey. One of the correspondents along stepped over the corpses to feed it some fruit. (Days later, I came back to the spot. The corpses were gone, but so was the monkey. There had been so many refugees and so little food then, and someone must have eaten him.) The Marines of 2/5 had secured almost all of the central south bank and were now fanning out to the west, fighting and clearing one of the major canals. We were waiting for some decision on whether or not U.S. Marines would be going into the Citadel itself, but no one had any doubts about what that decision would be. We sat there taking in the dread by watching the columns of smoke across the river, receiving occasional sniper rounds, infrequent bursts of .50-caliber, watching the Navy LCU's on the river getting shelled from the wall. One Marine next to me was saying that it was just a damned shame, all them poor people, all them nice-looking houses, they even had a Shell station there. He was looking at the black napalm blasts and the wreckage along the wall. "Looks like the Imperial City's had the schnitz," he said.

The courtyard of the American compound in Hue was filled with puddles from the rain, and the canvas tops of the jeeps and trucks sagged with the weight of the water. It was the fifth day of the fighting, and everyone was still amazed that the NVA or the Cong had not hit the compound on the first night. An enormous white goose had come into the compound that night, and now his wings were heavy with the oil that had formed on the surface of the puddles. Every time a vehicle entered the yard he would beat his wings in a fury and scream, but he never left the compound and, as far as I knew, no one ever ate him.

Nearly 200 of us were sleeping in the two small rooms that had been the compound's dining quarters. The Army was not happy about having to billet so many of the Marines that were coming through, and they were absolutely furious about all the correspondents who were hanging around now, waiting until the fighting moved north across the river, into the Citadel. You were lucky to find space enough on the floor to lie down on, luckier if you found an empty stretcher to sleep on, and luckiest of all if the stretcher was new. All night long the few unbroken windows would rattle from the airstrikes across the river, and a mortar pit just outside fired incessantly. At two or three in the morning, Marines would come in from their patrols. They'd cross the room, not much caring whether they stepped on anyone or not. They'd turn their radios on and shout across the room to one another. "Really, can't you fellows show a bit more consideration?" a British correspondent said, and their laughter woke anyone who was not already up.

One morning there was a fire in the prison camp across the road from the compound. We saw the black smoke rising over the barbed wire that topped the camp wall and heard automatic weapons' fire. The prison was full of captured NVA and Viet Cong or Viet Cong suspects, the guards said that they'd started the fire to cover an escape. The ARVN and a few Americans were shooting blindly into the flames, and the bodies were burning where they fell. Civilian dead lay out on the sidewalks only a block from the compound, and the park by the river was littered with dead. It was cold and the sun never came out once, but the rain did things to the corpses that were worse in their way than anything the sun could have done. It was on one of those days that I realized that the only corpse I couldn't bear to look at would be the one I would never have to see.

It stayed cold and dark like that for the next ten days, and that damp gloom was the background for all the footage that we took out of the Citadel. What little sunlight there was caught the heavy motes of dust that blew up from the wreckage of the east wall, held it until everything you saw was filtered through it. And you saw things from unaccustomed angles, quick looks from a running crouch, or up from flat out, hearing the hard dry rattle of shrapnel scudding against the debris around you. With all of that dust blowing around, the acrid smell of cordite would hang in the air for a long time after firefights, and there was the CS gas that we'd fired at the NVA blowing back in over our positions. It was impossible to get a clean breath with all of that happening, and there was that other smell too that came up from the shattered heaps of stone wherever an airstrike had come in. It held to the lining of your nostrils and worked itself into the weave of your fatigues, and weeks later, miles away, you'd wake up at night and it would be in the room with you. The NVA had dug themselves so deeply into the wall that airstrikes had to open it meter by meter, dropping napalm as close as a hundred meters from our positions. Up on the highest point of the wall, on what had once been a tower, I looked across the Citadel's moat and saw the NVA moving quickly across the rubble of the opposing wall. We were close enough to be able to see their faces. A rifle went off a few feet to my right, and one of the running figures jerked back and dropped. A Marine sniper leaned out from his cover and grinned at me.

Between the smoke and the mist and the flying dust inside the Citadel, it was hard to call that hour between light and darkness a true dusk, but it was the time when most of us would open our C rations. We were only meters away from the worst of the fighting, not more than a Vietnamese city block in distance, and yet civilians kept appearing, smiling, shrugging, trying to get back to their homes. The Marines would try to menace them away at rifle point, shouting, "Di, di, *di,* you sorry-ass motherfuckers, go on, get the hell away from here!" and the refugees would smile, half bowing, and flit up one of the shattered streets. A little boy of about ten came up to a bunch of Marines from Charlie Company. He was laughing and moving his head from side to side in a funny way. The fierceness in his eyes should have told everyone what it was, but it had never occurred to most of the grunts that a Vietnamese child could be driven mad too, and by the time they understood it the boy had begun to go for their eyes and tear at their fatigues, spooking everyone, putting everyone really uptight, until a black grunt grabbed him from behind and held his arm. "C'mon, poor li'l baby, 'fore one a these grunt mothers shoots you," he said, and carried the boy to where the corpsmen were.

On the worst days, no one expected to get through it alive. A despair set in among members of the battalion that the older ones, the veterans of two other wars, had never seen before. Once or twice, when the men from Graves Registration took the personal effects from the packs and pockets of dead Marines, they found letters from home that had been delivered days before and were still unopened.

We were running some wounded onto the back of a half-ton truck, and one of the young Marines kept crying from his stretcher. His sergeant held both of his hands, and the Marine kept saying, "Shit, Sarge, I ain' gone make it. Oh damn, I'm gone die, ain't I?" "No you ain't gonna die, for Christ's sake," the sergeant said. "Oh yeah, Sarge, yeah, I am." "Crowley," the sergeant said, "you ain't hurt that bad. I want you to just shut the fuck up. You ain't done a thing except bitch ever since we got to this fucking Hue City." But the sergeant didn't really know. The kid had been hit in the throat, and you couldn't tell about those. Throat wounds were bad. Everyone was afraid of throat wounds.

We lucked out on our connections. At the battalion aid station we got a chopper that carried us and a dozen dead Marines to the base at Phu Bai, and three minutes after we landed there we caught a C-130 to Danang. Hitching in from the airfield, we found a Psyops officer who felt sorry for us and drove us all the way to the press center. As we came in the gate we could see that the net was up and the daily volleyball game between the Marines assigned to the press center was on.

"Where the hell have *you* guys been?" one of them asked. We looked pretty fucked up.

The inside of the dining room was freezing with air-conditioning. I sat at a table and ordered a hamburger and a brandy from one of the peasant girls who waited tables. I sat there for a couple of hours and ordered four more hamburgers and at least a dozen brandies. It wasn't possible, just not possible, to have been where we'd been before and to be where we were now, all in the same afternoon. One of the correspondents who had come back with me sat at another table, also by himself, and we looked at each other, shook our heads and laughed. I went to my room and took my boots and fatigues off and got into the shower. The water was incredibly hot, for a moment I thought I'd gone insane from it, and I sat down on the concrete floor for a long time, shaving there, soaping myself over and over. I dressed and went back to the dining room. The net was down now, one of the Marines said hello and asked me if I knew what the movie was going to be that night. I ordered a steak and another long string of brandies. When I left the correspondent was still sitting alone. I got into bed and smoked a joint. I was going back in the morning, it was understood, but why was it understood? All of my stuff was in order, ready for the five-o'clock wake-up. I finished the joint and shuddered off into sleep.

By the end of the week the wall had cost the Marines roughly one casualty for every meter taken, a quarter of them KIA. 1/5, which came to be known as the Citadel Battalion, had been through every tough battle the Marines had had in the past six months, they'd even fought the same NVA units a few weeks before between Hai Vanh Pass and Phu Loc, and now three of its companies were below platoon strength. They all knew how bad it was, the novelty of fighting in a city had become a nasty joke, everyone wanted to get wounded.

At night in the CP, the major who commanded the battalion would sit reading his maps, staring vacantly at the trapezoid of the Citadel. It could have been a scene in a Norman farmhouse twenty-five years ago, with candles burning on the tables, bottles of red wine arranged along damaged shelves, the chill in the room, the high ceilings, the heavy ornate cross on the wall. The major had not slept for five nights, and for the fifth night in a row he assured us that tomorrow would get it for sure, the final stretch of wall would be taken and he had all the Marines he needed to do it. And one of his aides, a tough mustang first lieutenant, would pitch a hard, ironic smile above the major's stare, a smile that rejected good news, it was like hearing him say, "The major here is full of shit, and we both know it."

Sometimes a company would find itself completely cut off, and it would take hours for the Marines to get their wounded out. I remember one Marine with a headwound who finally made it to the Battalion CP when the jeep he was in stalled. He finally jumped out and started to push, knowing it was the only way out of there. Most of the tanks and trucks that carried casualties had to move up a long straight road without cover, and they began calling it Rocket Alley. Every tank the Marines had there had been hit at least once. An epiphany of Hue appeared in John Olson's great photograph for *Life*, the wounded from Delta Company hurriedly piled on a tank. Sometimes, on the way to the aid station the more seriously wounded would take on that bad color, the gray-blue fishbelly promise of death that would spread upward from the chest and cover the face. There was one Marine who had been shot through the neck, and all the way out the corpsmen massaged his chest. By the time they reached the station, though, he was so bad that the doctor triaged him, passed him over to treat the ones that he knew could still be saved, and when they put him into the green rubber body bag there was some chance that he was clinically alive. The doctor had never had to make choices like that before, and he wasn't getting used to it. During the lulls he'd step outside for some air, but it was no better out there. The bodies were stacked together and there was always a crowd of ARVN standing around staring, death-enthralled like all Vietnamese. Since they didn't know what else to do, and not knowing what it would look like to the Marines, they would smile at the bodies there, and a couple of ugly incidents occurred. The Marines who worked the body detail were overloaded and rushed and became snappish, ripping packs off of corpses angrily, cutting gear away with bayonets, heaving bodies into the green bags. One of the dead Marines had gone stiff and they had trouble getting him to fit. *"Damn,"* one of them said, "this fucker had big feet. Didn't this fucker have big feet," as he finally forced the legs inside. In the station there was the youngest-looking Marine I'd ever seen. He'd been caught in the knee by a large piece of shrapnel, and he had no idea of what they'd do with him now that he was wounded. He lay out on the stretcher while the doctor explained how he would be choppered back to Phu Bai hospital and then put on a plane for Danang and then flown back to the States for what would certainly be the rest of his tour. At first the boy was sure that the doctor was kidding him, then he started to believe it, and then he knew it was true, he was actually getting out, he couldn't stop smiling, and enormous tears ran down into his ears.

It was at this point that I began to recognize almost every

casualty, remember conversations we'd had days or even hours earlier, and that's when I left, riding a medevac with a lieutenant who was covered with blood-soaked bandages. He'd been hit in both legs, both arms, the chest and head, his ears and eyes were full of caked blood, and he asked a photographer in the chopper to get a picture of him like this to send to his wife.

But by then the battle for Hue was almost over. The Cav was working the northwest corner of the Citadel, and elements of the 101st had come in through what had formerly been an NVA re-supply route. (In five days these outfits lost as many men as the Marines had in three weeks.) Vietnamese Marines and some of the 1st ARVN Division had been moving the remaining NVA down toward the wall. The NVA flag that had flown for so long over the south wall had been cut down, and in its place an American flag had been put up. Two days later the Hoc Bao, Vietnamese Rangers, stormed through the walls of the Imperial Palace, but there were no NVA left inside. Except for a few bodies in the moat, most of their dead had been buried. When they'd first come into Hue the NVA had sat at banquets given for them by the people. Before they left, they'd skimmed all the edible vegetation from the surface of the moat. Seventy percent of Vietnam's one lovely city was destroyed, and if the landscape seemed desolate, imagine how the figures in that landscape looked.

There were two official ceremonies marking the expulsion of the NVA, both flag-raisings. On the south bank of the Perfume River, 200 refugees from one of the camps were recruited to stand, sullen and silent in the rain, and watch the GVN flag being run up. But the rope snapped, and the crowd, thinking the VC had shot it down, broke up in panic. (There was no rain in the stories that the Saigon papers ran, no trouble with the rope, and the cheering crowd numbered thousands.) As for the other ceremony, the Citadel was thought by most people to be insecure, and when the flag finally went up there was no one to watch it except for a handful of Vietnamese troops.

Major Trong bounced around in the seat of his jeep as it drove us over the debris scattered across the streets of Hue. His face seemed completely expressionless as we passed the crowds of Vietnamese stumbling over the fallen beams and powdered brick of their homes, but his eyes were covered by dark glasses and it was impossible to know what he was feeling. He didn't look like a victor, he was so small and limp in his seat I was afraid he was going to fly out of the jeep. His driver was a sergeant named Dang, one of the biggest Vietnamese I'd ever seen, and his English was better than the major's. The jeep would stall on rubble heaps from time to time, and Dang would turn to us and smile an apology. We were on our way to the Imperial Palace.

A month earlier the Palace grounds had been covered with dozens of dead NVA and the burned-over leavings of three weeks' siege and defense. There had been some reluctance about bombing the Palace, but a lot of the bombing nearby had done heavy damage, and there had been some shelling, too. The large bronze urns were dented beyond restoring, and the rain poured through a hole in the roof of the throne room, soaking the two small thrones where the old Annamese royalty had sat. In the great hall (great once you'd scaled it to the Vietnamese) the red lacquer work on the upper walls was badly chipped, and a heavy dust covered everything. The crown of the main gate had collapsed, and in the garden the broken branches of the old cay-dai trees lay like the forms of giant insects seared in a fire, wispy, delicate, dead. It was rumored during those days that the Palace was being held by a unit of student volunteers who had taken the invasion of Hue as a sign and had rushed to join the North Vietnamese. (Another rumor of those days, the one about some 5,000 "shallow graves" outside the city, containing the bodies from NVA executions, had just now been shown to be true.)

But once the walls had been taken and the grounds entered, there was no one left inside except for the dead. They bobbed in the moat and littered all the approaches. The Marines moved in then, and empty ration cans and muddied sheets from the *Stars and Stripes* were added to the litter. A fat Marine had been photographed pissing into the locked-open mouth of a decomposing North Vietnamese soldier.

"No good," Major Trong said. "No good. Fight here very hard, very bad."

I'd been talking to Sergeant Dang about the Palace and about the line of emperors. When we stalled one last time at the foot of a moat bridge, I'd been asking him the name of the last emperor to occupy the throne. He smiled and shrugged, not so much as if he didn't know, more like it didn't matter.

"Major Trong is emperor now," he said, and gunned the jeep into the Palace grounds.

Khe Sanh

I

During the bad maximum incoming days of the late winter of
1968 there was a young Marine at Khe Sanh whose Vietnam
tour had run out. Nearly five of his thirteen months in-
country had been spent there at the Khe Sanh Combat Base
with the 26th Marines, who had been slowly building to full
and then reinforced regimental strength since the previous
spring. He could remember a time, not long before, when the
26th considered themselves lucky to be there, when the guys
talked of it as though it were a reward for whatever their
particular outfits had been through. As far as this Marine
was concerned, the reward was for an ambush that fall on
the Cam Lo–Con Thien road, when his unit had taken 40
percent casualties, when he himself had taken shrapnel in the
chest and arms. (Oh, he'd tell you, but he had seen some shit
in this war.) That was when Con Thien was the name everyone knew, long before Khe Sanh had taken on the proportions of a siege camp and lodged itself as an obsession in the
heart of the Command, long before a single round had ever
fallen inside the perimeter to take off his friends and make his
sleep something indistinguishable from waking. He remembered when there was time to play in the streams below the
plateau of the base, when all anybody ever talked about were
the six shades of green that touched the surrounding hills,
when he and his friends had lived like human beings, above
ground, in the light, instead of like animals who were so
spaced out that they began taking pills called Diarrhea-Aid

to keep their walks to exposed latrines at a minimum. And on this last morning of his tour, he might have told you that he'd been through it all and hacked it pretty well.

He was a tall blond from Michigan, probably about twenty, although it was never easy to guess the ages of Marines at Khe Sanh since nothing like youth ever lasted in their faces for very long. It was the eyes: because they were always either strained or blazed-out or simply blank, they never had anything to do with what the rest of the face was doing, and it gave everyone the look of extreme fatigue or even a glancing madness. (And age. If you take one of those platoon photographs from the Civil War and cover everything but the eyes, there is no difference between a man of fifty and a boy of thirteen.) This Marine, for example, was always smiling. It was the kind of smile that verged on the high giggles, but his eyes showed neither amusement nor embarrassment nor nervousness. It was a little insane, but it was mostly esoteric in the way that so many Marines under twenty-five became esoterics after a few months in I Corps. On that young, nondescript face the smile seemed to come out of some old knowledge, and it said, "I'll tell you why I'm smiling, but it will make you crazy."

He had tattooed the name MARLENE on his upper arm, and up on his helmet there was the name JUDY, and he said, "Yeah, well, Judy knows all about Marlene. That's cool, there's no sweat there." On the back of his flak jacket he had once written, *Yea, though I walk through the Valley of the Shadow of Death I shall fear no Evil, because I'm the meanest motherfucker in the Valley,* but he had tried later, without much success, to scrub it off because, he explained, every damn dude in the DMZ had that written on their flak jackets. And he'd smile.

He was smiling on this last morning of his tour. His gear was straight, his papers in order, his duffel packed, and he was going through all of the last-minute business of going home, the back-slapping and goosing; the joshing with the Old Man ("Come on, you know you're gonna miss this place." "Yes sir. Oh wow!"); the exchanging of addresses; the odd, fragmented reminiscences blurted out of awkward silences. He had a few joints left, wrapped up in a plastic bag (he hadn't smoked them, because, like most Marines at Khe Sanh, he'd expected a ground attack, and he didn't want to be stoned when it came), and he gave these to his best friend, or, rather, his best surviving friend. His oldest friend had been blown away in January, on the same day that the ammo dump had been hit. He had always wondered whether Gunny, the company gunnery sergeant, had known about all the smoking. After three wars Gunny probably didn't care much; besides, they all knew that Gunny was into some pretty cool shit himself. When he dropped by the bunker they said goodbye, and then there wasn't anything to do with the morning but to run in and out of the bunker for a look at the sky, coming back in every time to say that it really ought to clear enough by ten for the planes to get in. By noon, when the goodbyes and take-cares and get-a-little-for-me's had gone on for too long by hours, the sun started to show through the mist. He picked up his duffel and a small AWOL bag and started for the airstrip and the small, deep slit trench on the edge of the strip.

Khe Sanh was a very bad place then, but the airstrip there was the worst place in the world. It was what Khe Sanh had instead of a V-ring, the exact, predictable object of the mortars and rockets hidden in the surrounding hills, the sure target of the big Russian and Chinese guns lodged in the side of CoRoc Ridge, eleven kilometers away across the Laotian border. There was nothing random about the shelling there, and no one wanted anything to do with it. If the wind was right, you could hear the NVA .50-calibers starting far up the valley whenever a plane made its approach to the strip, and the first incoming artillery would precede the landings by seconds. If you were waiting there to be taken out, there was nothing you could do but curl up in the trench and try to make yourself small, and if you were coming in on the plane, there was nothing you could do, nothing at all.

There was always the debris of one kind of aircraft or another piled up on or near the strip, and sometimes the damage would cause the strip to be closed off for hours while the Seabees or the 11th Engineers did the clearing. It was so bad, so predictably bad, that the Air Force stopped flying in their star transport, the C-130, and kept to the smaller, more maneuverable C-123. Whenever possible, loads were parachuted in on pallet drops from 1,500 feet, pretty blue-and-yellow chutes, a show, dropping down around the perimeter. But obviously, passengers had to be flown in or picked up on the ground. These were mostly replacements, guys going to or returning from R&R's, specialists of one kind or another, infrequent brass (most staff from Division and higher made their own travel arrangements for Khe Sanh) and a lot of correspondents. While a planeload of passengers tensed and sweated and made the run for the trench over and over in their heads, waiting for the cargo hatch to drop, ten to fifty Marines and correspondents huddled down in the trench, worked their lips futilely to ease the dryness, and then, at the exact same instant, they would all race, collide, stampede, exchanging places. If the barrage was a particularly heavy one, the faces would all distort in the most simple kind of panic, the eyes going wider than the eyes of horses caught in a fire. What you saw was a translucent blur, sensible only at the immediate center, like a swirly-chic photograph of Carnival, and you'd glimpse a face, a shell fragment cased in white sparks, a piece of gear somehow suspended in air, a drift of smoke, and you'd move around the flight crews working the heavy cargo strapping, over scout dogs, over the casually arranged body bags that always lay not far from the strip, covered with flies. And men would still be struggling on or off as the aircraft turned slowly to begin the taxi before the most accelerated take-off the machine had it in it to make. If you were on board, that first movement was an ecstasy. You'd all sit there with empty, exhausted grins, covered with the impossible red dust that laterite breaks down to, dust like scales, feeling the delicious afterchill of the fear, that one quick convulsion of safety. There was no feeling in the world as good as being airborne out of Khe Sanh.

On this last morning, the young Marine caught a ride from his company position that dropped him off fifty meters from the strip. As he moved on foot he heard the distant sound of the C-123 coming in, and that was all he heard. There was hardly more than a hundred-foot ceiling, scary, bearing down on him. Except for the approaching engines, everything was still. If there had been something more, just one incoming round, he might have been all right, but in that silence the sound of his own feet moving over the dirt was terrifying to him. He later said that this was what made him stop. He dropped his duffel and looked around. He watched the plane, his plane, as it touched down, and then he ran leaping over some discarded sandbags by the road. He lay out flat and listened as the plane switched loads and took off, listened until there was nothing left to listen to. Not a single round had come in.

Back at the bunker there was some surprise at his return, but no one said anything. Anyone can miss a plane. Gunny slapped him on the back and wished him a better trip the next time out. That afternoon he rode in a jeep that took him all the way to Charlie Med, the medical detachment for Khe Sanh that had been set up insanely close to the strip, but he never got himself past the sandbagging outside of the triage room.

"Oh no, you raggedy-assed bastard," Gunny said when he got back to the outfit. But he looked at him for a long while this time.

"Well," the kid said. "Well. . . ."

The next morning two of his friends went with him to the edge of the strip and saw him into the trench. ("Goodbye," Gunny said. "And that's an order.") They came back to say that he'd gotten out for sure this time. An hour later he came up the road again, smiling. He was still there the first time I left Khe Sanh, and while he probably made it out eventually, you can't be sure.

Such odd things happen when tours are almost over. It's the Short-Timer Syndrome. In the heads of the men who are really in the war for a year, all tours end early. No one expects much from a man when he is down to one or two weeks. He becomes a luck freak, an evil-omen collector, a diviner of every bad sign. If he has the imagination, or the experience of war, he will precognize his own death a thousand times a day, but he will always have enough left to do the one big thing, to Get Out.

Something more was working on the young Marine, and Gunny knew what it was. In this war they called it "acute environmental reaction," but Vietnam has spawned a jargon of such delicate locutions that it's often impossible to know even remotely the thing being described. Most Americans would rather be told that their son is undergoing acute environmental reaction than to hear that he is suffering from shell shock, because they could no more cope with the fact of shell shock than they could with the reality of what had happened to this boy during his five months at Khe Sanh.

Say that his legs just weren't working. It was clearly a medical matter, and the sergeant was going to have to see that something was done about it. But when I left, the kid was still there, sitting relaxed on his duffel and smiling, saying, "Man, when I get home, I'll have it knocked."

II

The terrain above II Corps, where it ran along the Laotian border and into the DMZ, was seldom referred to as the Highlands by Americans. It had been a matter of military expediency to impose a new set of references over Vietnam's older, truer being, an imposition that began most simply with the division of one country into two and continued—it had its logic—with the further division of South Vietnam into four clearly defined tactical corps. It had been one of the exigencies of the war, and if it effectively obliterated even some of the most obvious geographical distinctions, it made for clear communication, at least among members of the Mission and the many components of the Military Assistance Command, Vietnam, the fabulous MACV. In point of geographical fact, for example, the delta of Vietnam comprehends the Plain of Reeds and frames the Saigon River, but on all the charts and deep in all the sharp heads, it ended at the map line dividing III and IV Corps. Referentially, the Highlands were confined to II Corps, ending abruptly at the line which got drawn just below the coastal city of Chu Lai; everything between that and the DMZ was just I Corps. All in-country briefings, at whatever level, came to sound like a Naming of the Parts, and the language was used as a cosmetic, but one that diminished beauty. Since most of the journalism from the war was framed in that language or proceeded from the view of the war which those terms implied, it would be as impossible to know what Vietnam looked like from reading most newspaper stories as it would be to know how it smelled. Those Highlands didn't simply vanish at the corps border, but went all the way up into a section of North Vietnam that Navy fliers called the Armpit, running in a chain with the wonderful name of the Annamese Cordillera that spanned more than 1,700 miles from the Armpit to a point just below Pleiku, cutting through much of the North, through the DMZ, through the valley fastness (theirs) of the A Shau, and through the piedmont that was once the Marine Combat Base of Khe Sanh. And since the country it traversed was very special, with its special evocations, my insistence on placing Khe Sanh there is much more than some recondite footnote to a history of that sad place and the particular ways in which so many Americans suffered their part of the war there.

Because the Highlands of Vietnam are spooky, unbearably spooky, spooky beyond belief. They are a run of erratic mountain ranges, gnarled valleys, jungled ravines and abrupt plains where Montagnard villages cluster, thin and disappear as the terrain steepens. The Montagnards in all of their tribal components make up the most primitive and mysterious portion of the Vietnamese population, a population that has always confused Americans even in its most Westernized segments. Strictly speaking, the Montagnards are not really Vietnamese at all, certainly not *South* Vietnamese, but a kind of upgraded, demi-enlightened Annamese aborigine, often living in nakedness and brooding silence in their villages. Most Vietnamese and most Montagnards consider each other inferior, and while many Montagnards hired out as mercenaries to the American Special Forces, that older, racially based enmity often slowed down the Allied effort. Many Americans considered them to be nomadic, but the war had had more to do with that than anything in their temperament. We napalmed off their crops and flattened their villages, and then admired the restlessness in their spirit. Their nakedness, their painted bodies, their recalcitrance, their silent composure before strangers, their benign savagery and the sheer, awesome ugliness of them combined to make most Americans who were forced to associate with them a little uncomfortable over the long run. It would seem fitting, ordained, that they should live in the Highlands, among triple canopies, where sudden, contrary mists offered sinister bafflement, where the daily heat and the nighttime cold kept you perpetually, increasingly, on edge, where the silences were interrupted only by the sighing of cattle or the rotor-thud of a helicopter, the one sound I know that is both sharp and dull at the same time. The Puritan belief that Satan dwelt in Nature could have been born here, where even on the coldest, freshest mountaintops you could smell jungle and that tension between rot and genesis that all jungles give off. It is ghost-story country, and for Americans it had been the scene of some of the war's vilest surprises. The Ia Drang battles of late 1965 constituted the first and worst of these surprises. They marked the first wholesale appearance of North Vietnamese regulars in the South, and no one who was around then can ever forget the horror of it or, to this day, get over the confidence and sophistication with which entire battalions came to engage Americans in a war. A few correspondents, a few soldiers back for second and third tours still shuddered uncontrollably at what they remembered: impromptu positions held to the last man and then overrun; Americans and North Vietnamese stiff in one another's death embrace, their eyes wide open, their teeth bared or sunk deep into enemy flesh; the number of helicopters shot down (relief mission after relief mission after relief mission . . .); the NVA equipment hauls which included the first AK-47 assault rifles, the first RPG-7 rockets, the hundreds of aluminum grave markers. No, a lot of the ones who saw that, the toughest of them, didn't even like to talk about it. The very best of our divisions, the 1st Air Cavalry, was blooded in the Ia Drang that autumn, and while the official number of dead was released at around 300, I never met anyone who had been there, including officers of the Cav, who would settle for less than three or even four times that figure.

There is a point of view that says that the United States got involved in the Vietnam War, commitments and interests aside, simply because we thought it would be easy. But after the Ia Drang, that first arrogance sat less and less well about the shoulders of the Command; it never vanished. There was never again a real guerrilla war after Ia Drang, except in the Delta, and the old Giap stratagem of interdicting the South through the Highlands, cutting the country in two, came to be taken seriously, even obsessively, by many influential Americans.

Oh, that terrain! The bloody, maddening uncanniness of it! When the hideous Battle of Dak To ended at the top of Hill 875, we announced that 4,000 of them had been killed; it had been the purest slaughter, our losses were bad, but clearly it was another American victory. But when the top of the hill was reached, the number of NVA found was four. Four. Of course more died, hundreds more, but the corpses kicked and counted and photographed and buried numbered four. Where, Colonel? And how, and why? Spooky. Everything up there was spooky, and it would have been that way even if there had been no war. You were there in a place where you didn't belong, where things were glimpsed for which you would have to pay and where things went unglimpsed for which you would also have to pay, a place where they didn't play with the mystery but killed you straight off for trespassing. The towns had names that laid a quick, chilly touch on your bones: Kontum, Dak Mat Lop, Dak Roman Peng, Poli Klang, Buon Blech, Pleiku, Pleime, Plei Vi Drin. Just moving through those towns or being based somewhere above them spaced you out, and every time I'd have that vision of myself lying dead somewhere, it was always up there, in the Highlands. It was enough to make an American commander sink to his knees and plead, "O God! Just *once,* let it be our way. We have the strength, give us the terms!" Not even the Cav, with their style and courage and mobility, were able to penetrate that abiding Highland face. They killed a lot of Communists, but that was all they did, because the number of Communist dead meant nothing, changed nothing.

Sean Flynn, photographer and connoisseur of the Vietnam War, told me that he once stood on the vantage of a firebase up there with a battalion commander. It was at dusk, those ghastly mists were fuming out of the valley floor, ingesting light. The colonel squinted at the distance for a long time. Then he swept his hand very slowly along the line of jungle, across the hills and ridges running into Cambodia (the Sanctuary!). "Flynn," he said. "Somewhere out there . . . is the *entire First NVA Division."*

O dear God, just once!

III

Somewhere Out There, within artillery range of the Khe Sanh Combat Base, within a twenty-mile radius, a day's march, assuming the "attack posture," concealed and silent and ominous, lay five full divisions of North Vietnamese Regulars. This was the situation during the closing weeks of 1967:

Somewhere to the southwest was the 304th NVA Division.

Due east (somewhere) was the 320th. The 325C was deployed in an unknown fashion to the northwest, and the 324B (a cause for real alarm among enemy-division buffs) was somewhere to the northeast. There was also an unidentified division just the other side of the Laotian border, where their big artillery had been dug so deeply into the mountainsides that not even our B-52's could harm them. All of that terrain, all of that cover, ridge after ridge, murderous slides and gorges, all cloaked by triple canopy and thick monsoon mists. And whole divisions were out there in that.

Marine Intelligence (While I see many hoof-marks going in, I see none coming out), backed by the findings of increasing Air Force reconnaissance missions, had been watching and evaluating the build-up with alarm since spring. Khe Sanh had always been in the vicinity of major infiltration routes, "sat astride" them, as the Mission put it. That slight but definite plateau, rising abruptly from the foothills bridging Laos and Vietnam, had been of value for as long as the Vietnamese had been at war. The routes now used by the NVA had been used twenty years earlier by the Viet Minh. Khe Sanh's original value to the Americans might be gauged by the fact that in spite of the known infiltration all around it, we held it for years with nothing more than a Special Forces A Team; less than a dozen Americans and around 400 indigenous troops, Vietnamese and Montagnard. When the Special Forces first moved in there in 1962, they built their teamhouse, outbuildings, club and defenses over bunkers that had been left by the French. Infiltrating columns simply diverted their routes a kilometer or so away from the central Khe Sanh position. The Green Berets ran out regular, extremely cautious patrols. Since they were almost always surrounded by the infiltrators, Khe Sanh was not the most comfortable duty in Vietnam, but there was seldom anything more than the random ambush or the occasional mortaring that was standard for A Teams anywhere in-country. If the NVA had considered Khe Sanh tactically crucial or even important, they could have taken it at any time. And if we had thought of it as anything more than a token outpost—you can't have infiltrators running around without putting someone in there for a look—we could have created it as a major base. No one builds bases like Americans.

In the course of routine patrols during the early spring of 1966, Special Forces reported what appeared to be a significant increase in the number of enemy troops in the immediate Khe Sanh area, and a battalion of Marines was sent to reinforce the patrols. A year later, in April and May of 1967, during large but routine Search-and-Destroy operations, the Marines found and engaged battalion-strength units of North Vietnamese holding the tops of Hills 881 North and South, and a lot of people were killed on both sides. The battles grew into the bloodiest of the spring. The hills were taken and, weeks later, abandoned. The Marines that might have maintained the hills (Where better to observe infiltration than from a vantage of 881 meters?) were sent instead to Khe Sanh, where the 1st and 3rd Battalions of the 26th Marine Regiment rotated, increasing their harassment of the NVA, hoping, if not to drive them out of the sector, to at least force their movements into predictable patterns. The 26th, a hybrid regiment, was formed out of the TAOR of the 5th Marine Division, a numerical designation which remained on paper even after the actual command of the regiment became the responsibility of the 3rd Marine Division, headquartered at Dong Ha, nearby in the DMZ.

By summer, it became obvious that the battles for 881 North and South had engaged a relatively small number of the enemy thought to be in the area. Patrols were stepped up (they were now thought to be among the most dangerous in I Corps), and additional elements of the 26th Marines were airlifted into what was now being called the Khe Sanh Combat Base. The Seabees laid down a 600-meter tarmac airstrip. A beer hall and an air-conditioned officers' club were built, and the regimental command set up its Tactical Operations Center in the largest of the deserted French bunkers. Yet Khe Sanh continued to be only a moderate, private concern of the Marine Corps. A few old hands in the press corps knew vaguely about the base and about the small ville of about a thousand Montagnards which lay four kilometers to the south. It was not until November, when the regiment had grown to full and then reinforced strength (6,000 Marines, not including units added from the 9th Marine Regiment), with 600 Vietnamese Rangers, two detachments of Seabees, a helicopter squadron and a small Special Forces Compound, that the Marines began "leaking" the rather remarkable claim that by building up the base we had lured an unbelievable number of enemy to the area.

It was at about this time that copies of the little red British paperback edition of Jules Roy's *The Battle of Dienbienphu* began appearing wherever members of the Vietnam press corps gathered. You'd spot them around the terrace bar of the Continental Hotel, in L'Amiral Restaurant and Aterbea, at the 8th Aerial Port of Tan Son Nhut, in the Marine-operated Danang Press Center and in the big briefing room of JUSPAO in Saigon, where every afternoon at 4:45 spokesmen conducted the daily war briefing which was colloquially referred to as the Five O'Clock Follies, an Orwellian grope through the day's events as seen by the Mission. (It was very hard-line.) Those who could find copies were reading Bernard Fall's Dien Bien Phu book, *Hell in a Very Small Place,* which many considered the better book, stronger on tactics, more businesslike, with none of the high-level staff gossip that made the Roy book so dramatic. And as the first Marine briefings on Khe Sanh took place in Marine headquarters at Danang or Dong Ha, the name Dien Bien Phu insinuated itself like some tasteless ghost hawking bad news. Marines who had to talk to the press found references to the old French disaster irritating and even insulting. Most were not interested in fielding questions about it, and the rest were unequipped. The more irritated they became, the more the press would flaunt the irritant. For a while it looked like nothing that had happened on the ground during those weeks seemed as thrilling and sinister as the recollection of Dien Bien Phu. And it had to be admitted, the parallels with Khe Sanh were irresistible.

To begin with, the ratio between attackers and defenders was roughly the same, eight to one. The terrain was hauntingly similar, although Khe Sanh was only two square miles inside its perimeter, as opposed to the sprawl of Dien Bien Phu. The weather conditions were the same, with the monsoons favoring the attackers by keeping American air activity at a minimum. Khe Sanh was now encircled, as Dien Bien Phu had been, and where the initial attacks of March 1954 had been launched from Viet Minh trenches, the NVA had begun digging a network of trenches that would soon approach to within a hundred yards of the Marine wire. Dien Bien Phu had been the master plan of General Vo Nguyen Giap; rumors splintered from American Intelligence suggested that Giap himself was directing the Khe Sanh operation from a post somewhere above the DMZ. Given the fact that a lot of Marine officers did not understand what we were doing at Khe Sanh in the first place, the repeated evocations of Dien Bien Phu were unnerving. But then, on what briefers liked to call "our side of the ledger," there were important differences.

The base at Khe Sanh was raised, if only slightly, on a

plateau which would have slowed a ground attack and given the Marines a gentle vantage from which to fire. The Marines also had a massive reaction force to count on, or at least to hope for. For publication, this consisted of the 1st Air Cavalry Division and elements of the 101st Airborne, but in fact the force numbered almost a quarter of a million men, men at support firebases across the DMZ, planners in Saigon (and Washington) and, most important of all, pilots and crews from headquarters as far away as Udorn, Guam, and Okinawa, men whose energies and attentions became fixed almost exclusively on Khe Sanh missions. Air support was everything, the cornerstone of all our hopes at Khe Sanh, and we knew that once the monsoons lifted, it would be nothing to drop tens of thousands of tons of high explosives and napalm all around the base, to supply it without strain, to cover and reinforce the Marines.

It was a comfort, all of that power and precision and exquisitely geared clout. It meant a lot to the thousands of Marines at Khe Sanh, to the Command, to correspondents spending a few days and nights at the base, to officials in the Pentagon. We could all sleep easier for it: lance corporals and General Westmoreland, me and the President, Navy medics and the parents of all the boys inside the wire. All any of us had to worry about was the fact that Khe Sanh was vastly outnumbered and entirely surrounded; that, and the knowledge that all ground evacuation routes, including the vital Route 9, were completely controlled by the NVA, and that the monsoons had at least six weeks more to run.

There was a joke going around that went like this: "What's the difference between the Marine Corps and the Boy Scouts?" "The Boy Scouts have adult leadership." Dig it! the grunts would say, digging it just as long as they didn't have to hear it from outsiders, from "non-essential personnel" like the Army or the Air Force. For them it was only good as a joke when it also had that touch of fraternal mystery. And what a fraternity! If the war in I Corps was a matter for specialization among correspondents, it was not because it was inherently different as war, but because it was fought almost exclusively by the Marines, whose idiosyncrasies most reporters found intolerable and even criminal. (There was a week in the war, one week, when the Army lost more men killed, proportionately, than the Marines, and Army spokesmen had a rough time hiding their pride, their absolute glee.) And in the face of some new variation on old Marine disasters, it didn't much matter that you knew dozens of fine, fine officers. Something almost always went wrong somewhere, somehow. It was always something vague, unexplainable, tasting of bad fate, and the results were always brought down to their most basic element—the dead Marine. The belief that one Marine was better than ten Slopes saw Marine squads fed in against known NVA platoons, platoons against companies, and on and on, until whole battalions found themselves pinned down and cut off. That belief was undying, but the grunt was not, and the Corps came to be called by many the finest instrument ever devised for the killing of young Americans. There were always plenty of stories about entire squads wiped out (their mutilated bodies would so enrage Marines that they would run out "vengeance patrols" which often enough ended the same way), companies taking 75 percent casualties, Marines ambushing Marines, artillery and airstrikes called in on our own positions, all in the course of routine Search-and-Destroy operations. And you knew that, sooner or later, if you went with them often enough, it would happen to you too.

And the grunts themselves knew: the madness, the bitterness, the horror and doom of it. They were hip to it, and more: they savored it. It was no more insane than most of what was going down, and often enough it had its refracted logic. "Eat the apple, fuck the Corps," they'd say, and write it up on their helmets and flak jackets for their officers to see. (One kid tattooed it on his shoulder.) And sometimes they'd look at you and laugh silently and long, the laugh on them and on you for being with them when you didn't have to be. And what could be funnier, really, given all that an eighteen-year-old boy could learn in a month of patrolling the Z? It was that joke at the deepest part of the blackest kernel of fear, and you could die laughing. They even wrote a song, a letter to the mother of a dead Marine, that went something like, "Tough shit, tough shit, your kid got greased, but what the fuck, he was just a grunt. . . ." They got savaged a lot and softened a lot, their secret brutalized them and darkened them and very often it made them beautiful. It took no age, seasoning or education to make them know exactly where true violence resided.

And they were killers. Of course they were; what would anyone expect them to be? It absorbed them, inhabited them, made them strong in the way that victims are strong, filled them with the twin obsessions of Death and Peace, fixed them so that they could never, never again speak lightly about the Worst Thing in the World. If you learned just this much about them, you were never quite as happy (in the miserable-joyous way of covering the war) with other outfits. And, naturally, the poor bastards were famous all over Vietnam. If you spent some weeks up there and afterward joined an Army outfit of, say, the 4th or 25th Division, you'd get this:

"Where you been? We ain't seen you."

"Up in I Corps."

"With the *Marines?*"

"That's what's up there."

"Well, all I got to say is Good Luck! Marines. Fuck that."

"Khe Sanh is the Western Anchor of our defense," the Commanding General offered.

"Who told you that?" the Examining Angels replied.

"Why . . . everybody!"

No Marine ever called it that, not even those officers who believed in it tactically, just as no Marine ever called what happened there for seventy-six days a "siege." Those were MACV conceits, often taken up by the press, and they angered Marines. As long as the 26th Marines could maintain a battalion outside the wire (the garrison at Khesanville was withdrawn and the town bombed flat, but Marines still patrolled beyond the perimeter and lived on nearby hilltops), as long as planes could re-supply the base, it could not be a siege. Marines may get beleaguered, but not besieged. Whatever one chose to call it, by the time of the Tet Offensive, a week after the shelling of Khe Sanh began, it looked as though both sides had committed themselves on such a scale that engagement was inevitable. No one I knew doubted that it would come, probably in the form of a massive ground attack, and that when it came it would be terrible and great.

Tactically, its value to the Command was thought so great that General Westmoreland could announce that the Tet Offensive was merely Phase II of a brilliant Giap strategy. Phase I had been revealed in the autumn skirmishes between Loc Ninh and Dak To. Phase III ("the capstone," the general called it) was to be Khe Sanh. It seems impossible that anyone, at any time, even in the chaos of Tet, could have actually called something as monumental (and decisive?) as that offensive a mere diversion for something as negligible as Khe Sanh, but all of that is on record.

And by then, Khe Sanh was famous, one of the very few place names in Vietnam that was recognized by the American public. Khe Sanh said "siege," it said "encircled Marines" and "heroic defenders." It could be understood by newspaper readers quickly, it breathed Glory and War and Honored Dead. It seemed to make sense. It was good stuff. One can only imagine the anxiety which the Commander in Chief suffered over it. Lyndon Johnson said it straight out, he did not want "any damn Dinbinfoo," and he did something unprecedented in the history of warfare. The Joint Chiefs of Staff were summoned and made to sign a statement "for the public reassurance," asserting that Khe Sanh could and would be held at all costs. (Apparently, *Coriolanus* had never been required reading at the Point. Noncoms in the field, even grunts with no career ambitions, felt the professional indignity of the President's gambit, talked of it as something shameful.) Perhaps Khe Sanh would be held, perhaps not; the President had his statement now, and it was signed clearly. If Khe Sanh stood, he would presumably be available for a grin in the victory picture. If it fell, it would not be on his head.

More than any other Americans in Vietnam, Khe Sanh's defenders became hostages, nearly 8,000 Americans and Vietnamese who took their orders not from the regimental commander in the TOC, nor from General Cushman in Danang nor General Westmoreland in Saigon, but from a source which one Intelligence officer I knew always called "Downtown." They were made to sit and wait, and Marines defending are like antichrists at vespers. Somehow, digging in seems a soft thing to do, fighting from a hole is like fighting on your knees. ("Digging," General Cushman said, "is not the Marine way.") Most of the defenses against artillery were built entirely or substantially reinforced after the heavy shelling began, when the Tet Offensive diverted supply from the air and made Khe Sanh even more isolated. They were built on the scrounge and so haphazardly that the lines of sandbagging had a sensuous, plastic drift to them as they stretched away into the filtered light of mist and dust, the shapes growing dimmer in the distance. If all of the barbed wire and all of the sandbags were taken away, Khe Sanh would have looked like one of those Colombian valley slums whose meanness is the abiding factor, whose despair is so palpable that for days after you leave you are filled with a vicarious shame for the misery you have just tripped through. At Khe Sanh most bunkers were nothing more than hovels with inadequate overhead cover, and you could not believe that Americans were living this way, even in the middle of a war. The defenses were a scandal, and everywhere you could smell that sour reek of obsolescence that followed the Marines all over Vietnam. If they could not hear their own dead from Con Thien, only three months past, how could they ever be expected to hear the dead from Dien Bien Phu?

Not a single round had fallen inside the perimeter. The jungled slopes running up from the bowl of the base were not yet burned over and hung with the flare chutes that looked like infants' shrouds. Six shades of green, motherfucker, tell me that ain't something beautiful. There were no heaps of shredded, blood-soaked jungle fatigues outside the triage room, and the wires were not cluttered each dawn with their dead. None of it had happened yet when Khe Sanh became lost forever as a tactical entity. It is impossible to fix the exact moment in time when it happened, or to know, really, why. All that was certain was that Khe Sanh had become a passion, the false love object in the heart of the Command. It cannot even be determined which way the passion traveled. Did it proceed from the filthiest ground-zero slit trench and proceed outward, across I Corps to Saigon and on (taking the true perimeter with it) to the most abstract reaches of the Pentagon? Or did it get born in those same Pentagon rooms where six years of failure had made the air bad, where optimism no longer sprang from anything viable but sprang and sprang, all the way to Saigon, where it was packaged and shipped north to give the grunts some kind of reason for what was about to happen to them? In its outlines, the promise was delicious: Victory! A vision of as many as 40,000 of them out there in the open, fighting it out on our terms, fighting for once like men, fighting to no avail. There would be a battle, a set-piece battle where he could be killed by the numbers, killed wholesale, and if we killed enough of him, maybe he would go away. In the face of such a promise, the question of defeat could not even be considered, no more than the question of whether, after Tet, Khe Sanh might have become militarily unwise and even absurd. Once it was all locked in place, Khe Sanh became like the planted jar in Wallace Stevens' poem. It took dominion everywhere.

IV

When I think of it quickly, just seeing the name somewhere or being asked what it was like, I see a flat, dun stretch of ground running out in an even plane until the rim of the middle distance takes on the shapes and colors of jungled hills. I had the strangest, most thrilling kind of illusion there, looking at those hills and thinking about the death and mystery that was in them. I would see the thing I knew I actually saw: the base from the ground where I stood, figures moving across it, choppers rising from the pad by the strip, and the hills above. But at the same time I would see the other, too; the ground, the troops and even myself, all from the vantage of the hills. It was a double vision that came to me more than once there. And in my head, sounding over and over, were the incredibly sinister words of the song we had all heard for the first time only days before. "The Magical Mystery Tour is waiting to take you away," it promised, "Coming to take you away, dy-ing to take you away. . . ." That was a song about Khe Sanh; we knew it then, and it still seems so. Inside the bunker, one of the grunts has been saying hideous things in his sleep, laughing a bad laugh and then going more silent than even deep sleep permits before starting it up again, and it is more terrible in there than any place I can even imagine. I got up then and went outside, any place at all was better than this, and stood in the dark smoking a cigarette, watching the hills for a sign and hoping none would come because, shit, what could be revealed except more fear? Three in the morning, and my blood is intimate with the chill, host to it, and very willing too. From the center of the earth there is a tremor that shakes everything, running up through my legs and body, shaking my head, yet no one in the bunker wakes up. We called them "Archlights," he called them Rolling Thunder, and it was incessant during the nights. The bombs would release at 18,000 feet and the planes would turn and fly back to Udorn or Guam. Dawn seems to last until late morning, dusk falls at four. Everything I see is blown through with smoke, everything is on fire everywhere. It doesn't matter that memory distorts; every image, every sound comes back out of smoke and the smell of things burning.

Some of it, like smoke from an exploding round in the air, breaks cleanly and at a comfortable distance. Some of it pours out of large tubs of shit being burned off with diesel fuel, and it hangs, hangs, taking you full in the throat even though you are used to it. Right there on the strip a fuel ship has been hit, and no one who has heard that can kill the shakes for an hour. (What woke you? . . . What woke you?) A picture comes in, absolutely still for a moment, and then resumes the motion it once had: a heat tablet, burning in high intensity, covered by a tiny, blackened stove a Marine had made for me two weeks before in Hue out of the small dessert can from a ration box. From this little bit of light I can see the outlines of a few Marines, all of us in a bunker filling with the acrid smoke of the tablet, glad for it because the rations will be hot tonight, glad because we know how safe the bunker is and because we are both private and together, and find a lot of things to laugh about. I brought the tablets with me, stole them from a colonel's aide in Dong Ha, supercilious prick, and these guys hadn't had any in days, weeks. I also have a bottle. ("Oh man, you are welcome here. You are *definitely* welcome. Let's wait for Gunny.") The beef and potatoes, the meatballs and beans, the ham and Mothers, all that good stuff, will be hot tonight, and who really gives a fuck about tomorrow night anyway? Somewhere above ground now, in full afternoon light, there is a four-foot stack of C-ration cartons, the cardboard burned away from the metal binding wire, the cans and utility packs lying all around, and on top of it all there is the body of a young ARVN Ranger who had just come over to Bravo Recon to scrounge a few cans of American food. If he'd succeeded, he would have gone back to his unit a celebrity, but as it was he didn't make out. Three rounds had come in very quickly, neither killing nor wounding any of the Marines, and now two lance corporals are arguing. One wants to put the dead Ranger into a green body bag, the other just wants to cover the body somehow, anyhow, and run it over to the Dink compound. He's very pissed off. "We keep tellin' them fuckin' people to stay with their own fuckin' outfits," he says, over and over. Fires eat at everything. There are fires at night, the trees on hillsides kilometers away erupting in smoke, burning. At late morning, the sun burns off the last of the chill and early mist, making the base visible from above until late afternoon, when the chill and the mists return. Then it is night again, and the sky beyond the western perimeter is burning with slowly dropping magnesium flares. Heaps of equipment are on fire, terrifying in their jagged black massiveness, burning prehistoric shapes like the tail of a C-130 sticking straight up in the air, dead metal showing through the gray-black smoke. God, if it can do that to metal, what will it do to me? And then something very near me is smoldering, just above my head, the damp canvas coverings on the sandbags lining the top of a slit trench. It is a small trench, and a lot of us have gotten into it in a hurry. At the end farthest from me there is a young guy who has been hit in the throat, and he is making the sounds a baby will make when he is trying to work up the breath for a good scream. We were on the ground when those rounds came, and a Marine nearer the trench had been splattered badly across the legs and groin. I sort of took him into the trench with me. It was so crowded I couldn't help leaning on him a little, and he kept saying, "You motherfucker, you cocksucker," until someone told him that I wasn't a grunt but a reporter. Then he started to say, very quietly, "Be careful, Mister. Please be careful." He'd been wounded before, and he knew how it would hurt in a few minutes. People would just get ripped up in the worst ways there, and things were always on fire. Far up the road that skirted the TOC was a dump where they burned the gear and uniforms that nobody needed anymore. On top of the pile I saw a flak jacket so torn apart that no one would ever want it again. On the back, its owner had listed the months that he had served in Vietnam. *March, April, May* (each month written out in a tentative, spidery hand), *June, July, August, September, Octobler, Novembler, Decembler, Janurary, Feburary*, the list ending right there like a clock stopped by a bullet. A jeep pulled up to the dump and a Marine jumped out carrying a bunched-up fatigue jacket held out away from him. He looked very serious and scared. Some guy in his company, some guy he didn't even know, had been blown away right next to him, all over him. He held the fatigues up and I believed him. "I guess you couldn't wash them, could you?" I said. He really looked like he was going to cry as he threw them into the dump. "Man," he said, "you could take and scrub them fatigues for a million years, and *it would never happen.*"

I see a road. It is full of ruts made by truck and jeep tires, but in the passing rains they never harden, and along the road there is a two-dollar piece of issue, a poncho which had just been used to cover a dead Marine, a blood-puddled, mud-wet poncho going stiff in the wind. It has reared up there by the road in a horrible, streaked ball. The wind doesn't move it, only setting the pools of water and blood in the dents shimmering. I'm walking along this road with two black grunts, and one of them gives the poncho a vicious, helpless kick. "Go easy, man," the other one says, nothing changing in his face, not even a look back. "That's the American flag you gettin' your foot into."

During the early morning of February 7 something so horrible happened in the Khe Sanh sector that even those of us who were in Hue when we heard news of it had to relinquish our own fear and despair for a moment to acknowledge the horror and pay some tribute to it. It was as though the very worst dream any of us had ever had about the war had come true; it anticipated nightmares so vile that they could take you off shuddering in your sleep. No one who heard it was able to smile that bitter, secret survivor's smile that was the reflex to almost all news of disaster. It was too awful even for that.

Five kilometers southwest of the Khe Sanh Combat Base, sitting above the river which forms the border with Laos, there was a Special Forces A Camp. It was called Langvei, taking its name from the small Montagnard village nearby which had been mistakenly bombed a year before by the Air Force. The camp was larger than most Special Forces camps, and much better built. It was set on twin hills about 700 meters apart, and the vital bunkers holding most of the troops were on the hill nearest the river. It was manned by twenty-four Americans and over 400 Vietnamese troops. Its bunkers were deep, solid, with three feet of reinforced concrete overhead, seemingly impregnable. And sometime after midnight, the North Vietnamese came and took it. They took it with a style that had been seen only once before, in the Ia Drang, attacking with weapons and tactics which no one imagined they had. Nine light tanks, Soviet T-34's and 76's, were deployed east and west, closing on the camp so suddenly that the first sound of them was mistaken by the Americans for a malfunction of the camp generator. Satchel charges, bangalore torpedoes, tear gas and—ineffable horror—napalm were all hurled into the machine-gun slits and air vents of the bunkers. It took very little time. An American colonel who had come on an inspection visit to Langvei was seen charging the tanks with nothing but hand grenades before he was cut down. (He survived. The word "miracle" doesn't even apply.) Somewhere between ten and fifteen Americans were killed, and as many as 300 of the indigenous troops. The survivors traveled all night, most of them on foot through NVA positions (some were picked up later by choppers), arriving at Khe Sanh after dawn, and it was said that some of them had become insane. At the same time that Langvei was being overrun, Khe Sanh received the most brutal artillery barrage of the war: 1,500 rounds that night, six rounds a minute for more minutes than anyone could bear to count. The Marines at Khe Sanh saw the Langvei survivors come in. They saw them and heard about them up in their Special Forces compound, holding off all visitors at rifle point, saw their faces and their unfocused stares, and they talked quietly among themselves about it. Jesus, they had tanks. Tanks! . . . After Langvei, how could you look out of your perimeter at night without hearing the treads coming? How could you patrol in the dark without remembering every story you ever heard about ghostly enemy helicopters flying the fringes of the Z? About the trails cut in the floor of the A Shau Valley, big enough to hold trucks? About the complete fanaticism of attackers who were doped to the eyeballs (sure they smoke dope, it gets them crazy), who ran pushing civilian shields forward, who chained themselves to their machine guns and died right there rather than fail, who had No Regard For Human Life?

Officially, the Marines admitted no relevance between the Langvei attack and Khe Sanh. Confidentially, they said something awful about Langvei having been bait—bait which the poor, desperate bastards took, exactly as we hoped they would. But everyone knew better, much better, and the majors and colonels who had to tell reporters about it were met with embarrassed silence. One hated to bring it up, one never really did, but there was a question that had everything in the world to do with Khe Sanh after Langvei fell. I wanted to ask it so badly that my hesitance made me mad for months. Colonel (I wanted to ask), this is purely hypothetical, I hope you understand. But what if all of those gooks that you think are out there are *really* out there? And what if they attack before the monsoons blow south, some mist-clogged night when our planes just cannot get up there?

What if they really want Khe Sanh, want it so badly that they are willing to maneuver over the triple lines of barbed wire, the German razor wire too; over barricades formed by their own dead (a tactic, Colonel, favored by your gook in Korea), coming in waves, *human* waves, and in such numbers that the barrels of our .50-calibers overheat and melt and all the M-16's are jammed, until all of the death in all of the Claymore mines on our defenses has been spent and absorbed? What if they are still coming, moving toward the center of a base so smashed by their artillery that those pissy little trenches and bunkers that *your* Marines half got up are useless, coming as the first MIG's and IL-28's ever seen in this war bomb out the TOC and the strip, the med tent and the control tower (People's Army my ass, right, Colonel?), coming at you 20,000 to 40,000 strong? And what if they pass over every barricade we can put in their way . . . and kill every living thing, defending or retreating . . . and take Khe Sanh?

Some strange things would happen. One morning, at the height of the monsoons, the sun came up brightly at dawn and shone all day. The early-morning skies were a clean, brilliant blue, the only time before April that anyone saw that at Khe Sanh, and instead of waking and coming out shivering from their bunkers, the grunts stripped down to boots, pants and flak jackets; biceps, triceps and tattoos all out for breakfast. Probably because the NVA knew that American surveillance and bombers would be working overtime on a morning like this, there was almost no shelling, and we all knew we could count on it. For those few hours Khe Sanh had the atmosphere of reprieve. I remember passing a chaplain named Stubbe on the road and seeing his incredible pleasure at the miracle of this morning. The hills did not seem like the same hills that had given off so much fear the night before and all of the days and nights before that. In the early-morning light they looked sharp and tranquil, as though you could take some apples and a book and go up there for an afternoon.

I was walking around by myself in the 1st Battalion area. It was before eight in the morning, and as I walked I could hear someone walking behind me, singing. At first I couldn't hear what it was, only that it was a single short phrase being sung over and over at short intervals, and that every time someone else would laugh and tell the singer to shut up. I slowed down and let them catch up.

" 'I'd rather be an Oscar Mayer weiner,' " the voice sang. It sounded very plaintive and lonely.

Of course I turned around. There were two of them, one a big Negro with a full mustache that drooped over the corners of his mouth, a mean, signifying mustache that would have worked if only there had been the smallest trace of meanness anywhere on his face. He was at least six-three and quarter-back thick. He was carrying an AK-47. The other Marine was white, and if I'd seen him first from the back I would have said that he was eleven years old. The Marines must have a height requirement; whatever it is, I don't see how he made it. Age is one thing, but how do you lie about your height? He'd been doing the singing, and he was laughing now because he'd made me turn around. His name was Mayhew, it was written out in enormous red letters across the front of his helmet: MAYHEW—*You'd better believe it!* I'd been walking with my flak jacket open, a stupid thing to do even on this morning, and they could see the stitched tag above my left breast pocket with the name of my magazine written on it.

"Correspondent?" the Negro said.

Mayhew just laughed. " 'I'd-a rather be—a Oscar Mayer

. . . weenieeee,' " he sang. "You can write that, man, tell 'em all I said so."

"Don't pay no attention to him," the Negro said. "That's Mayhew. He's a crazy fucker, ain't you, Mayhew?"

"I sure hope so," Mayhew said. " 'I'd rather be a Oscar Mayer weiner. . . .' "

He was young, nineteen, he later told me, and he was trying to grow a mustache. His only luck with it so far was a few sparse, transparent blond clumps set at odd intervals across his upper lip, and you couldn't see that unless the light was right. The Negro was called Day Tripper. It was on his helmet, along with DETROIT CITY. And on the back, where most guys just listed the months of their tours, he had carefully drawn a full calendar where each day served was marked off with a neat X. They were both from Hotel Company of the 2nd Battalion, which was dug in along the northern perimeter, but they were taking advantage of the day to visit a friend of theirs, a mortar man with 1/26.

"The lieutenant ever hear 'bout this, he know what to do," Day Tripper said.

"Fuck the lieutenant," Mayhew said. "You remember from before he ain't wrapped too tight."

"Well, he wrapped tight enough to tear *you* a new asshole."

"Now what's he gonna do to me? Send me to Vietnam?"

We walked past the battalion CP, piled five feet high with sandbags, and then we reached a giant ring of sandbagging, the mortar pit, and climbed down. In the center was a large four-oh-deuce mortar piece, and the inside of the pit was stacked completely around with ammunition, piled from the ground to just below the sandbags. A Marine was stretched out in the dust with a war comic spread over his face.

"Hey, where's Evans?" Mayhew said. "You know a guy named Evans?"

The Marine took the comic off of his face and looked up. He'd been asleep.

"Shit," he said. "I thought you was the Old Man for a second. Beg your pardon."

"We're looking for this guy Evans," Mayhew said. "You know him?"

"I—uh—no, I don't guess so. I'm pretty new."

He looked it. He was the kind of kid that would go into the high-school gym alone and shoot baskets for the half-hour before the basketball team took it over for practice, not good enough yet for the team but determined.

"The rest of the crew'll be down here right away. You can wait if you want." He looked at all the rounds. "It's probably not too cool," he said, smiling. "But you can if you want."

Mayhew unbuttoned one of the pockets in the leg of his fatigues and took out a can of crackers and Cheddar-cheese spread. He took the P-38 opener from a band around his helmet and sat down.

"Might as well eat some shit while we wait. You get hungry, it ain't so bad. I'd give my left ball for a can of fruit now."

I always scrounged fruit from rear areas to bring forward, and I had some in my pack. "What kind do you like?" I asked.

"Any kind's good," he said. "Fruit cocktail's really good."

"No, man," Day Tripper said. "Peaches, baby, peaches. All that syrup. Now that's some good shit."

"There you go, Mayhew," I said, tossing him a fruit cocktail. I gave a can of peaches to Day Tripper and kept a can for myself.

We talked while we ate. Mayhew told me about his father, who "got greased in Korea," and about his mother, who worked in a department store in Kansas City. Then he started to tell about Day Tripper, who got his name because he was afraid of the night—not the dark, but the night—and who didn't mind who knew it. There wasn't anything he wouldn't do during daylight, but if there was any way at all to fix it he liked to be deep in his bunker by nightfall. He was always volunteering for the more dangerous daylight patrols, just to make sure he got in by dusk. (This was before daylight patrols, in fact almost all patrols around Khe Sanh, were discontinued.) There were a lot of white guys, especially junior officers trying to be cool, who were always coming on to Day Tripper about his hometown, calling it Dodge City or Motown and laughing. ("Why they think somethin's special about Detroit?" he said. "Ain't nothin' special, ain't nothin' so funny, neither.") He was a big bad spade gone wrong somehow, and no matter how mean he tried to look something constantly gentle showed. He told me he knew guys from Detroit who were taking mortars back, breaking them down so that each one could get a piece into his duffel and then reassembling them when they got together back on the block. "You see that four-oh-deuce?" he said. "Now, that'll take out a police station for you. I don't need all that hassle. But maybe nex' year I gonna need it."

Like every American in Vietnam, he had his obsession with Time. (No one ever talked about When-this-lousy-war-is-over. Only "How much time you got?") The degree of Day Tripper's obsession, compared with most of the others, could be seen in the calendar on his helmet. No metaphysician ever studied Time the way he did, its components and implications, its per-second per seconds, its shadings and movement. The Space-Time continuum, Time-as-Matter, Augustinian Time: all of that would have been a piece of cake to Day Tripper, whose brain cells were arranged like jewels in the finest chronometer. He had assumed that correspondents in Vietnam *had* to be there. When he learned that

I had asked to come here he almost let the peaches drop to the ground.

"Lemmee . . . lemmee jus' hang on that a minute," he said. "You mean you don' *have* to be here? An' you're *here?*"

I nodded.

"Well, they gotta be payin' you some tough bread."

"You'd get depressed if I told you."

He shook his head.

"I mean, they ain' *got* the bread that'd get me here if I didn' have t' be here."

"Horse crap," Mayhew said. "Day Tripper loves it. He's short now, but he's comin' back, ain't you, Day Tripper?"

"Shit, my momma'll come over here and pull a tour before I fuckin' come back."

Four more Marines dropped into the pit.

"Where's Evans?" Mayhew demanded. "Any of you guys know Evans?"

One of the mortar men came over.

"Evans is over in Danang," he said. "He caught a little shit the other night."

"That right?" Mayhew said. "Evans get wounded?"

"He hurt bad?" Day Tripper asked.

"Not bad enough," the mortar man said, laughing. "He'll be back in ten days. Just some stuff in the legs."

"He's real lucky," another one said. "Same round got him killed a guy."

"Yeah," someone said. "Greene got killed." He wasn't talking to us, but to the crew, who knew it already. "Remember Greene?" Everyone nodded.

"Wow, Greene," he said. "Greene was all fixed to get out. He's jerkin' off thirty times a day, that fuckin' guy, and they's all set to give him a medical. And out."

"That's no shit," the other one said. "Thirty times a day. Dis*gus*ting, man. That sombitch had come all over his pants, that fuckin' Greene. He was waitin' outside to see the major about gettin' sent home, an' the major comes out to find him an' he's just sittin' there jerkin' off. Then he gets blown away the night before."

"Well," Day Tripper said quietly to Mayhew, "see what happens if you jerk off?"

A Chinook, forty feet long with rotors front and back, set down on the airstrip by Charlie Med, looking like a great, gross beast getting a body purchase on some mud, blowing bitter gusts of dust, pebbles and debris for a hundred yards around. Everywhere within that circle of wind men turned and crouched, covering their necks against the full violence of it. The wind from those blades could come up strong enough to blow you over, to tear papers from your hands, to lift tarmac sections weighing a hundred pounds in the air. But it was mostly the sharp fragments, the stinging dirt, the muddy, pissed-in water, and you acquired a second sense of when it would reach you, learned to give it only your back and your helmet. The Chinook had flown in with its rear hatch down and a gunner with a .50-caliber machine gun stretched out flat on his stomach peering over the edge of the hatch. Neither he nor the door gunners would relax their weapons until the chopper touched the strip. Then they let go, the barrels of the big guns dropping down like dead weights in their mounts. A bunch of Marines appeared on the edge of the strip and ran to the chopper, through the ring of harsh, filthy wind, toward the calm at the center. Three mortar rounds came in at three-second intervals, all landing in a cluster 200 meters down the strip. No one around the chopper stopped. The noise from the Chinook drowned out the noise of the rounds, but we could see the balls of white smoke blowing out away from the strip in the wind, and the men were still running for the chopper. Four full litters were carried at a run from the rear of the Chinook to the med tent. Some walking wounded came out and headed for the tent, some walking slowly, unaided, others moving uncertainly, one being supported by two Marines. The empty litters were returned and loaded with four poncho-covered figures, which were set down near some sandbagging in front of the tent. Then the Chinook reared up abruptly, dipped horribly, regained its flight and headed north and west, toward the covering hills.

"One-nine," Mayhew said. "I'll bet anything."

Four kilometers northwest of Khe Sanh was Hill 861, the hardest-hit of all the sector outposts after Langvei, and it seemed logical to everyone that the 1st Battalion of the 9th Marine Regiment should have been chosen to defend it. Some even believed that if anyone but 1/9 had been put there, 861 would never have been hit. Of all the hard-luck outfits in Vietnam, this was said to be the most doomed, doomed in its Search-and-Destroy days before Khe Sanh, known for a history of ambush and confusion and for a casualty rate which was the highest of any outfit in the entire war. That was the kind of reputation that takes hold most deeply among the men of the outfit itself, and when you were with them you got a sense of dread that came out of something more terrible than just a collective loss of luck. All the odds seemed somehow sharply reduced, estimates of your own survival were revised horribly downward. One afternoon with 1/9 on 861 was enough to bend your nerves for days, because it took only a few minutes up there to see the very worst of it: the stumbles, the simple motions of a walk suddenly racked by spasms, mouths sand-dry seconds after drinking, the dreamy smiles of total abdication. Hill 861 was the home of the thousand-yard stare, and I prayed hard for a chopper to come and get me away from there, to fly me over the ground fire and land me in the middle of a mortar barrage on the Khe Sanh pad—whatever! Anything was better than this.

On a night shortly after the Langvei attack an entire platoon of 1/9 was ambushed during a patrol and wiped out. Hill 861 had been hit repeatedly, once for three days straight during a perimeter probe that turned into a siege that really *was* a siege. For reasons that no one is certain of, Marine helicopters refused to fly missions up there, and 1/9 was cut off from support, re-supply or medical evacuation. It was bad, and they had to get through it any way they could, alone. (The stories from that time became part of the worst Marine legends; the story of one Marine putting a wounded buddy away with a pistol shot because medical help was impossible, or the story of what they did to the NVA prisoner taken beyond the wire—stories like that. Some of them may even have been true.) The old hostility of the grunt toward Marine Air became total on 861: when the worst of it was over and the first Ch-34 finally showed over the hilltop, the door gunner was hit by enemy ground fire and fell out of the chopper. It was a drop of over 200 feet, and there were Marines on the ground who cheered when he hit.

Mayhew, Day Tripper and I were walking near the triage tent of Charlie Med. In spite of all the shrapnel that had fallen into that tent, no way had been found to protect it. The sandbagging around it was hardly more than five feet high, and the top was entirely exposed. It was one reason why grunts feared even the mildest of the Going Home wounds. Someone ran out of the tent and took photographs of the four dead Marines. The wind from the Chinook had blown the ponchos from two of them, and one had no face left at all. A Catholic chaplain on a bicycle rode up to the entrance of the tent and walked inside. A Marine came out and stood by the flap for a moment, an unlighted cigarette hanging from his mouth. He had neither a flak jacket nor a helmet. He let the cigarette drop from his lips, walked a few steps to the sandbags and sat down with his legs drawn up and his head hanging down between his knees. He threw one limp arm over his head and began stroking the back of his neck, shaking his head from side to side violently, as though in agony. He wasn't wounded.

We were here because I had to pass this way to reach my bunker, where I had to pick up some things to take over to Hotel Company for the night. Day Tripper wasn't liking the route. He looked at the bodies and then at me. It was that look which said, "See? You see what it does?" I had seen that look so many times during the past months that I must have had it too now, and neither of us said anything. Mayhew wasn't letting himself look at anything. It was as though he were walking by himself now, and he was singing in an odd, quiet voice. " 'When you get to San Francisco,' " he sang, " 'be sure and wear some flowers in your hair.' "

We passed the control tower, that target that was its own aiming stake, so prominent and vulnerable that climbing up there was worse than having to run in front of a machine gun. Two of them had already been hit, and the sandbags running up the sides didn't seem to make any difference. We went by the grimy admin buildings and bunkers, a bunch of deserted "hardbacks" with crushed metal roofs, the TOC, the command latrine and a post-office bunker. There was the now roofless beer hall and the collapsed, abandoned officers' club. The Seabee bunker was just a little farther along the road.

It was not like the other bunkers. It was the deepest, safest, cleanest place in Khe Sanh, with six feet of timbers, steel and sandbags overhead, and inside it was brightly lit.

The grunts called it the Alamo Hilton and thought it was candy-assed, while almost every correspondent who came to Khe Sanh tried to get a bed there. A bottle of whiskey or a case of beer would be enough to get you in for a few nights, and once you became a friend of the house, gifts like that were simply a token and very deeply appreciated. The Marines had set up a press "facility" very, very near the strip, and it was so bad that a lot of reporters thought there was a conscious conspiracy working to get some of us killed off. It was nothing more than a narrow, flimsily covered, rat-infested hole, and one day when it was empty an incoming 152 shell sewed part of it up.

I went down into the Seabee bunker, picked up a bottle of Scotch and a field jacket, and told one of the Seabees to give my rack to anyone who needed it that night.

"You ain't mad at us or anything?" he said.

"Nothing like that. I'll see you tomorrow."

"Okay," he said as I left. "If you think so."

As the three of us walked toward the 2/26 positions, two batteries of Marine artillery started firing 105's and 155's from the other side of the base. Every time a round was fired I'd flinch a little, and Mayhew would laugh.

"Them're outgoing," he said.

Day Tripper heard the deep sliding whistle of the other shells first. "*That* ain' no outgoin'," he said, and we ran for a short trench a few yards away.

"That ain't outgoing," Mayhew said.

"Now what I jus' say?" Day Tripper yelled, and we reached the trench as a shell landed somewhere between the 37th ARVN Rangers compound and the ammo dump. A lot of them were coming in, some mortars too, but we didn't count them.

"Sure was some nice mornin'," Day Tripper said. "Oh, man, why they can' jus' leave us alone one time?"

" 'Cause they ain't gettin' paid to leave us alone," Mayhew said, laughing. " 'Sides, they do it 'cause they know how it fucks you all up."

"Tell me *you* ain' scared shit!"

"You'll never see *me* scared, motherfucker."

"Oh no. Three nights ago you was callin' out for your *momma* while them fuckers was hittin' our wire."

"Boo-sheeit! I ain't never gettin' hit in Vietnam."

"Oh no? Okay, mothafucker, why not?"

" 'Cause," Mayhew said, "it don't exist." It was an old joke, but this time he wasn't laughing.

By now, the trenchline circled the camp almost completely. Most of the northern perimeter was held down by the 2nd Battalion of the 26th Marine Regiment, and Hotel Company was along this sector. In its westernmost part it was opposed by North Vietnamese trenches that ended just 300 meters away. Farther to the east it sat above a narrow river, and beyond that was Hill 950, three kilometers to the north, which was held by the NVA and whose highest ridge ran exactly parallel to the Khe Sanh airstrip. The bunkers and connecting trenchworks sat on a rise that ran up from the riverbank, and the hills began a couple of hundred meters from the far side of the river. Two hundred meters away, facing the Marine trenches, there was an NVA sniper with a .50-caliber machine gun who shot at the Marines from a tiny spider hole. During the day he fired at anything that rose above the sandbags, and at night he fired at any lights he could see. You could see him clearly from the trench, and if you were looking through the scope of a Marine sniper's rifle you could even see his face. The Marines fired on his position with mortars and recoilless rifles, and he would drop into his hole and wait. Gunships fired rockets at him, and when they were through he would come up again and fire. Finally, napalm was called in, and for ten minutes the air above the spider hole was black and orange from the strike, while the ground around it was galvanized clean of every living thing. When all of it cleared, the sniper popped up and fired off a single round, and the Marines in the trenches cheered. They called him Luke the Gook, and after that no one wanted anything to happen to him.

Mayhew had a friend named Orrin from somewhere in Tennessee, from the mountains there where his family owned three small trucks and did a short-haul business. On the morning that Mayhew and Day Tripper had gone over to 1/26 to find Evans, Orrin received a letter from his wife. It told him straight off that her pregnancy was not seven months along, as he had believed, but only five. It made all the difference in the world to Orrin. She had felt so awful all the time (she wrote) that she went to see the minister, and the minister had finally convinced her that the Truth was God's one sure key to a beautiful conscience. She would not tell him who the father was (and Honey, don't you never, never try and make me tell), except to mention that it was someone Orrin knew well.

When we got back to the company, Orrin was sitting on top of the sandbags above the trench, alone and exposed, looking out toward the hills and Luke the Gook. He had a beefy, sulky kid's face, a perpetual mean squint and a pouting mouth that would break into a dull smile and then a dry, soundless laugh. It was the face of someone who would hunt the winter out and then let the meat go to rot, a mean Southland aberration of a face. He just sat there, working the bolt of a freshly cleaned .45. No one in the trench would go near him or say anything to him, except to yell out, "Come on down, Orrin. You'll get greased for sure, motherfucker." Finally, the gunnery sergeant came along and said, "If you don't get your ass down off that berm I'll shoot you myself."

"Listen," Mayhew said. "Maybe you better go and see the chaplain."

"Real good," Orrin said. "What's that cocksucker gone do for me?"

"Maybe you could get an emergency leave."

"No," someone said. "There's gotta be a death in the family before you'll get out like that."

"Oh, don't worry," Orrin said. "There's gone be a death in my family. Just soon's I git home." And then he laughed.

It was a terrible laugh, very quiet and intense, and it was the thing that made everyone who heard it believe Orrin. After that, he was the crazy fucking grunt who was going to get through the war so he could go home and kill his old lady. It made him someone special in the company. It made a lot of guys think that he was lucky now, that nothing could happen to him, and they stayed as close to him as they could. I even felt some of it, enough to be glad that we would be in the same bunker that night. It made sense. I believed it too, and I would have been really surprised if I had heard later that anything had happened to him. But that was the kind of thing you seldom heard after you left an outfit, the kind of thing you avoided hearing if you could. Maybe he was killed or maybe he changed his mind, but I doubt it. When I remembered Orrin, all I could think of was that there was going to be a shooting in Tennessee.

Once on a two-day pass to Danang, Mayhew had gone off limits and into the black market looking for grass and an air mattress. He never found the grass, and he had been scared to death when he finally bought the mattress. He told me that nothing that had ever happened at Khe Sanh had scared him the way he had been scared that day. I don't know what he had been told the MP's would do to him if they caught him in the market, but as he told the story it had been the best adventure he'd had since the day two years back when the game warden had used a helicopter to chase him and a friend out of the woods after deer season had closed. We were sitting in the mingy damp of the eight-man bunker where Mayhew and Day Tripper both slept. Mayhew had been trying to make me use his mattress for the night and I'd refused it. He said that if I didn't sleep on it he was just going to take it and throw it outside into the trench and leave it there until morning. I told him that if I'd wanted an air mattress I could have picked one up anytime in Danang, and that the MP's wouldn't have even bothered me about it. I said I liked sleeping on the ground; it was good training. He said that that was all horsecrap (he was right), and he swore to God, the mattress would just lie out there all night with the rest of the rubbish that collects on trench floors. Then he got very mysterious and told me to think about it while he was gone. Day Tripper tried to find out where he was going, but Mayhew wouldn't tell him.

During those brief moments when the ground all around you was not rumbling, when there were no airstrikes on the hills, no incoming or outgoing or firing from the perimeter, you could sit inside and listen to the rats running across the bunker floor. A lot of them had been poisoned, shot, caught in traps or killed by the lucky toss of a combat boot, and they were here in the bunker too. There was the smell of urine, of old, old sweat, C-ration decay, moldy canvas and private crud, and that mixing up of other smells that were special to combat zones. A lot of us believed that exhaustion and fear could be smelled and that certain dreams gave off an odor.

(We were regular Hemingway gypsies about some things. No matter how much wind a chopper would put out as it landed, you could always tell when there were body bags around an lz, and the tents where the Lurps lived smelled unlike any other tents anywhere in Vietnam.) This bunker was at least as bad as any I'd ever been in, and I gagged in there once, the first time. Because there was almost no light, you had to imagine most of what you smelled, and that became something like a pastime. I hadn't realized how black Day Tripper was until we walked inside the bunker.

"It *def*initely stinks somethin' fierce in here," he said. "I gotta be gettin' me a mo'—uh—*eff*ective deodorant."

He paused.

"Any kinda shit come up tonight, you jus' keep with me. You be lucky Mayhew don' think you a Zip an' blast your fuckin' head off. He'll go pretty crazy sometimes."

"You think we'll be hit?"

He shrugged. "He might try an' do a probe. He did that number 'gainst us three nights ago an' kill one boy. Kill a Brother.

"But this here's a real good bunker. We took some shit right on top here. All kindsa dirt come down on top our heads, but we'se all right."

"Are guys sleeping in their flak jackets?"

"Some do. I don'. Mayhew, crazy fucker, he sleep bare-ass. He so tough, man, li'l fucker, the hawk is out, an' he's in here bare-ass."

"What's that? About the hawk?"

"That means it's a co-o-old Mother Fucker."

Mayhew had been gone for more than an hour now, and when Day Tripper and I stepped out on the ammo-crate planking that made the trench floor we saw him outside talking to some grunts. He started walking toward us, laughing, looking like a little boy dressed in a man's combat gear, swimming in his flak jacket, and the grunts sang after him, "Mayhew's a lifer. . . . 'Ray for him."

"Hey, Day Tripper!" he called. "Hey, you hear it, motherfucker?"

"I hear *what?*"

"I just went over and extended."

The smile vanished on Day Tripper's face. He looked like he didn't understand for a second, and then he looked angry, almost dangerous.

"Say again?"

"Yeah," Mayhew said. "I just saw the Old Man about it."

"Uh-huh. How long you extend for?"

"Just four months."

"Jus' four months. Tha's real fine, Jim."

"Hey, man . . ."

"Don' talk to me, Jim."

"Oh come on, Day Tripper, don't be a hard-on. It gets me outta the Corps three months early."

"Whatever. Jim."

"Oh man, don't call me that." He looked at me. "Every time he gets pissed off he calls me that. Listen, motherfucker, I get outta the *Marine Corps* early. And I get a home leave. The Old Man says I can go next month."

"You *can't* be talkin' to *me*. I jus' don' hear nonna that. I don' hear one word you sayin', Jim."

"Aw . . ."

"You jus' another dumb grunt. What I gotta talk to you for? It's like you never hear one word I say to you, ever. Not one word. An' I *know* . . . oh man, I jus' *know* you already sign that paper."

Mayhew didn't say anything. It was hard to believe that the two were around the same age.

"What I gonna do with you, poor fucker? Why . . . why

you jus' don' go runnin' out over th' wire there? Let 'em gun
you down an' get it over with. Here, man, here's a grenade.
Why you jus' don' go up backa the shithouse an' pull the pin
an' lie down on it?"

"You're fuckin' unbe*lie*vable. Man, it's just four months!"

"Four months? Baby, four *seconds* in this whorehouse'll
get you greased. An' after your poppa an' all that. An' you
jus' ain' *learned*. You're the sorriest, *sorriest* grunt mother I
ever seen. No, man, but the *sorriest!* Fuckin' Mayhew, man.
I feel sorry for you."

"Day Tripper? Hey, it'll be okay. Y'know?"

"Sure, baby. Jus' don' talk to me right away. Clean your
rifle. Write your momma. Do *somethin'*. Talk to me later."

"We can smoke some bullshit."

"Okay, baby. Say later." He walked back into the bunker
and lay down. Mayhew took off his helmet and scratched out
something written on the side. It had read *20 April and*
OUTTA SIGHT!

Sometimes you'd step from the bunker, all sense of time passing having left you, and find it dark out. The far side of the
hills around the bowl of the base was glimmering, but you
could never see the source of the light, and it had the look of
a city at night approached from a great distance. Flares were
dropping everywhere around the fringes of the perimeter,
laying a dead white light on the high ground rising from the
piedmont. There would be dozens of them at once sometimes, trailing an intense smoke, dropping white-hot sparks,
and it seemed as though anything caught in their range
would be made still, like figures in a game of living statues.
There would be the muted rush of illumination rounds, fired
from 60-mm. mortars inside the wire, dropping magnesium-
brilliant above the NVA trenches for a few seconds, outlin-

ing the gaunt, flat spread of the mahogany trees, giving the landscape a ghastly clarity and dying out. You could watch mortar bursts, orange and gray-smoking, over the tops of trees three and four kilometers away, and the heavier shelling from support bases farther east along the DMZ, from Camp Carrol and the Rockpile, directed against suspected troop movements or NVA rocket and mortar positions. Once in a while—I guess I saw it happen three or four times in all—there would be a secondary explosion, a direct hit on a supply of NVA ammunition. And at night it was beautiful. Even the incoming was beautiful at night, beautiful and deeply dreadful.

I remembered the way a Phantom pilot had talked about how beautiful the surface-to-air missiles looked as they drifted up toward his plane to kill him, and remembered myself how lovely .50-caliber tracers could be, coming at you as you flew at night in a helicopter, how slow and graceful, arching up easily, a dream, so remote from anything that could harm you. It could make you feel a total serenity, an elevation that put you above death, but that never lasted very long. One hit anywhere in the chopper would bring you back, bitten lips, white knuckles and all, and then you knew where you were. It was different with the incoming at Khe Sanh. You didn't get to watch the shells very often. You knew if you heard one, the first one, that you were safe, or at least saved. If you were still standing up and looking after that, you deserved anything that happened to you.

Nights were when the air and artillery strikes were heaviest, because that was when we knew that the NVA was above ground and moving. At night you could lie out on some sandbags and watch the C-47's mounted with Vulcans doing their work. The C-47 was a standard prop flareship, but many of them carried .20- and .762-mm. guns on their doors,

Mike-Mikes that could fire out 300 rounds per second, Gatling style, "a round in every square inch of a football field in less than a minute," as the handouts said. They used to call it Puff the Magic Dragon, but the Marines knew better: they named it Spooky. Every fifth round fired was a tracer, and when Spooky was working, everything stopped while that solid stream of violent red poured down out of the black sky. If you watched from a great distance, the stream would seem to dry up between bursts, vanishing slowly from air to ground like a comet tail, the sound of the guns disappearing too, a few seconds later. If you watched at a close range, you couldn't believe that anyone would have the courage to deal with that night after night, week after week, and you cultivated a respect for the Viet Cong and NVA who had crouched under it every night now for months. It was awesome, worse than anything the Lord had ever put down on Egypt, and at night, you'd hear the Marines talking, watching it, yelling, "Get some!" until they grew quiet and someone would say, "Spooky understands." The nights were very beautiful. Night was when you really had the least to fear and feared the most. You could go through some very bad numbers at night.

Because, really, what a choice there was; what a prodigy of things to be afraid of! The moment that you understood this, really understood it, you lost your anxiety instantly. Anxiety was a luxury, a joke you had no room for once you knew the variety of deaths and mutilations the war offered. Some feared head wounds, some dreaded chest wounds or stomach wounds, everyone feared the wound of wounds, the Wound. Guys would pray and pray—Just you and me, God. Right?—offer anything, if only they could be spared that: Take my legs, take my hands, take my eyes, take my fucking *life*, You Bastard, but please, please, please, don't take *those*.

Whenever a shell landed in a group, everyone forgot about the next rounds and skipped back to rip their pants away, to check, laughing hysterically with relief even though their legs might be shattered, their kneecaps torn away, kept upright by their relief and shock, gratitude and adrenaline.

There were choices everywhere, but they were never choices that you could hope to make. There was even some small chance for personal style in your recognition of the one thing you feared more than any other. You could die in a sudden bloodburning crunch as your chopper hit the ground like dead weight, you could fly apart so that your pieces would never be gathered, you could take one neat round in the lung and go out hearing only the bubble of the last few breaths, you could die in the last stage of malaria with that faint tapping in your ears, and that could happen to you after months of firefights and rockets and machine guns. Enough, too many, were saved for that, and you always hoped that no irony would attend your passing. You could end in a pit somewhere with a spike through you, everything stopped forever except for the one or two motions, purely involuntary, as though you could kick it all away and come back. You could fall down dead so that the medics would have to spend half an hour looking for the hole that killed you, getting more and more spooked as the search went on. You could be shot, mined, grenaded, rocketed, mortared, sniped at, blown up and away so that your leavings had to be dropped into a sagging poncho and carried to Graves Registration, that's all she wrote. It was almost marvelous.

And at night, all of it seemed more possible. At night in Khe Sanh, waiting there, thinking about all of them (40,000, some said), thinking that they might really try it, could keep you up. If they did, when they did, it might not matter that you were in the best bunker in the DMZ, wouldn't matter

that you were young and had plans, that you were loved, that
you were a noncombatant, an observer. Because if it came, it
would be in a bloodswarm of killing, and credentials would
not be examined. (The only Vietnamese many of us knew
was the words "Bao Chi! Bao Chi!"—Journalist! Journalist!
or even "Bao Chi Fap!"—French journalist!, which was the
same as crying, Don't shoot! Don't shoot!) You came to love
your life, to love and respect the mere fact of it, but often
you became heedless of it in the way that somnambulists are
heedless. Being "good" meant staying alive, and sometimes
that was only a matter of caring enough at any given moment. No wonder everyone became a luck freak, no wonder
you could wake at four in the morning some mornings and
know that tomorrow it would finally happen, you could stop
worrying about it now and just lie there, sweating in the
dampest chill you ever felt.

But once it was actually going on, things were different.
You were just like everyone else, you could no more blink
than spit. It came back the same way every time, dreaded
and welcome, balls and bowels turning over together, your
senses working like strobes, free-falling all the way down to
the essences and then flying out again in a rush to focus, like
the first strong twinge of tripping after an infusion of psilo-
cybin, reaching in at the point of calm and springing all the
joy and all the dread ever known, *ever* known by *everyone*
who *ever* lived, unutterable in its speeding brilliance, touching all the edges and then passing, as though it had all been
controlled from outside, by a god or by the moon. And
every time, you were so weary afterward, so empty of everything but being alive that you couldn't recall any of it, except
to know that it was like something else you had felt once
before. It remained obscure for a long time, but after enough
times the memory took shape and substance and finally re-

vealed itself one afternoon during the breaking off of a fire-fight. It was the feeling you'd had when you were much, much younger and undressing a girl for the first time.

The Coleman lantern had been down to its minimum light for an hour, and now it was off for good. A lieutenant came in and flashed a sharp light around quickly, looking for someone who was supposed to be up on the wire. Then the canvas flap dropped shut, closing out the flarelight from the middle ground between their trenches and ours, and there were only cigarette ends and the light from Mayhew's radio.

"Let's talk about tracers," the announcer was saying. "Sure, they're fun to shoot. They light up the sky! But did you know that tracers leave *deposits* on your barrel? Deposits that often lead to mal*functions* and even *jamming* . . ."

"Hey Mayhew, turn that fuckin' thing off."

"Right after Sports," Mayhew said. He was naked now, sitting up in his bed and hunched over the radio as though the light and the voice were a miracle for him. He was cleaning his face with some Wash 'n Dri's.

"It's been proven!" someone said. "You take and put a Chevvy in a Ford and a Ford in a Chevvy and they *both* go faster. It's been proven!"

We were all ready for sleep. Mayhew was the only one with his boots off. Two Marines that I hadn't even met before nightfall had gone out on the scrounge and come back with a new stretcher for me to sleep on, giving it to me without looking at me, as if to say, Shit, it ain't anything, we *like* walking around above ground. They were always doing things like that for you, the way Mayhew had tried to give me his mattress, the way grunts in Hue one day had tried to give me their helmets and flak jackets because I had turned up without my own. If you tore your fatigues on the wire or trying to crawl for cover, you'd have new or at least fresh ones within minutes and never know where they came from. They always took care of you.

". . . so next time," the announcer said, *"think* about it. It *might* just save your life." Another voice came on: "All right, then, moving right along here with our fabulous Sounds of the Sixties, AFVN, Armed Forces Radio Network, Vietnam, and for all you guys in the First of the Forty-fourth, and especially for the Soul Brother in the Orderly Room, here's Otis Redding—the *immortal* Otis Redding, singing 'Dock of the Bay.' "

"All right, my man," Day Tripper said.

"Listen," one of the Marines said. "When you think of all the guys in this fucked-up war, them casualties don't mean nothing. *Nothing!* Shit, your chances are better here than on the L.A. Freeway."

"Cold comfort," I muttered to myself.

Mayhew jumped up. "Hey, man, you cold? Whyn't you say so before? Here, my old lady sent me this. I ain't hardly used it." I didn't have a chance to say a word, he threw over a silvery square that fell against my hands like a sheet of India paper. It was a space blanket.

"Your ol' lady!" Day Tripper said.

"Yeah, my mother."

"Mayhew's momma," Day Tripper said. "What else your momma send you, Hand Job?"

"Well, she sent me them Christmas cookies that you scarfed up before I hardly got the fuckin' paper off."

Day Tripper laughed and lit another cigarette.

"Man," Mayhew said, "I'm so horny . . ." We waited for the rest of it, but there wasn't any.

"Hey, Mayhew," someone called, "you ever been laid? Your first don't count."

"Oh, yeah," Day Tripper said. "Mayhew got himself a little number down at China Beach, little chickie workin' the scivvie houses there, she jus' *love* Mayhew. Don't she?"

"That's a Rog," Mayhew said. He was grinning like an old illustration of Puck. "She loves it."

"Bullshit," Orrin said. "Ain't a Slope bitch in this whole fucked-up country that loves it."

"Okay, Jim," Mayhew said, and Day Tripper started to giggle.

The radio delivered a dramatized warning against losing pay vouchers and currency-exchange slips, and then the disc jockey came on again. "This one's a request for Hard-Core Paul and the Fire Team, and for our groovy CO, Fred the Head. . . ."

"Hey, Mayhew, turn that up. Turn it on up."

"Hey, cocksuck, you just tol' me to turn it off."

"Come on, man, that's an outtasight song."

Mayhew turned it up. It still wasn't very loud, but it filled the bunker. It was a song that had been on the radio a lot that winter.

There's something happening here,
What it is ain't exactly clear.
There's a man with a gun over there,
Tellin' me I've got to beware.
I think it's time we stopped, children,
What's that sound?
Everybody look what's goin' down. . . .

"Know what I heard over at the captain's hootch?" Mayhew said. "Some kid tol' me the Cav's comin' in here."

"Right," someone said. "They're coming tomorrow."

"What *time* tomorrow?"

"All right," Mayhew said. "Don't believe me. This kid was

a clerk. He's over to the TOC yesterday and he heard 'em talking."

"What's the Cav gonna do here? Make this a fuckin' parking lot for helicopters?"

The Marines did not like the Cav, the 1st Cavalry Division (Airmobile), they liked them even less than they liked the rest of the Army, and at the same time members of the Cav were beginning to feel as though their sole mission in Vietnam was to bail out Marines in trouble. They had come to help the Marines a dozen times in the past six months, and the last time, during the battle of Hue, they had taken almost as many casualties as the Marines had. There had been rumors about a relief operation for Khe Sanh since February, and by now they were being taken about as seriously as the rumors of attack which would attach themselves to particular dates thought to be significant to the North Vietnamese. (March 13, the anniversary of the initial Dien Bien Phu attacks, was the only one of those dates which anyone believed in. No one wanted to be anywhere near Khe Sanh on that day, and, as far as I know, the only correspondent who stayed through it was John Wheeler of the Associated Press.) If the rumors involved attack, everyone chose to ignore them. If they involved relief, no matter how farfetched they seemed, the Marines would embrace them privately while laughing them away publicly.

"Man, ain' no Cav goin' anywhere *near* this motherfucker."

"Okay, I don' give a shit," Mayhew said. "I'm just tellin' you what this kid tol' me."

"Thanks, Mayhew. Now shut the fuck up and let's get some fuckin' sleep."

That's what we did. Sometimes, sleeping at Khe Sanh was like sleeping after a few pipes of opium, a floating and a drifting in which your mind still worked, so that you could ask yourself whether you were sleeping even while you slept, acknowledging every noise above ground, every explosion and every running tremor in the earth, cataloging the specifics of each without ever waking. Marines would sleep with their eyes open, with their knees raised and rigid, often standing up on the doze as though touched by a spell. You took no pleasure from sleep there, no real rest. It was a commodity, it kept you from falling apart, the way cold, fat-caked C rations kept you from starving. That night, probably sleeping, I heard the sound of automatic-weapons fire outside. I had no real sense of waking, only of suddenly seeing three cigarettes glowing in the dark without any memory of their having been lighted.

"Probe," Mayhew said. He was leaning over me, completely dressed again, his face almost touching mine, and for a second I had the idea that he might have run over to cover me from any possible incoming. (It would not have been the first time that a grunt had done that.) Everyone was awake, all of our poncho liners were thrown back, I reached for my glasses and helmet and realized that I'd already put them on. Day Tripper was looking at us. Mayhew was grinning.

"Listen to that fucker, listen to that, that fucker's gonna burn out the barrel for sure."

It was an M-60 machine gun and it was not firing in bursts, but in a mad, sustained manner. The gunner must have seen something; maybe he was firing cover for a Marine patrol trying to get back in through the wire, maybe it was a three- or four-man probe that had been caught in the flarelight, something standing or moving, an infiltrator or a rat, but it sounded like the gunner was holding off a division. I couldn't tell whether there was answering fire or not, and then, abruptly, the firing stopped.

"Let's go see," Mayhew said, grabbing his rifle.

"Don' you go messin' with that out there," Day Tripper said. "They need us, they be sendin' for us. Fuckin' Mayhew."

"Man, it's all over. Listen. Come on," he said to me. "See if we can get you a story."

"Give me a second." I put on my flak jacket and we left the bunker, Day Tripper shaking his head at us, saying, "Fuckin' Mayhew. . . ."

Before, the fire had sounded as though it were coming from directly above the bunker, but the Marines on watch there said that it had been from a position forty meters farther down the trenchline. We walked that way in the dark, figures appearing and disappearing in the mist around us, odd, floating presences; it seemed like a long walk and then Mayhew bumped helmets with someone.

"You wanna watch where the fuck you're goin'," he said.

"That's 'You want to watch where the fuck you're going, *Sir*.'" It was a lieutenant, and he was laughing.

"Sorry, Sir."

"Mayhew?"

"Yes, Sir."

"What the fuck are you doing over here?"

"We heard some shit."

"Who's that man? Where's his rifle?"

"He's a reporter, Sir."

"Oh . . . Hello."

"Hello," I said.

"Well," the lieutenant said, "you missed the good part. You should have been here five minutes ago. We caught three of them out there by the first wire."

"What were they trying to do?" I asked.

"Don't know. Maybe cut the wires. Maybe lay in a mine, steal some of our Claymores, throw grenades, harass us some, don't know. Won't know, now."

We heard then what sounded at first like a little girl crying, a subdued, delicate wailing, and as we listened it became louder and more intense, taking on pain as it grew until it was a full, piercing shriek. The three of us turned to each other, we could almost feel each other shivering. It was terrible, absorbing every other sound coming from the darkness. Whoever it was, he was past caring about anything except the thing he was screaming about. There was a dull pop in the air above us, and an illumination round fell drowsily over the wire.

"Slope," Mayhew said. "See him there, see there, on the wire there?"

I couldn't see anything out there, there was no movement, and the screaming had stopped. As the flare dimmed, the sobbing started up and built quickly until it was a scream again.

A Marine brushed past us. He had a mustache and a piece of camouflaged parachute silk fastened bandana-style around his throat, and on his hip he wore a holster which held an M-79 grenade-launcher. For a second I thought I'd hallucinated him. I hadn't heard him approaching, and I tried now to see where he might have come from, but I couldn't. The M-79 had been cut down and fitted with a special stock. It was obviously a well-loved object; you could see the kind of work that had gone into it by the amount of light caught from the flares that glistened on the stock. The Marine looked serious, dead-eyed serious, and his right hand hung above the holster, waiting. The screaming had stopped again.

"Wait," he said. "I'll fix that fucker."

His hand was resting now on the handle of the weapon. The sobbing began again, and the screaming; we had the pattern now, the North Vietnamese was screaming the same thing over and over, and we didn't need a translator to tell us what it was.

"Put that fucker away," the Marine said, as though to himself. He drew the weapon, opened the breach and dropped in a round that looked like a great swollen bullet, listening very carefully all the while to the shrieking. He placed the M-79 over his left forearm and aimed for a second before firing. There was an enormous flash on the wire 200 meters away, a spray of orange sparks, and then everything was still except for the roll of some bombs exploding kilometers away and the sound of the M-79 being opened, closed again and returned to the holster. Nothing changed on the Marine's face, nothing, and he moved back into the darkness.

"Get some," Mayhew said quietly. "Man, did you *see* that?"

And I said, Yes (lying), it was something, really something.

The lieutenant said he hoped that I was getting some real good stories here. He told me to take her easy and disappeared. Mayhew looked out at the wire again, but the silence of the ground in front of us was really talking to him now. His fingers were limp, touching his face, and he looked like a kid at a scary movie. I poked his arm and we went back to the bunker for some more of that sleep.

V

On the higher levels of Command, the Khe Sanh situation was being regarded with great optimism, the kind that had seen us through Tet, smiling in the shambles. This often led to misunderstandings between the press and ranking Marine officers, particularly when it caused heavy casualties to be announced as light, routs and ambushes to be described as temporary tactical ploys, and filthy weather to be characterized as good and even excellent. It is hard to be there in the coastal warmth of Danang and be told by some Marine PIO that the DMZ, from which you have just that day returned, is enjoying the same warmth, especially when a hot shower and a change of clothes have failed to remove the damp chill of three days from your buttocks. You don't have to be a seasoned tactician to realize that your ass is cold.

Interviews with the commander of the 26th Marine Regiment, Colonel David Lownds, seemed to reveal a man who was utterly insensible to the gravity of his position, but Lownds was a deceptively complicated man with a gift (as one of his staff officers put it) for "jerking off the press." He could appear as a meek, low-keyed, distracted and even stupid man (some reporters referred to him privately as "The Lion of Khe Sanh"), as though he had been carefully picked for just these qualities by a cynical Command as a front for its decisions. When confronted with the possible odds against a successful defense of Khe Sanh, he would say things like "I do not plan on reinforcements" or "I'm not worried. I've got Marines." He was a small man with vague, watery eyes, slightly reminiscent of a rodent in a fable, with one striking feature: a full, scrupulously attended regimental mustache.

His professed ignorance of Dien Bien Phu drove correspondents crazy, but it was a dodge. Lownds knew very well about Dien Bien Phu and what had happened there, knew more about it than most of the interviewers. When I first met him, I brought a two-week-old message to Khe Sanh from his son-in-law, a Marine captain whom I'd met in Hue. He had been badly wounded in the fighting along the canals southwest of the Citadel, and the message amounted to little more than personal regards. Being a colonel commanding a regiment, Lownds of course had all the current information on the captain's condition, but he seemed glad for the chance to talk to someone who'd been there, who had seen him. He was proud of his son-in-law and very touched by the remembrance. He was also growing tired of reporters and of the criticism which most of the questions addressed to him implied, and I couldn't help but feel a sympathy for him. There were policies and attitudes at Khe Sanh that were getting grunts killed, but I doubted that they were the colonel's. He was really sort of a grunt himself, he had been there for a long time now, and it was beginning to tell on his face. The stories published about him never bothered to mention his personal courage or the extreme and special caution with which he risked the lives of his men.

No, to find the really mindless optimism, the kind that rejected facts and killed grunts wholesale and drove you into mad, helpless rages, you had to travel outward from Khe Sanh. The morale of the men at Khe Sanh was good (they were surviving, most of them; they were hacking it), but that didn't give any general the right to claim that they were anxious for a fight, eager for the attack to come. During a five-day trip across the DMZ at the end of February and the beginning of March, that seemed to be the only kind of talk that any of them was capable of. "Excellent," "real fine," "outstanding," "first rate": talk like that poured over you until it was all you could do to keep from seizing one graying crew-cut head or another and jamming it deep into the nearest tactical map.

On that trip I traveled with Karsten Prager of *Time*. Prager was in his early thirties and had been covering the war on and off for over three years. He was a German who had come to the States to attend college, and had lost all traces of his original accent. What replaced it was a gruff, clipped, Brooklyn-docks way of speaking. I once asked him how it was that he had been speaking English for such a short time and yet lost his German accent. "Well," he said, "I got dis tuhriffic eah fuh langwidjis." He had tough, shrewd eyes that matched his voice and a disdain for Command bravado that could be unsettling in an interview.

We flew the DMZ together from Quang Tri to Camp Carrol and the Rockpile, hitting each of the firebases that had been set up or converted to firing missions supporting Khe Sanh. We flew in beat-up Marine choppers, clumsy H-34's (Screw metal fatigue, we decided; the 34 had a lot of heart), over the cold, shattered, mist-bound hills, the same hills that had received over 120,000,000 pounds of explosives from B-52 raids in the previous three weeks, terrain like moonscapes, cratered and pitted and full of skilled North Vietnamese gunners. From past experience and the estimates of our meteorologists, the monsoons should be ending now, blowing south, clearing the DMZ skies and leaving the hills warm, but it wasn't happening, the monsoon held ("The weather?" some colonel would say. "The weather is increasingly advantageous!"), we were freezing, you could barely piss on those hilltop firebases, and the ceilings were uniformly low before noon and after three. On the last part of the trip, flying into Dong Ha, the aluminum rod that held the seats broke, spilling us to the floor and making the exact sound that a .50-caliber round will make when it strikes a chopper, giving us all a bad scare and then a good, good laugh. A couple of times the pilots thought they saw something moving on the hilltops and we went down, circling five or six times while we all groaned and giggled from fear and the cold. The crew chief was a young Marine who moved around the chopper without a safety line hooked to his flight suit, so comfortable with the rolling and shaking of the ship that you couldn't even pause to admire his daredevil nerve; you cut straight through to his easy grace and control, marveling as he hunkered down by the open door to rig the broken seat up again with pliers and a length of wire. At 1,500 feet he stood there in the gale-sucking door (Did he ever think about stepping off? How often?), his hands resting naturally on his hips, as though he were just standing around on a street corner somewhere, waiting. He knew he was good, an artist, he knew we were digging it, but it wasn't for us at all; it was his, private; he was the man who was never going to fall out of any damn helicopter.

At Dong Ha, after days without a bath or a shave or a change of fatigues, we went to the headquarters of the 3rd Marine Division, where Prager requested an immediate interview with General Tompkins, the commander. The general's aide was a brisk dude of a first lieutenant, scrubbed and shaved and polished to a dull glow, and he stared at us in disbelief. That initial distaste was mutual, and I didn't think we'd ever get beyond it, but a moment later he led us reluctantly into the general's office.

General Tompkins was seated behind his desk dressed in an OD sweatshirt, and he gave us a smile that made us feel slightly lunatic, standing there in our stubble and dirt and wrecked fatigues. When the lieutenant left the room, it was as though a great door had been slammed against the chill, and the general asked us to be seated. In spite of his hard good health and his taut, weathered face, he reminded me of Everett Dirksen. It was something sly and amused in his smile, a lurking wit behind the eyes, a soft gravel in his voice, each sentence rounding out in a grand deliberateness. Behind him several flags hung in their standards, and across the length of one entire wall there was a remarkable relief map of the DMZ, with several small sectors covered over, obscured from the eyes of unauthorized personnel.

We sat down, the general offered us cigarettes (by the pack) and Prager began the questioning. It was all stuff I'd heard before, a synthesis of everything Prager had gotten together during the past four days. I'd never seen any point in asking generals heavy questions about anything; they were officials too, and the answers were almost always what you expected them to be. I half listened, tuning in and out, and Prager began a long, involved question dealing with weather variants, air capability, elevation and range of our big guns, his big guns, problems of supply and reinforcement and (apologetically) disengagement and evacuation. The general touched his fingertips together as the question developed, smiled and nodded as it went into its third minute, he looked impressed by Prager's grasp of the situation and, finally, when the question ended, he placed his hands on the desk. He was still smiling.

"What?" he said.

Prager and I looked at each other quickly.

"You'll have to excuse me, boys. I'm a little hard of hearing. I don't always catch it all."

So Prager did it again, speaking unnaturally loud, and my mind went back to the map, into it really, so that the sound of outgoing artillery beyond the general's windows and the smell of burning shit and wet canvas brought in on the cold air put my head back at Khe Sanh for a moment.

I thought about the grunts who had sat in a circle one night with a guitar, singing "Where Have All the Flowers Gone?" Jack Laurence of CBS News had asked them if they knew what that song meant to so many people, and they said, Yes, yes, they knew. I thought about the graffiti that John Wheeler had discovered on a latrine wall there, "I think I'm falling in love with Jake," and about the grunts who had gone running up the trenchline to find a stretcher for me to sleep on, about Mayhew's space blanket, about the kid who had mailed a gook ear home to his girl and could not understand now why she had stopped writing to him. I thought of the thirteen Marine maneuver battalions deployed across the Z and of the brutality and sweetness they contained, all the ways they had of saying their thanks, even though they knew you were crazy for being there. I thought about the Marines at Khe Sanh on this night; it would be about the forty-fifth night of the shelling, the Flood had not lasted this long. Prager was still talking, the general was still nodding and touching his fingertips together and the question was almost finished. "General," Prager said, "what I want to know is, *what if* he decides to attack at Khe Sanh and, at the same time, he attacks at every single base the Marines have set up to support Khe Sanh, all across the DMZ?"

And I thought, Please, General, say "God forbid!" Let your hands fly up, let involuntary shudders rack your spare, tough frame. Remember Langvei. Remember Mayhew.

The general smiled, the crack trapper anticipating something good, past all doubting. "*That* . . . is *exactly* . . . what we . . . *want* him to do," he said.

We thanked him for his time and cigarettes and went out to look for a place to sleep that night.

On the afternoon of the day that we returned to Danang an important press conference was held at the Marine-operated, Marine-controlled press center, a small compound on the river where most correspondents based themselves whenever they covered I Corps. A brigadier general from III MAF, Marine Headquarters, was coming over to brief us on developments in the DMZ and Khe Sanh. The colonel in charge of "press operations" was visibly nervous, the dining room was being cleared for the meeting, microphones set up, chairs arranged, printed material put in order. These official briefings usually did the same thing to your perception of the war that flares did to your night vision, but this one was supposed to be special, and correspondents had come in from all over I Corps to be there. Among us was Peter Braestrup of the

Washington Post, formerly of *The New York Times.* He had
been covering the war for nearly three years. He had been a
captain in the Marines in Korea; ex-Marines are like ex-
Catholics or off-duty Feds, and Braestrup still made the Marines a special concern of his. He had grown increasingly
bitter about the Marines' failure to dig in at Khe Sanh, about
their shocking lack of defenses against artillery. He sat
quietly as the colonel introduced the general and the briefing
began.

The weather was excellent: "The sun is up over Khe Sanh
by ten every morning." (A collective groan running through
the seated journalists.) "I'm glad to be able to tell you that
Route Nine is now open and completely accessible." (Would
you drive Route 9 into Khe Sanh, General? You bet you
wouldn't.)

"What about the Marines at Khe Sanh?" someone asked.

"I'm glad we've come to that," the general said. "I was at
Khe Sanh for several hours this morning, and I want to tell
you that those Marines there are *clean!"*

There was a weird silence. We all knew we'd heard him,
the man had said that the Marines at Khe Sanh were clean
("Clean? He said 'clean,' didn't he?"), but not one of us
could imagine what he'd meant.

"Yes, they're bathing or getting a good wash every other
day. They're shaving every day, every single day. Their
mood is good, their spirits are fine, morale is excellent and
there's a twinkle in their eye!"

Braestrup stood up.

"General."

"Peter?"

"General, what about the defenses at Khe Sanh? Now, you
built this wonderful, air-conditioned officers' club, and that's
a complete shambles. You built a beer hall there, and *that's*

been blown away." He had begun calmly, but now he was having trouble keeping the anger out of his voice. "You've got a medical detachment there that's a disgrace, set up right on the airstrip, exposed to hundreds of rounds every day, and *no* overhead cover. You've had men at the base since July, you've expected an attack at least since November, they've been shelling you heavily since January. General, why haven't those Marines *dug in?*"

The room was quiet. Braestrup had a fierce smile on his face as he sat down. When the question had begun, the colonel had jerked suddenly to one side of his chair, as though he'd been shot. Now, he was trying to get his face in front of the general's so that he could give out the look that would say, "See, General? See the kind of peckerheads I have to work with every day?" Braestrup was looking directly at the general now, waiting for his answer—the question had not been rhetorical—and it was not long in coming.

"Peter," the general said, "I think you're hitting a small nail with an awfully big hammer."

VI

The door gunner was leaning out, looking down, and he started to laugh. He wrote out a note and handed it to me. It read, "We sure brang some pee down to bear on them hills."

The monsoons were breaking, a hard heat was coming back to I Corps and the ordeal at Khe Sanh was almost over. Flying across the westernmost stretches of the DMZ, you could read the history of that terrible winter just by looking at the hills.

For most of the time that the North Vietnamese had controlled Route 9 and kept the Marines isolated at Khe Sanh, all that anyone could see of the hills had been what little the transient mists allowed, a desolated terrain, cold, hostile, all colors deadened by the rainless monsoon or secreted in the fog. Now they were full and voluptuous in the new spring light.

Often you'd hear Marines talking about how beautiful those hills must have been, but that spring they were not beautiful. Once they had been the royal hunting grounds of the Annamese emperors. Tigers, deer and flying squirrels had lived in them. I used to imagine what a royal hunt must have been like, but I could only see it as an Oriental children's story: a conjuring of the emperor and empress, princes and princelings, court favorites and emissaries, all caparisoned for the hunt; slender figures across a tapestry, a promise of bloodless kills, a serene frolic complete with horseback flirtations and death-smiling game. And even now you could hear Marines comparing these hills with the hills around their homes, talking about what a pleasure it would be to hunt in them for anything other than men.

But mostly, I think, the Marines hated those hills; not from time to time, the way many of us hated them, but constantly, like a curse. Better to fight the war in the jungles or along the dry flats that lined the Cua Viet River than in those hills. I heard a grunt call them "angry" once, probably something he'd picked up from a movie or a television series, but from his point of view he was right, the word was a good one. So when we decimated them, broke them, burned parts of them so that nothing would ever live on them again, it must have given a lot of Marines a good feeling, an intimation of power. They had humped those hills until their legs were in an agony, they'd been ambushed in them and blown apart on their trails, trapped on their barren ridges, lain under fire clutching the foliage that grew on them, wept alone in fear and exhaustion and shame just knowing the kind of terror that night always brought to them, and now, in April, something like revenge had been achieved.

We never announced a scorched-earth policy; we never announced any policy at all, apart from finding and destroying the enemy, and we proceeded in the most obvious way. We used what was at hand, dropping the greatest volume of explosives in the history of warfare over all the terrain within the thirty-mile sector which fanned out from Khe Sanh. Employing saturation-bombing techniques, we delivered more than 110,000 tons of bombs to those hills during the eleven-week containment of Khe Sanh. The smaller foothills were often quite literally turned inside out, the steeper of them were made faceless and drawless, and the bigger hills were left with scars and craters of such proportions that an observer from some remote culture might see in them the obsessiveness and ritual regularity of religious symbols, the blackness at the deep center pouring out rays of bright, overturned earth all the way to the circumference; forms like Aztec sun figures, suggesting that their makers had been men who held Nature in an awesome reverence.

Once on a Chinook run from Cam Lo to Dong Ha, I sat next to a Marine who took a Bible from his pack and began reading even before we took off. He had a small cross sketched in ballpoint on his flak jacket and another, even less obtrusive, on his helmet cover. He was an odd-looking guy for a combat Marine in Vietnam. For one thing, he was never going to tan, no matter how many months he spent in the sun. He would just go red and blotchy, even though his hair was dark. He was also very heavy, maybe twenty pounds overweight, although you could see from his boots and fatigues that he'd humped it a lot over here. He wasn't a chaplain's assistant or anything, just a grunt who happened to be fat, pale and religious. (You didn't meet that many who were deeply religious, although you expected to, with so many kids from the South and the Midwest, from farms and small rural towns.) We strapped in and he started reading, getting very absorbed, and I leaned out the door and looked at the endless progression of giant pits which were splashed over the ground, at the acre-sized scars where napalm or chemical spray had eaten away the cover. (There was a special Air Force outfit that flew defoliation missions. They were called the Ranch Hands, and their motto was, "Only we can prevent forests.") When I held out some cigarettes to offer him one, he looked up from the Bible and shook his head, getting off that quick, pointless laugh that told me for sure that he'd seen a lot of action. Maybe he had even been at Khe Sanh, or up on 861 with the 9th. I don't think he realized that I wasn't a Marine, I had on a Marine flak jacket which covered the correspondent's identification tags sewn on my fatigues, but he saw the offer of a cigarette as a courtesy and he wanted to return it. He passed over the open Bible, almost giggling now, and pointed to a passage. It was Psalms 91:5, and it said,

Thou shalt not be afraid for the terror by night; nor for the arrow that flieth by day.

Nor for the pestilence that walketh in darkness; nor for the destruction that wasteth at noonday.

A thousand shall fall at thy side, and ten thousand at thy right hand; but it shall not come nigh thee.

Okay, I thought, that's good to know. I wrote the word "Beautiful!" out on a piece of paper and handed it back to him, and he jerked his thumb up, meaning that he thought so too. He went back to the book and I went back to the door, but I had a nasty impulse all the way into Dong Ha to run through Psalms and find a passage which I could offer him, the one that talked about those who were defiled with their own works and sent a-whoring with their own inventions.

The relief of Khe Sanh began on April 1. It was code-named Operation Pegasus, and while it included over 10,000 Marines and three full battalions of ARVN, it took its name and its style from the 1st Cavalry Division (Airmobile). A week earlier, 18,000 members of the Cav had left their base at Camp Evans, near Dong Ha, and moved to a point in a river valley eleven miles northeast of Khe Sanh, just beyond the range of the big guns that were dug into the Laotian mountains. The Cav had plenty of helicopters, choppers were what the Cav was all about; and Sky Cranes lifted in earth-moving equipment, Chinooks brought in the heavier artillery pieces, and within days there was a forward operational base that looked better than most permanent installations in I Corps, complete with a thousand-meter airstrip and deep, ventilated bunkers. They named it LZ Stud, and once it was finished Khe Sanh ceased to be the center of its own sector; it became just another objective.

It was almost as though the war had ended. The day before Pegasus began, President Johnson had announced the suspension of airstrikes against the North and put a closing date on his own Administration. The Marines' 11th Engineers had begun moving down Route 9, deactivating mines and repairing bridges, and they had met with no resistance. The shelling of Khe Sanh had become a matter of a few scattered rounds a day, and it had been more than two weeks now since General Westmoreland had revealed that, in his opinion, the attack on Khe Sanh would never come. The 304th NVA Division had left the area, and so had the 325C. Now, it seemed that all but a token force of NVA had vanished. And now, everywhere you went, you could see the most comforting military insignia in all of Vietnam, the yellow-and-black shoulder patch of the Cav. You were with the pro's now, the elite. LZ's and firebases were being established at a rate of three and four a day, and every hour brought them closer to Khe Sanh.

Really, it was almost too good, and by the third day something odd attended Pegasus. As an operation, it revealed the tastes of the Cav's commander, Major General John Tolson, a general of uncommon intelligence and subtlety. Its precision and speed were unbelievable, especially to anyone who had just spent the better part of three months with the Marines. Pegasus was almost elegant in its tactics and scope. Stendhal would have loved it (he would have called it "an affair of outposts"), but it soon came to look more like a spectacle than a military operation, a non-operation devised to non-relieve the non-siege of Khe Sanh. When I told General Tolson that I had no real grasp of what the Cav was doing, he laughed and told me that I was probably brighter about it than I knew. Pegasus was objectiveless, he said. Its purpose was to engage. But engage what?

Perhaps, as we claimed, the B-52's had driven them all away, broken the back of their will to attack. (We claimed 13,000 NVA dead from those raids.) Maybe they'd left the Khe Sanh area as early as January, leaving the Marines pinned down, and moved across I Corps in readiness for the Tet Offensive. Many people believed that a few battalions, clever enough and active enough, could have kept the Marines at Khe Sanh inside the wire and underground for all of those weeks. Maybe they'd come to see reasons why an attack would be impossible, and gone back into Laos. Or A Shau. Or Quang Tri. Or Hue. We didn't know. They were somewhere, but they were not around Khe Sanh anymore.

Incredible arms caches were being found, rockets still

crated, launchers still wrapped in factory paper, AK-47's still packed in Cosmoline, all indicating that battalion-strength units had left in a hurry. The Cav and the Marines above Route 9 were finding equipment suggesting that entire companies had fled. Packs were found on the ground in perfect company formations, and while they contained diaries and often poems written by the soldiers, there was almost no information about where they had gone or why. Considering the amount of weapons and supplies being found (a record for the entire war), there were surprisingly few prisoners, although one prisoner did tell his interrogators that 75 percent of his regiment had been killed by our B-25's, nearly 1,500 men, and that the survivors were starving. He had been pulled out of a spider hole near Hill 881 North, and had seemed grateful for his capture. An American officer who was present at the interrogation actually said that the boy was hardly more than seventeen or eighteen, and that it was hideous that the North was feeding such young men into a war of aggression. Still, I don't remember anyone, Marine or Cav, officer or enlisted, who was not moved by the sight of their prisoners, by the sudden awareness of what must have been suffered and endured that winter.

For the first time in eleven weeks, Marines at Khe Sanh left their perimeter, walked two miles to Hill 471, and took it, after what amounted to the one serious battle of those weeks. (LZ's, including Stud, were sporadically rocketed and mortared; the Cav lost some ships to NVA gunners; there were small often sharp firefights almost every day. One or two body bags waited for removal at most landing zones on most afternoons, but it was different, and that was the trouble. After the slaughter of the winter, you were afraid of this unaccustomed mercy, afraid of becoming lax or afraid of having the Joke played on you. It was one thing, if it had to happen, to have it happen in Hue or Khe Sanh, but something else to be one of the few. WHY ME? was a common piece of helmet graffiti.) You'd hear a trooper of the Cav say something like, "I hear the Marines stepped into the shit above Route Nine," but what he really meant was, Of *course* the Marines stepped into the shit, what *else* would they be doing in this war? The Cav's attitude acknowledged that they might die too, but never the way the Marines did. A story circulated around the Pegasus TAOR about a Marine who had been staked to a hillside by the NVA: Marine choppers refused to pick him up, so the Cav went down and got him. Whether it was true or not, it revealed the complexities of the Marine–Cav rivalry, and when the Cav sent an outfit to relieve the Marines on 471, it killed off one of the last surviving romances about war left over from the movies: there was no shouting, no hard kidding, no gleeful obscenities, or the old "Hey, where you from? Brooklyn!? No kiddin'! Me too!" The departing and arriving files passed one another without a single word being spoken.

The death of Martin Luther King intruded on the war in a way that no other outside event had ever done. In the days that followed, there were a number of small, scattered riots, one or two stabbings, all of it denied officially. The Marine recreational facility in China Beach in Danang was put off-limits for a day, and at Stud we stood around the radio and listened to the sound of automatic-weapons fire being broadcast from a number of American cities. A southern colonel on the general's staff told me that it was a shame, a damn shame, but I had to admit (didn't I?) that he'd been a long time asking for it. A black staff sergeant in the Cav who had taken me over to his outfit for dinner the night before cut me dead on the day that we heard the news, but he came over to the press tent later that night and told me that it shouldn't happen that way. I got a bottle of Scotch from my pack and we went outside and sat on the grass, watching the flares dropping over the hillside across the river. There were still some night mists. In the flarelight it looked like heavy snow, and the ravines looked like ski trails.

He was from Alabama and he had all but decided on a career in the Army. Even before King's murder he had seen what this might someday mean, but he'd always hoped to get around it somehow.

"Now what I gonna do?" he said.

"I'm a great one to ask."

"But dig it. Am I gonna take 'n' turn them guns aroun' on my own people? Shit!"

That was it, there was hardly a black NCO anywhere who wasn't having to deal with that. We sat in the dark, and he told me that when he'd walked by me that afternoon it had made him sick. He couldn't help it.

"Shit, I can't do no twenny in this Army. They ain' no way. All's I hope is I can hang back when push comes t' shove. An' then I think, Well, fuck it, why should I? Man, home's jus' gonna be a hassle."

There was some firing on the hill, a dozen M-79 rounds and the dull bap-bap-bap of an AK-47, but that was over there, there was an entire American division between that and us. But the man was crying, trying to look away while I tried not to look.

"It's just a bad night for it," I said. "What can I tell you?"

He stood up, looked at the hill and then started to leave. "Oh, man," he said. "This war gets old."

At Langvei we found the two-month-old corpse of an American stretched out on the back of a wrecked jeep. This was on the top of the small hill that opposed the hill containing the Special Forces bunkers taken by the NVA in February. They were still in there, 700 meters away. The corpse was the worst thing we'd ever seen, utterly blackened now, the skin on the face drawn back tightly like stretched leather, so that all of his teeth showed. We were outraged that he had not been buried or at least covered, and we moved away and set up positions around the hill. Then the ARVN moved out toward the bunkers and were turned back by machine-gun fire. We sat on the hill and watched while napalm was dropped against the bunkers, and then we set up a recoilless rifle and fired at the vents. I went back to Stud. The next day a company of the Cav tried it, moving in two files on high and low ground approaching the bunkers, but the terrain between the hills offered almost no cover, and they were turned back. That night they were rocketed heavily, but took no serious casualties. I came back on the third day with Rick Merron and John Lengle of the Associated Press. There had been heavy airstrikes against the bunkers that night, and now two tiny helicopters, Loaches, were hovering a few feet above the slits, pouring in fire.

"Man, one Dink with a forty-five could put a hurtin' on those Loaches they'd never come back from," a young captain said. It was incredible, those little ships were the most beautiful things flying in Vietnam (you had to stop once in a while and admire the machinery), they just hung there above those bunkers like wasps outside a nest. "That's sex," the captain said. "That's pure sex."

One of the Loaches rose suddenly and flew over the hill, crossed the river and darted into Laos. Then it circled quickly, dipped, flew directly over us and hung there. The pilot radioed the captain.

"Sir, there's a gook di-di-ing down the trail into Laos. Permission to kill him."

"Permission given."

"Thank you," the pilot said, and the ship broke its suspended motion and sped toward the trail, clearing its guns.

A rocket whistled by, missing the hill, and we ran for the bunkers. Two more came in, both missing, and then we moved out for the opposite hill one more time, watching the machine-gun slits for fluttering blips of light with one eye and checking the ground for booby traps with the other. But they had abandoned it during the night, and we took it without a shot, standing on top of the bunkers, looking down into Laos, past the remains of two bombed-out Russian tanks, feeling relieved, victorious and silly. When Merron and I flew back to Stud that afternoon, the two-month-old corpse rode with us. No one had covered him until ten minutes before the chopper had picked us up, and the body bag swarmed with flies until the motion of the rising chopper shook them off. We got out at Graves Registration with it, where one of the guys opened the bag and said, "Shit, this is a *gook!* What'd they bring him *here* for?"

"Look, Jesus, he's got on our uniform."

"I don't give a fuck, that ain't no American, that's a fucking *gook!*"

"Wait a minute," the other one said. "Maybe it's a spade. . . ."

The chopper that brought us back to Khe Sanh had barely touched the strip, and we were running again. I must have seen the Marines playing softball there, lounging around, hanging up laundry, but I rejected it and ran anyway. It was the only way I knew to behave there. I knew where the trench was, and went for it.

"Must be Airborne trainin'," some grunt called, and I slowed down.

"Ain' no hurry-up no more," a black Marine said. They all had their fatigue shirts off, there must have been hundreds of them, all around the field. It didn't seem possible, but I knew it must be all right; I had noticed the weight of my flak jacket and pack as I'd run. Nearly 500 Vietnamese Rangers sat near the strip with all of their gear around them. One of them ran up to an American, probably an advisor, and embraced him tightly. They were being taken out that morning. Colonel Lownds' replacement was due at the base any hour now, and some of the 26th had already been lifted out and moved to Hoi An, south of Danang. The new Charlie Med triage room had just been completed, deep underground and well lighted, but only a few men a day were being treated there. I went over to Hotel Company's position, but they were gone; a company of the Cav was there instead. They had cleaned out the trench floor all along the perimeter there, and the old bunker smelled now as though it had been dug that morning. It was no wonder that the Marines called the Cav dudes and got uncomfortable whenever they were around. I was relieving myself on the ground by one of the dumps when a Marine sergeant came up to me.

"You wanna please use the piss tube next time," he said.

It hadn't even occurred to me; I couldn't remember ever having seen a piss tube at Khe Sanh.

"Has the Cav taken over most of the perimeter?" I asked.

"Hmmmm."

"It must be a relief not to have to worry about that anymore."

"Shit, I'd feel a whole lot better if we had *Marines* here still. Damn Cav, all's they do is sleep on watch."

"Have you seen that?"

"No, but that's what they do."

"You don't like the Cav much?"

"I wouldn't say that."

Far up the strip, 400 meters away, there was a man sitting on some ammo crates. He was by himself. It was the colonel. I hadn't seen him in nearly six weeks, and he looked tired now. He had the same stare that the rest of the Marines here had, and the corners of his mustache had been rolled tortuously into two tight points that were caked with dried creamed coffee. Yes, he said, it sure would be good to get out of this place. He sat there looking at the hills, and I think that he was all but hypnotized by them now; they were not the same hills that had surrounded him for most of the past ten months. They had held such fearful mystery for so long that when they were suddenly found to be peaceful again, they were transformed as greatly as if a flood had swept over them.

A token American force was kept at Khe Sanh for the next month, and the Marines went back to patrolling the hills, as they had done a year before. A great many people wanted to know how the Khe Sanh Combat Base could have been the Western Anchor of our Defense one month and a worthless piece of ground the next, and they were simply told that the situation had changed. A lot of people suspected that some kind of secret deal had been made with the North; activity along the DMZ all but stopped after Khe Sanh was abandoned. The Mission called it a victory, and General Westmoreland said that it had been "a Dien Bien Phu in reverse." In early June engineers rolled up the airstrip and transported the salvaged tarmac back to Dong Ha. The bunkers were filled with high explosives and then blown up. The sandbagging and wire that remained were left to the jungle, which grew with a violence of energy now in the Highland summer, as though there was an impatience somewhere to conceal all traces of what had been left by the winter.

Postscript: China Beach

It was a great curving stretch of beachfront that faced the Bay of Danang. Even during the monsoons the afternoons were warm and clear, but now, in August, the dry, hot winds blew the sharp grit of the sand across the beach, into your eyes, hurling it stinging against your skin. Every Marine in I Corps got to spend a few days at China Beach at least once during their thirteen-month tours. It was a place where they could go swimming or surfing, get drunk, get stoned, get laid, get straight, groove in the scivvie houses, rent sailboats, or just sleep on the beach. Sometimes it was just an in-country R&R, a vacation, and sometimes it was a reward for outstanding service, exceptional bravery. Some Marines, the ones who were more than just good in a firefight, would get here as often as once a month because their company commanders did not like having them around between operations. With their medals and commendations, they would get three days out, a reprieve that promised them hot food, hot showers, time to goof and miles of beach. Sometimes choppers from the Cav would fly low along the beach, buzzing the Marines, and once, when a beautiful girl in a bikini was sighted, one of them actually landed. But you saw very few women here, mostly just Marines, and on some days there were thousands of them. They would splash in the surf, giggling and shouting, riding beach disks along the shoreline, playing like kids. Sometimes they would just lie asleep, half in the water and half in the sand. This was not the war for such images, you knew better, but they were Marines, and there was something terrible about seeing them there, limp in the wash of the tide.

Up from the beach there was a long, airless concrete building that served as a cafeteria. It had the best jukebox in Vietnam, and black Marines would spend more time there than on the beach, jiving around the room, carrying stacks of greasy hamburgers, dank french fries, giant paper cups full of malted milk, grape drink or (because it was so pretty, one of them told me) tomato juice. You'd sit at the tables there listening to the music, glad to be out of the sun, and every once in a while some grunts would recognize you from an operation and come over to talk. It was always nice to see them, but it always brought bad news, and sometimes the sight of what the war had done to them was awful. The two who came up to me now looked all right.

"You're a reporter, ain't you?"

I nodded.

"We seen you one time at Khe Sanh."

They were from the 26th Marines, Hotel Company, and they told me all about what had happened to the outfit since April. They weren't from the same platoon as Orrin and Day Tripper, but they knew that both of them had made it home. One of the guys who had run out to bring me a stretcher to sleep on was in a big hospital in Japan. I couldn't remember the name of the one grunt I most wanted to hear about, I was probably afraid of what they'd say, but I described him. He was a little cat with blond hair, and he was trying to grow a mustache.

"Oh, you mean Stoner."

"No, it wasn't that. He was always hanging out with Day Tripper. The guy I mean extended back in March, A crazy, funny little guy."

They looked at each other, and I was sorry I'd asked.

"I know the guy you mean," one of them said. "He was always running around singing real crazy shit? Yeah, I know. He got killed. What was that little fucker's name?"

"I don't know which one," the other Marine said.

"Shit, yes, he got greased out on that *brilliant* fuckin' operation down from Hoi An. 'Member, in May?"

"Oh yeah. Him."

"Took a fuckin' RPG round right in the chest. God *damn*, I'll think of his name."

But I already remembered it now, and I sat there playing with a bottle of suntan lotion.

"It was Montefiori," one of them said.

"No, but it started with an M," the other one said.

"Winters!"

"No, dumb shit, now does Winters start with an M?"

"That kid Morrisey."

"You're just fuckin' with me now. Morrisey got sent home last week. . . ."

They went on like that, they really couldn't remember it. It was just a matter of pride or politeness for them to come up with the name of a dead buddy, they were going to try, but when they thought I wasn't watching, they looked at each other and smiled.

Illumination Rounds

We were all strapped into the seats of the Chinook, fifty of us, and something, someone was hitting it from the outside with an enormous hammer. How do they do that? I thought, we're a thousand feet in the air! But it had to be that, over and over, shaking the helicopter, making it dip and turn in a horrible out-of-control motion that took me in the stomach. I had to laugh, it was so exciting, it was the thing I had wanted, almost what I had wanted except for that wrenching, resonant metal-echo; I could hear it even above the noise of the rotor blades. And they were going to fix that, I knew they would make it stop. They had to, it was going to make me sick.

They were all replacements going in to mop up after the big battles on Hills 875 and 876, the battles that had already taken on the name of one great battle, the battle of Dak To. And I was new, brand new, three days in-country, embarrassed about my boots because they were so new. And across from me, ten feet away, a boy tried to jump out of the straps and then jerked forward and hung there, his rifle barrel caught in the red plastic webbing of the seat back. As the chopper rose again and turned, his weight went back hard against the webbing and a dark spot the size of a baby's hand showed in the center of his fatigue jacket. And it grew—I knew what it was, but not really—it got up to his armpits and then started down his sleeves and up over his shoulders at the same time. It went all across his waist and down his legs, covering the canvas on his boots until they were dark like everything else he wore, and it was running in slow, heavy drops off of his fingertips. I thought I could hear the drops hitting the metal strip on the chopper floor. Hey! . . . Oh, but this isn't anything at all, it's not real, it's just some *thing* they're going through that isn't real. One of the door gunners was heaped up on the floor like a cloth dummy. His hand had the bloody raw look of a pound of liver fresh from the butcher paper. We touched down on the same lz we had just left a few minutes before, but I didn't know it until one of the guys shook my shoulder, and then I couldn't stand up. All I could feel of my legs was their shaking, and the guy thought I'd been hit and helped me up. The chopper had taken eight hits, there was shattered plastic all over the floor, a dying pilot up front, and the boy was hanging forward in the straps again, he was dead, but not (I knew) really dead.

It took me a month to lose that feeling of being a spectator to something that was part game, part show. That first afternoon, before I'd boarded the Chinook, a black sergeant had tried to keep me from going. He told me I was too new to go near the kind of shit they were throwing around up in those hills. ("You a reporter?" he'd asked, and I'd said, "No, a writer," dumbass and pompous, and he'd laughed and said, "Careful. You can't use no eraser up where you wanna go.") He'd pointed to the bodies of all the dead Americans lined in two long rows near the chopper pad, so many that they could not even cover all of them decently. But they were not real then, and taught me nothing. The Chinook had come in, blowing my helmet off, and I grabbed it up and joined the replacements waiting to board. "Okay, man," the sergeant said. "You gotta go, you gotta go. All's I can say is, I hope you get a clean wound."

The battle for Hill 875 was over, and some survivors were being brought in by Chinook to the landing strip at Dak To. The 173rd Airborne had taken over 400 casualties, nearly 200 killed, all on the previous afternoon and in the fighting that had gone on all through the night. It was very cold and wet up there, and some girls from the Red Cross had been sent up from Pleiku to comfort the survivors. As the troops filed out of the helicopters, the girls waved and smiled at them from behind their serving tables. "Hi, soldier! What's your name?" "Where you from, soldier?" "I'll bet some hot coffee would hit the spot about now."

And the men from the 173rd just kept walking without answering, staring straight ahead, their eyes rimmed with red from fatigue, their faces pinched and aged with all that had happened during the night. One of them dropped out of line and said something to a loud, fat girl who wore a Peanuts sweatshirt under her fatigue blouse and she started to cry. The rest just walked past the girls and the large, olive-drab coffee urns. They had no idea of where they were.

A senior NCO in the Special Forces was telling the story: "We was back at Bragg, in the NCO Club, and this school-teacher comes in an' she's real good-lookin'. Dusty here grabs her by the shoulders and starts runnin' his tongue all over her face like she's a fuckin' ice-cream cone. An' you know what she says? She says, 'I like you. You're different.' "

At one time they would have lighted your cigarette for you on the terrace of the Continental Hotel. But those days are almost twenty years gone, and anyway, who really misses them? Now there is a crazy American who looks like George Orwell, and he is always sleeping off his drinks in one of the wicker chairs there, slumped against a fable, starting up with violence, shouting and then going back to sleep. He makes everyone nervous, especially the waiters; the old ones who had served the French and the Japanese and the first American journalists and OSS types ("those noisy bastards at the Continental," Graham Greene called them) and the really young ones who bussed the tables and pimped in a modest way. The little elevator boy still greets the guests each morning with a quiet "*Ça va?*" but he is seldom answered, and the old baggage man (he also brings us grass) will sit in the lobby and say, "How are you tomorrow?"

"Ode to Billy Joe" plays from speakers mounted on the terrace's corner columns, but the air seems too heavy to carry the sound right, and it hangs in the corners. There is an exhausted, drunk master sergeant from the 1st Infantry Division who has bought a flute from the old man in khaki shorts and pith helmet who sells instruments along Tu Do Street. The old man will lean over the butt-strewn flower boxes that line the terrace and play "Frère Jacques" on a wooden stringed instrument. The sergeant has bought the flute, and he is playing it quietly, pensively, badly.

The tables are crowded with American civilian construction engineers, men getting $30,000 a year from their jobs on government contracts and matching that easily on the black market. Their faces have the look of aerial photos of silicone pits, all hung with loose flesh and visible veins. Their mistresses were among the prettiest, saddest girls in Vietnam. I always wondered what they had looked like before they'd made their arrangements with the engineers. You'd see them at the tables there, smiling their hard, empty smiles into those rangy, brutal, scared faces. No wonder those men all looked alike to the Vietnamese. After a while they all looked alike to me. Out on the Bien Hoa Highway, north of Saigon, there is a monument to the Vietnamese war dead, and it is one of the few graceful things left in the country. It is a modest pagoda set above the road and approached by long flights of gently rising steps. One Sunday, I saw a bunch of these engineers gunning their Harleys up those steps, laughing and shouting in the afternoon sun. The Vietnamese had a special name for them to distinguish them from all other Americans; it translated out to something like "The Terrible Ones," although I'm told that this doesn't even approximate the odium carried in the original.

There was a young sergeant in the Special Forces, stationed at the C Detachment in Can Tho, which served as the SF headquarters for IV Corps. In all, he had spent thirty-six months in Vietnam. This was his third extended tour, and he planned to come back again as soon as he possibly could after this current hitch was finished. During his last tour he had lost a finger and part of a thumb in a firefight, and he had been generally shot up enough times for the three Purple Hearts which mean that you don't have to fight in Vietnam anymore. After all that, I guess they thought of him as a combat liability, but he was such a hard charger that they gave him the EM Club to manage. He ran it well and seemed happy, except that he had gained a lot of weight in the duty, and it set him apart from the rest of the men. He loved to horse around with the Vietnamese in the compound, leaping on them from behind, leaning heavily on them, shoving them around and pulling their ears, sometimes punching them a little hard in the stomach, smiling a stiff small smile that was meant to tell them all that he was just being playful. The Vietnamese would smile too, until he turned to walk away. He loved the Vietnamese, he said, he really *knew* them after three years. As far as he was concerned, there was no place in the world as fine as Vietnam. And back home in North Carolina he had a large, glass-covered display case in which he kept his medals and decorations and citations, the photographs taken during three tours and countless battles, letters from past commanders, a few souvenirs. The case stood in the center of the living room, he said, and every night his wife and three kids would move the kitchen table out in front of it and eat their dinner there.

At 800 feet we knew we were being shot at. Something hit the underside of the chopper but did not penetrate it. They weren't firing tracers, but we saw the brilliant flickering blips of light below, and the pilot circled and came down very fast, working the button that released fire from the flex guns mounted on either side of the Huey. Every fifth round was a tracer, and they sailed out and down, incomparably graceful, closer and closer, until they met the tiny point of light coming from the jungle. The ground fire stopped, and we went on to land at Vinh Long, where the pilot yawned and said, "I think I'll go to bed early tonight and see if I can wake up with any enthusiasm for this war."

A twenty-four-year-old Special Forces captain was telling me about it. "I went out and killed one VC and liberated a prisoner. Next day the major called me in and told me that I'd killed fourteen VC and liberated six prisoners. You want to see the medal?"

There was a little air-conditioned restaurant on the corner of Le Loi and Tu Do, across from the Continental Hotel and the old opera house which now served as the Vietnamese Lower House. Some of us called it the Graham Greene Milk Bar (a scene in *The Quiet American* had taken place there), but its name was Givral. Every morning they baked their own baguettes and croissants, and the coffee wasn't too bad. Sometimes, I'd meet there with a friend of mine for breakfast.

He was a Belgian, a tall, slow-moving man of thirty who'd been born in the Congo. He professed to know and love war, and he affected the mercenary sensibility. He'd been photographing the Vietnam thing for seven or eight years now, and once in a while he'd go over to Laos and run around the jungles there with the government, searching for the dreaded Pathet Lao, which he pronounced "Paddy Lao." Other people's stories of Laos always made it sound like a lotus land where no one wanted to hurt anyone, but he said that whenever he went on ops there he always kept a grenade taped to his belly because he was a Catholic and knew what the Paddy Lao would do to him if he were captured. But he was a little crazy that way, and tended to dramatize his war stories.

He always wore dark glasses, probably even during operations. His pictures sold to the wire services, and I saw a few of them in the American news magazines. He was very kind in a gruff, offhanded sort of way, kindness embarrassed him, and he was so graceless among people, so eager to shock, that he couldn't understand why so many of us liked him. Irony was the effect he worked for in conversation, that and a sense of how exquisite the war could be when all of its machinery was running right. He was explaining the finish of an operation he'd just been on in War Zone C, above Cu Chi.

"There were a lot of dead VC," he said. "Dozens and dozens of them! A lot of them were from that same village that has been giving you so much trouble lately. VC from top to bottom—Michael, in that village the fucking *ducks* are VC. So the American commander had twenty or thirty of the dead flown up in a sling load and dropped into the village. I should say it was a drop of at least two hundred feet, all those dead Viet Congs, right in the middle of the village."

He smiled (I couldn't see his eyes).

"Ah, Psywar!" he said, kissing off the tips of his fingers.

Bob Stokes of *Newsweek* told me this: In the big Marine hospital in Danang they have what is called the "White Lie Ward," where they bring some of the worst cases, the ones who can be saved but who will never be the same again. A young Marine was carried in, still unconscious and full of morphine, and his legs were gone. As he was being carried into the ward, he came out of it briefly and saw a Catholic chaplain standing over him.

"Father," he said, "am I all right?"

The chaplain didn't know what to say. "You'll have to talk about that with the doctors, son."

"Father, are my legs okay?"

"Yes," the chaplain said. "Sure."

By the next afternoon the shock had worn off and the boy knew all about it. He was lying on his cot when the chaplain came by.

"Father," the Marine said, "I'd like to ask you for something."

"What, son?"

"I'd like to have that cross." And he pointed to the tiny silver insignia on the chaplain's lapel.

"Of course," the chaplain said. "But why?"

"Well, it was the first thing I saw when I came to yesterday, and I'd like to have it."

The chaplain removed the cross and handed it to him. The Marine held it tightly in his fist and looked at the chaplain. "You lied to me, Father," he said. "You cocksucker. You lied to me."

His name was Davies, and he was a gunner with a helicopter group based at Tan Son Nhut airport. On paper, by the regulations, he was billeted in one of the big "hotel" BEQ's in Cholon, but he only kept his things there. He actually lived in a small two-story Vietnamese house deeper inside of Cholon, as far from the papers and the regulations as he could get. Every morning he took an Army bus with wire-grille windows out to the base and flew missions, mostly around War Zone C, along the Cambodian border, and most nights he returned to the house in Cholon where he lived with his "wife" (whom he'd found in one of the bars) and some other Vietnamese who were said to be the girl's family. Her mamma-san and her brother were always there, living on the first floor, and there were others who came and went. He seldom saw the brother, but every few days he would find a pile of labels and brand names torn from cardboard cartons, American products that the brother wanted from the PX.

The first time I saw him he was sitting alone at a table on the Continental terrace, drinking a beer. He had a full, drooping mustache and sharp, sad eyes, and he was wearing a denim workshirt and wheat jeans. He also carried a Leica and a copy of *Ramparts*, and I just assumed at first that he was a correspondent. I didn't know then that you could buy *Ramparts* at the PX, and after I'd borrowed and returned it we began to talk. It was the issue that featured left-wing Catholics like Jesus Christ and Fulton Sheen on the cover. *"Catholique?"* one of the bar girls said later that night. *"Moi aussi,"* and she kept the magazine. That was when we were walking around Cholon in the rain trying to find Hoa, his wife. Mamma-san had told us that she'd gone to the movies with some girlfriends, but Davies knew what she was doing.

"I hate that shit," he said. "It's so uncool."

"Well, don't put up with it."

"Yeah."

Davies' house was down a long, narrow alley that became nothing more than a warren at the end, smelling of camphor smoke and fish, crowded but clean. He would not speak to Mamma-san, and we walked straight up to the second floor. It was one long room that had a sleeping area screened off in an arrangement of filmy curtains. At the top of the stairs there was a large poster of Lenny Bruce, and beneath it, in a shrine effect, was a low table with a Buddha and lighted incense on it.

"Lenny," Davies said.

Most of one wall was covered with a collage that Davies had done with the help of some friends. It included glimpses of burning monks, stacked Viet Cong dead, wounded Marines screaming and weeping, Cardinal Spellman waving from a chopper, Ronald Reagan, his face halved and separated by a stalk of cannabis; pictures of John Lennon peering through wire-rimmed glasses, Mick Jagger, Jimi Hendrix, Dylan, Eldridge Cleaver, Rap Brown; coffins draped with American flags whose stars were replaced by swastikas and dollar signs; odd parts clipped from *Playboy* pictures, newspaper headlines (FARMERS BUTCHER HOGS TO PROTEST PORK PRICE DIP), photo captions (*President Jokes with Newsmen*), beautiful girls holding flowers, showers of peace symbols; Ky standing at attention and saluting, a small mushroom cloud forming where his genitalia should have been; a map of the western United States with the shape of Vietnam reversed and fitted over California and one large, long figure that began at the bottom with shiny leather boots and rouged knees and ascended in a microskirt, bare breasts, graceful shoulders and a long neck, topped by the burned, blackened face of a dead Vietnamese woman.

By the time Davies' friends showed up, we were already stoned. We could hear them below, laughing and rapping with Mama, and then they came up the stairs, three spades and two white guys.

"It sure do smell *peculiar* up here," one of them said.

"Hi, you freaky li'l fuckers."

"This grass is Number Ten," Davies said. "Every time I smoke this grass over here it gives me a bad trip."

"Ain' nuthin' th' matter with that grass," someone said. "It ain't the grass."

"Where's Hoa?"

"Yeah, Davies, where's your ole lady at?"

"She's out hustling Saigon tea, and I'm fucking sick of it." He tried to look really angry, but he only looked unhappy.

One of them handed off a joint and stretched out. "Hairy day today," he said.

"Where'd you fly?"

"Bu Dop."

"Bu Dop!" one of the spades said, and he started to move toward the joint, jiving and working his shoulders, bopping his head. "Bu Dop, budop, bu dop dop *dop!*"

"Funky funky Bu Dop."

"Hey, man, can you OD on grass?"

"I dunno, baby. Maybe we could get jobs at the Aberdeen Proving Grounds smokin' dope for Uncle Sugar."

"Wow, I'm stoned. Hey, Davies, you stoned?"

"Yeah," Davies said.

It started to rain again, so hard that you couldn't hear drops, only the full force of the water pouring down on the metal roof. We smoked a little more, and then the others started to leave. Davies looked like he was sleeping with his eyes open.

"That goddamn pig," he said. "Fuckin' whore. Man, I'm paying out all this bread for the house and those people downstairs. I don't even know who they are, for Christ's sake. I'm really . . . I'm getting sick of it."

"You're pretty short now," someone said. "Why don't you cut out?"

"You mean just split?"

"Why not?"

Davies was quiet for a long time.

"Yeah," he finally said. "This is bad. This is really bad. I think I'm going to get out of here."

A bird colonel, commanding a brigade of the 4th Infantry Division: "I'll bet you always wondered why we call 'em Dinks up in this part of the country. I thought of it myself. I'll tell you, I never *did* like hearing them called Charlie. See, I had an uncle named Charlie, and I liked him too. No, Charlie was just too damn good for the little bastards. So I just thought, What are they *really* like? and I came up with rinky-dink. Suits 'em just perfect, Rinky-Dink. 'Cept that was too long, so we cut it down some. And that's why we call 'em Dinks."

One morning before dawn, Ed Fouhy, a former Saigon bureau chief for CBS, went out to 8th Aerial Port at Tan Son Nhut to catch the early military flight to Danang. They boarded as the sun came up, and Fouhy strapped in next to a kid in rumpled fatigues, one of those soldiers you see whose weariness has gone far beyond physical exhaustion, into that state where no amount of sleep will ever give him the kind of rest he needs. Every torpid movement they make tells you that they are tired, that they'll stay tired until their tours are up and the big bird flies them back to the World. Their eyes are dim with it, their faces almost puffy, and when they smile you have to accept it as a token.

There was a standard question you could use to open a conversation with troops, and Fouhy tried it. "How long you been in-country?" he asked.

The kid half lifted his head; that question could *not* be serious. The weight was really on him, and the words came slowly.

"All   fuckin'   day," he said.

"You guys ought do a story on me suntahm," the kid said. He was a helicopter gunner, six-three with an enormous head that sat in bad proportion to the rest of his body and a line of picket teeth that were always on show in a wet, uneven smile. Every few seconds he would have to wipe his mouth with the back of his hand, and when he talked to you his face was always an inch from yours, so that I had to take my glasses off to keep them dry. He was from Kilgore, Texas, and he was on his seventeenth consecutive month in-country.

"Why should we do a story about you?"

" 'Cause I'm so fuckin' good," he said, " 'n' that ain' no shit, neither. Got me one hunnert 'n' fifty-se'en gooks kilt. 'N' fifty caribou." He grinned and stanched the saliva for a second. "Them're all certified," he added.

The chopper touched down at Ba Xoi and we got off, not unhappy about leaving him. "Lis'n," he said, laughing, "you git up onna ridgeline, see y' keep yer head down. Y'heah?"

"Say, how'd you get to be a co-respondent an' come ovah to this raggedy-ass motherfucker?"

He was a really big spade, rough-looking even when he smiled, and he wore a gold nose-bead fastened through his left nostril. I told him that the nose-bead blew my mind, and he said that was all right, it blew everybody's mind. We were sitting by the chopper pad of an lz above Kontum. He was trying to get to Dak To, I was heading for Pleiku, and we both wanted to get out of there before nightfall. We took turns running out to the pad to check the choppers that kept coming in and taking off, neither of us was having any luck, and after we'd talked for an hour he laid a joint on me and we smoked.

"I been here mor'n eight months now," he said. "I bet I been in mor'n twenny firefights. An' I ain' hardly fired back once."

"How come?"

"Shee-it, 1 go firin' back, I might kill one a th' Brothers, you dig it?"

I nodded, no Viet Cong ever called *me* honky, and he told me that in his company alone there were more than a dozen Black Panthers and that he was one of them. I didn't say anything, and then he said that he wasn't just a Panther; he was an agent for the Panthers, sent over here to recruit. I asked him what kind of luck he'd been having, and he said fine, real fine. There was a fierce wind blowing across the lz, and the joint didn't last very long.

"Hey, baby," he said, "that was just some shit I tol' you. Shit, I ain' no Panther. I was just fuckin' with you, see what you'd say."

"But the Panthers have guys over here. I've met some."

"Tha' could be," he said, and he laughed.

A Huey came in, and he jogged out to see where it was headed. It was going to Dak To, and he came back to get his gear. "Later, baby," he said. "An' luck." He jumped into the chopper, and as it rose from the strip he leaned out and laughed, bringing his arm up and bending it back toward him, palm out and the fist clenched tightly in the Sign.

One day I went out with the ARVN on an operation in the rice paddies above Vinh Long, forty terrified Vietnamese troops and five Americans, all packed into three Hueys that dropped us up to our hips in paddy muck. I had never been in a rice paddy before. We spread out and moved toward the marshy swale that led to the jungle. We were still twenty feet from the first cover, a low paddy wall, when we took fire from the treeline. It was probably the working half of a crossfire that had somehow gone wrong. It caught one of the ARVN in the head, and he dropped back into the water and disappeared. We made it to the wall with two casualties. There was no way of stopping their fire, no room to send in a flanking party, so gunships were called and we crouched behind the wall and waited. There was a lot of fire coming from the trees, but we were all right as long as we kept down. And I was thinking, Oh man, so this is a rice paddy, yes, wow! when I suddenly heard an electric guitar shooting right up in my ear and a mean, rapturous black voice singing, coaxing, "Now c'mon baby, stop actin' so crazy," and when I got it all together I turned to see a grinning black corporal hunched over a cassette recorder. "Might's well," he said. "We ain' goin' *no*where till them gunships come."

That's the story of the first time I ever heard Jimi Hendrix, but in a war where a lot of people talked about Aretha's "Satisfaction" the way other people speak of Brahms' Fourth, it was more than a story; it was Credentials. "Say, that Jimi Hendrix is my main man," someone would say. "He has *defi*nitely got his shit together!" Hendrix had once been in the 101st Airborne, and the Airborne in Vietnam was full of wiggy-brilliant spades like him, really mean and really good, guys who always took care of you when things got bad. That music meant a lot to them. I never once heard it played over the Armed Forces Radio Network.

I met this kid from Miles City, Montana, who read the *Stars and Stripes* every day, checking the casualty lists to see if by some chance anybody from his town had been killed. He didn't even know if there was anyone else from Miles City in Vietnam, but he checked anyway because he knew for sure that if there *was* someone else and they got killed, he would be all right. "I mean, can you just see *two* guys from a raggedy-ass town like Miles City getting killed in Vietnam?" he said.

The sergeant had lain out near the clearing for almost two hours with a wounded medic. He had called over and over for a medevac, but none had come. Finally, a chopper from another outfit, a LOH, appeared, and he was able to reach it by radio. The pilot told him that he'd have to wait for one of his own ships, they weren't coming down, and the sergeant told the pilot that if he did not land for them he was going to open fire from the ground and fucking well *bring* him down. So they were picked up that way, but there were repercussions.

The commander's code name was Mal Hombre, and he reached the sergeant later that afternoon from a place with the call signal Violent Meals.

"God *damn* it, Sergeant," he said through the static, "I thought you were a professional soldier."

"I waited as long as I could, Sir. Any longer, I was gonna lose my man."

"This outfit is perfectly capable of taking care of its own dirty laundry. Is that clear, Sergeant?"

"Colonel, since when is a wounded trooper 'dirty laundry'?"

"At ease, Sergeant," Mal Hombre said, and radio contact was broken.

There was a spec 4 in the Special Forces at Can Tho, a shy Indian boy from Chinle, Arizona, with large, wet eyes the color of ripe olives and a quiet way of speaking, a really nice way of putting things, kind to everyone without ever being stupid or soft about it. On the night that the compound and the airstrip were hit, he came and asked me if there was a chaplain anywhere around. He wasn't very religious, he said, but he was worried about tonight. He'd just volunteered for a "suicide squad," two jeeps that were going to drive across the airstrip with mortars and a recoilless rifle. It looked bad, I had to admit it; there were so few of us in the compound that they'd had to put me on the reaction force. It might be bad. He just had a feeling about it, he'd seen what always happened to guys whenever they got that feeling, at least he *thought* it was that feeling, a bad one, the worst he'd ever had.

I told him that the only chaplains I could think of would be in the town, and we both knew that the town was cut off.

"Oh," he said. "Look, then. If I get it tonight . . ."

"It'll be okay."

"Listen, though. If it happens . . . I think it's going to . . . will you make sure the colonel tells my folks I was looking for a chaplain anyway?"

I promised, and the jeeps loaded and drove off. I heard

later that there had been a brief firefight, but that no one had been hurt. They didn't have to use the recoilless. They all drove back into the compound two hours later. The next morning at breakfast he sat at another table, saying a lot of loud, brutal things about the gooks, and he wouldn't look at me. But at noon he came over and squeezed my arm and smiled, his eyes fixed somewhere just to the right of my own.

For two days now, ever since the Tet Offensive had begun, they had been coming by the hundreds to the province hospital at Can Tho. They were usually either very young or very old or women, and their wounds were often horrible. The more lightly wounded were being treated quickly in the hospital yard, and the more serious cases were simply placed in one of the corridors to die. There were just too many of them to treat, the doctors had worked without a break, and now, on the second afternoon, the Viet Cong began shelling the hospital.

One of the Vietnamese nurses handed me a cold can of beer and asked me to take it down the hall where one of the Army surgeons was operating. The door of the room was ajar, and I walked right in. I probably should have looked first. A little girl was lying on the table, looking with wide dry eyes at the wall. Her left leg was gone, and a sharp piece of bone about six inches long extended from the exposed stump. The leg itself was on the floor, half wrapped in a piece of paper. The doctor was a major, and he'd been working alone. He could not have looked worse if he'd lain all night in a trough of blood. His hands were so slippery that I had to hold the can to his mouth for him and tip it up as his head went back. I couldn't look at the girl.

"Is it all right?" he said quietly.

"It's okay now. I expect I'll be sick as hell later on."

He placed his hand on the girl's forehead and said, "Hello, little darling." He thanked me for bringing the beer. He probably thought that he was smiling, but nothing changed anywhere in his face. He'd been working this way for nearly twenty hours.

The Intel report lay closed on the green field table, and someone had scrawled "What does it all mean?" across the cover sheet. There wasn't much doubt about who had done that; the S-2 was a known ironist. There were so many like him, really young captains and majors who had the wit to cut back their despair, a wedge to set against the bittterness. What got to them sooner or later was an inability to reconcile their love of service with their contempt for the war, and a lot of them finally had to resign their commissions, leave the profession.

We were sitting in the tent waiting for the rain to stop, the major, five grunts and myself. The rains were constant now, ending what had been a dry monsoon season, and you could look through the tent flap and think about the Marines up there patrolling the hills. Someone came in to report that one of the patrols had discovered a small arms cache.

"An arms cache!" the major said. "What happened was, one of the grunts was out there running around, and he tripped and fell down. That's about the only way we ever find any of this shit."

He was twenty-nine, young in rank, and this was his second tour. The time before, he had been a captain commanding a regular Marine company. He knew all about grunts and patrols, arms caches and the value of most Intelligence.

It was cold, even in the tent, and the enlisted Marines seemed uncomfortable about lying around with a stranger, a correspondent there. The major was a cool head, they knew that; there wasn't going to be any kind of hassle until the rain stopped. They talked quietly among themselves at the far end of the tent, away from the light of the lantern. Reports kept coming in: reports from the Vietnamese, from recon, from Division, situation reports, casualty reports, three casualty reports in twenty minutes. The major looked them all over. "Did you know that a dead Marine costs eighteen thousand dollars?" he said. The grunts all turned around and looked at us. They knew how the major had meant that because they knew the major. They were just seeing about me.

The rain stopped, and they left. Outside, the air was still cool, but heavy, too, as though a terrible heat was coming on. The major and I stood by the tent and watched while an F-4 flew nose-down, released its load against the base of a hill, leveled and flew upward again.

"I've been having this dream," the major said. "I've had it two times now. I'm in a big examination room back at Quantico. They're handing out questionnaires for an aptitude test. I take one and look at it, and the first question says, 'How many kinds of animals can you kill with your hands?' "

We could see rain falling in a sheet about a kilometer away. Judging by the wind, the major gave it three minutes before it reached us.

"After the first tour, I'd have the goddamndest nightmares. You know, the works. Bloody stuff, bad fights, guys dying, *me* dying . . . I thought they were the worst," he said. "But I sort of miss them now."

Colleagues

I

There's a candle end burning in a corner of the bunker, held to the top of a steel helmet by melted wax, the light guttering over a battered typewriter, and the Old Guy is getting one off: "Tat-tat-tat, tatta-tatta-tat like your kid or your brother or your sweetheart maybe never wanted much for himself never asked for anything except for what he knew to be his some men have a name for it and they call it Courage when the great guns are still at last across Europe what will it matter maybe after all that this one boy from Cleveland Ohio won't be coming back-a-tat-tat." You can hear shellfire landing just outside, a little gravel falls into the typewriter, but the candle burns on, throwing its faint light over the bowed head and the few remaining wisps of white hair. Two men, the Colonel and the Kid, stand by the door watching. "Why, Sir?" the Kid asks. "What makes him do it? He could be sitting safe in London right now." "I don't know, son," the Colonel says. "Maybe he figures he's got a job to do, too. Maybe it's because he's somebody who really cares. . . ."

I never knew a member of the Vietnam press corps who was insensible to what happened when the words "war" and "correspondent" got joined. The glamour of it was possibly empty and lunatic, but there were times when it was all you had, a benign infection that ravaged all but your worst fears and deepest depressions. Admitting, for argument's sake, that we were all a little crazy to have gone there in the first place, there were those whose madness it was not to know always which war they were actually in, fantasizing privately about other, older wars, Wars I and II, air wars and desert wars and island wars, obscure colonial actions against countries whose names have since changed many times, punitive wars and holy wars and wars in places where the climate was so cool that you could wear a trench coat and look good; in other words, wars which sounded old and corny to those of us for whom the war in Vietnam was more than enough. There were correspondents all around who could break you up with their bad style and self-consciousness, but those aberrations were hardly ever beyond your understanding. Over there, all styles grew in their way out of the same haunted, haunting romance. Those Crazy Guys Who Cover The War.

In any other war, they would have made movies about us too, *Dateline: Hell!*, *Dispatch from Dong Ha,* maybe even *A Scrambler to the Front,* about Tim Page, Sean Flynn and Rick Merron, three young photographers who used to ride in and out of combat on Hondas. But Vietnam is awkward, everybody knows how awkward, and if people don't even want to hear about it, you know they're not going to pay money to sit there in the dark and have it brought up. (*The Green Berets* doesn't count. That wasn't really about Vietnam, it was about Santa Monica.) So we have all been compelled to make our own movies, as many movies as there are correspondents, and this one is mine. (One day at the battalion aid station in Hue a Marine with minor shrapnel wounds in his legs was waiting to get on a helicopter, a long wait with all of the dead and badly wounded going out first, and a couple of sniper rounds snapped across the airstrip, forcing us to move behind some sandbagging. "I *hate* this movie," he said, and I thought, "Why not?") My movie, my friends, my colleagues. But meet them in context:

There was a ridge called Mutter's Ridge that ran the crest of one of those DMZ hills which the Americans usually named according to height in meters, Hill Three Hundred Whatever. The Marines had been up there since early morning, when Kilo Company and four correspondents were choppered into a sparse landing zone on the highest rise of the ridge. If this had been an Army operation, we would have been digging now, correspondents too, but the Marines didn't do that, their training taught them more about fatal gesture than it did about survival. Everyone was saying that Charlie was probably just over there on the next hill scoping on us, but the grunts were keeping it all in the open, walking out along the ridge "coordinating," setting up positions and cutting out a proper lz with battery-powered saws and chunks of explosive. Every few minutes one or another of them would shag down to the spot below the lz where the correspondents were sitting and warn us indifferently about the next blast, saying, "Uh, listen, there's fire in the hole, so you guys wanna just turn your backs and sort of cover over your heads?" He'd hang in there for a moment to give us a good look, and then run back up to the lz site to tell the others about us.

"Hey, see them four guys there? Them're reporters."

"Bullshit, reporters."

"Okay, motherfucker, go on down and see. Next time we blast."

There were some Marines stretched out a few feet from us, passing around war comics and talking, calling each other Dude and Jive, Lifer and Shitkick and Motherfucker, touching this last with a special grace, as though it were the tenderest word in their language. A suave black grunt, identified on his helmet cover as LOVE CHILD, was studying an exhausted copy of *Playboy*, pausing to say, "Oh . . . *man!* She can sure come sit on my face *any*time. Any . . . time . . . at . . . all." But none of them were talking to us yet, they were sort of talking for us, trying to make us out, maintaining that odd delicacy of theirs that always broke down sooner or later. It was like a ritual, all the preliminary forms had to be observed and satisfied, and it wasn't simply because they were shy. As far as any of them knew, we were crazy, maybe even dangerous. It made sense: They *had* to be here, they knew that. We did *not* have to be here, and they were sure enough of that too. (The part that they never realized until later was that our freedom of movement was a door that swung both ways; at that very moment, the four of us were giving each other that Nothing Happening look and talking about getting out.) A GI would walk clear across a firebase for a look at you if he'd never seen a correspondent before because it was like going to see the Geek, and worth the walk.

Besides, there were four of us sitting there in a loose professional knot, there was another one flying in the command helicopter trying to get a long view of the operation, and a sixth, AP photographer Dana Stone, was walking up the hill now with a platoon that had been chosen to scout the trail. It was one thing for a lone reporter to join an outfit before an operation because the outfit, if it was a company or larger, could absorb him and the curiosity that his presence always set working, and when the operation was over most of the troops would never even know that he'd been along. But when six correspondents turned up on the eve of an operation, especially when it fell during a long period of light contact, the effect was so complicated that the abiding ambivalence of all troops and commanders toward all reporters didn't even begin to explain it. Everyone from the colonel to the lowest-ranking grunt felt a new importance about what he was going into, and to all appearances, as far as they were in touch with it, they were glad to see you. But our presence was also unnerving, picking at layers of fear that they might never have known about otherwise. ("Why us? I mean, *six* of those bastards, where the hell are we *going?*") When it came all the way down to this, even the poorest-connected free-lancer had the power on him, a power which only the most pompous and unfeeling journalists ever really wanted, throwing weird career scares into the staff and laying a cutting edge against each Marine's gut estimates of his own survival. Then, it didn't matter that we were dressed exactly as they were and would be going exactly where they were going; we were as exotic and as fearsome as black magic, coming on with cameras and questions, and if we promised to take the anonymity off of what was about to happen, we were also there to watchdog the day. The very fact that we had chosen *them* seemed to promise the most awful kind of engagement, because they were all certain that war correspondents never wasted time. It was a joke we all dug.

It was August now, when the heat in I Corps forgave nothing. That year the northern monsoons had been almost dry (so many stories had run the phrase "grim reminders of a rainless monsoon" that it became a standard, always good for a laugh), and across the raw spaces between hills you could see only the faintest traces of green in the valleys and draws, the hills rising from pale brown to sunbleached yellow and gaping like dark, dried sores wherever the winter air-strikes had torn their sides out. Very little had happened in this sector since early spring, when an odd disengagement had been effected at Khe Sanh and when a multi-division operation into the A Shau Valley had ended abruptly after two weeks, like a speech cut at mid-sentence. The A Shau held the North's great supply depot, they had tanks and trucks and heavy anti-aircraft guns dug in there, and while the American Mission had made its reflexive claims of success for the operation, they were made for once without much enthusiasm, indicating that even the Command had to acknowledge the inviolability of that place. It was admitted at the time that a lot of our helicopters had been shot down, but this was spoken of as an expensive equipment loss, as though our choppers were crewless entities that held to the sky by themselves, spilling nothing more precious than fuel when they crashed.

Between then and now, nothing larger than company-size sweeps had worked the western Z, generally without contact. Like all of the war's quieter passages, the spring-summer lull had left everyone badly strung out, and a lot of spooky stories began going around, like the ones about NVA helicopters (a Marine patrol supposedly saw one touch down on the abandoned Marine base at Khe Sanh and wait while a dozen men got out and walked around the perimeter, "like they was just checking things out"). It had been a mild season for Vietnam correspondents too (the lull aside, home offices were beginning to make it clear to their Saigon bureaus that the story was losing the old bite, what with Johnson's abdication, the spring assassinations and the coming elections), and we were either talking about how the Vietnam thing was really finished or bitching about getting shot at only to wind up on page nine. It was a good time to cruise the country, a day here and a week there, just hanging out with troops; a good time to make leisurely investigations into the smaller, darker pockets of the war. Now word had come down that a large mass of NVA was moving across the DMZ, possibly building for a new offensive against Hue, and battalions of the 5th Marines were deploying in rough conjunction with battalions of the 9th to find and kill them. It had the feel of what we always called a "good operation," and the six of us had gone up for it.

But there was nothing here now, no dreaded Cong, no shelling, no pictures for the wires, no stories for the files, no sign that anyone had been on this scalding ridge for at least six months. (A few miles north and a little east, a company of the 9th was in the middle of an evil firefight that would last until nightfall, leaving eleven of them dead and nearly thirty wounded, but we knew nothing about that now. If we had, we might possibly have made an effort at getting to it, some of us at least, explaining it later in cold professional terms and leaving all the other reasons unspoken, understood between us. If a Marine had ever expressed a similar impulse, we would probably have called him psychotic.) The only violence on Mutter's Ridge was in the heat and whatever associations with that terrible winter you could take from the view, from Cam Lo, Route 9 into Khe Sanh, the Rockpile. A few more Marines had joined the group around us, but they were being cool, pausing to read the tags sewn on our fatigue shirts as though to themselves, but out loud, just to show us that they knew we were here.

"Associated Press, yeah, and UPI, uh-huh, and *Esquire,* wow, *they* got a guy over here, what the fuck for, you tell 'em what we're wearing? And—hey, man, what's *that* supposed to be?" (Sean Flynn had only the words "Bao Chi" on his tags, Vietnamese for "journalist.") "That's pretty far out, what's that, in case you're captured or something?"

Actually, Bao Chi was all the affiliation that Flynn needed or wanted in Vietnam, but he didn't go into that. Instead, he explained that when he had first begun taking pictures here in 1965, most operations had been conducted by the South Vietnamese, and reporters would identify themselves this way so that they would not be mistaken for American advisors and shot by the ARVN during the routine hysteria of routine retreats.

"Boy, if that ain't just like the Slopes," one of the Marines said, walking away from us.

Flynn was cleaning his camera lens with a length of Australian sweat scarf that he always wore into the field, but the least movement sent up a fine-grained dust that seemed to hang there without resettling, giving the light a greasy quality and caking in the corners of your eyes. The Marines were looking hard at Flynn and you could see that he was blowing their minds, the way he blew minds all over Vietnam.

He was (indeed) the Son of Captain Blood, but that didn't mean much to the grunts since most of them, the young ones, had barely even heard of Errol Flynn. It was just apparent to anyone who looked at him that he was what the Marines would call "a dude who definitely had his shit together." All four of us on the ridge looked more or less as though we belonged there; the AP's John Lengle had covered every major Marine operation of the past eighteen months, Nick Wheeler of UPI had been around for two years, I'd had the better part of a year in now, we were all nearly young enough to be mistaken for grunts ourselves, but Flynn was special. We all had our movie-fed war fantasies, the Marines too, and it could be totally disorienting to have this outrageously glamorous figure intrude on them, really unhinging, like looking up to see that you've been sharing a slit trench with John Wayne or William Bendix. But you got used to that part of Flynn quickly.

When he'd first arrived in Vietnam in the summer of 1965, he had been considered news himself, and a lot of stories were written about his early trips into combat. Most of them managed to include all the clichés, all of them called him "swashbuckling." There were still a lot of easy things to say about him, and a lot of people around who were more than willing to say them, but after you knew him all of that talk just depressed you. There were a number of serious (heavy) journalists who could not afford to admit that anyone who looked as good as Flynn looked could possibly have anything more going for him. They chose not to take him as seriously as they took themselves (which was fine with Sean), and they accused him of coming to Vietnam to play, as though the war was like Africa had been for him, or the South of France or one of the places he'd gone to make those movies that people were always judging him by. But there were a lot of people in Vietnam who were playing, more than the heavies cared to admit, and Flynn's playing was done only on the most earnest levels. He wasn't much different from the rest; he was deeply fascinated by war, by *this* war, but he admitted it, knew where he stood in it, and he behaved as though it was nothing to be ashamed of. It gave him a vision of Vietnam that was profound, black and definitive, a knowledge of its wildness that very few of his detractors would have understood. All of this was very obvious in his face, particularly the wildness, but those people only saw it as handsome, making you realize that, as a group, newspapermen were not necessarily any more observant or imaginative than accountants. Flynn moved on and found his friends among those who never asked him to explain himself, among the GI's and the Apaches of the press corps, and he established his own celebrity there. (There would be occasional intrusions: embarrassingly deferential information officers, or a run-in with Colonel George Patton, Jr., who put him through one of those my-father-knew-your-father trials.) The grunts were always glad to see him. They'd call him "Seen," a lot of them, and tell him that they'd caught one of his flicks on R&R in Singapore or Taiwan, something that only a grunt could bring up and get away with, since all of that was finished for Flynn, the dues-paying and the accom-

modations, and he didn't like to talk about it. Sometime during his years in Vietnam, he realized that there really were
people whom he cared for and could trust, it must have been
a gift he'd never expected to have, and it made him someone
who his father, on the best day he ever had, could have
envied.

It was still a little too soon for the Marines to just sit down
and start talking, they would have to probe a little more first,
and we were getting bored. By the time they had finished
cutting the lz there was no cover left from the sun, and we
were all anxious for the scouting platoon to reach the top so
that we could get together with Dana Stone, put a little pressure on for a helicopter and get out. The trip back to the
press center in Danang could take two hours or two days,
depending on what was flying, but it was certain to go faster
with Stone along because he had friends at every airfield and
chopper pad in I Corps. Danang was Soul City for many of
us, it had showers and drinks, flash-frozen air-freighted
steaks, air-conditioned rooms and China Beach and, for
Stone, a real home—a wife, a dog, a small house full of
familiar possessions. Mutter's Ridge had sickening heat, a
rapidly vanishing water supply and boredom, so there really
wasn't any choice. Judging by the weathered, blackened bits
of ammunition casing (theirs and ours) that littered the
ground around us, the ridge also had a history, and Dana
had told us something about it.

Stone was a lapsed logger from Vermont (he always spoke
about going back to that, especially after a bad day in the
field, screw all this bullshit), twenty-five years old with sixty-
year-old eyes set in deep behind wire-rimmed glasses, their
shrewdness and experience almost lost in the lean anglings of
his face. We knew for certain that he would be walking well
ahead of the rest of the platoon on the trail, standard Dana
and a break for the Marines, since he was easily the best-

equipped man in the party for spotting booby traps or ambushes. But that had nothing to do with his being on point. Dana was the man in motion, he just couldn't slow himself down; he was the smallest man on the trail, but his engines would drive him up it as though the incline ran the other way. GI's who had forgotten his name would describe him for you as "that wiry little red-headed cat, *crazy* motherfucker, funny as a bastard," and Stone *was* funny, making you pay for every laugh he gave you. Hard mischief was his specialty—a thumb stuck abruptly into your egg yolk at breakfast or your brandy at dinner, rocks lobbed onto the metal roof of your room at the press center, flaming trails of lighter fluid rampaging across the floor toward you, a can of ham and limas substituted for peaches in syrup when you were practically dying of thirst—all Dana's way of saying hello, doing you good by doing you in. He'd wake you at dawn, shaking you violently and saying, "Listen, I need your glasses for just a minute, it's really important," splitting with them for an hour. He also took beautiful pictures (he called them "snaps" in accordance with the wire-service ethic which said you must never reveal your pride in good work) and in almost three years as a combat photographer he'd spent more time on operations than anyone else I knew, getting his cameras literally blown off his back more than once but keeping otherwise unhurt. By now, there was nothing that could happen around him in the field that he hadn't seen before, and if his joking was belligerent and even ghastly, you knew at least where it came from, saw the health that it carried. And that morning, waiting by the base-camp airstrip for the assault to begin, he started to tell us about the other time he'd been up on Mutter's Ridge, in the days before it even had a name. It had been, in fact, two years ago *to the day*, he'd said, on that *exact same ridge*. He'd gone up there with the 9th that time, and they'd *really stepped in deep shit*.

(It was true, we all knew it was true, he was doing it to us again, and a smile showed for just an instant on his face.) They had been pinned down on the ridge all night long without support or re-supply or medevac, and the *casualties* had been *unbelievable,* running somewhere around 70 percent. Flynn laughed and said, "Dana, you bastard," but Stone would have gone on like that in his flat Vermont voice, telling it to those of us about to go up there as though it were nothing more than the history of a racehorse, except that he looked up and saw that we weren't alone; a few of the guys from Kilo Company had come over to ask questions about our cameras or something, and they'd heard some of it. Stone turned a deep red, as he always did when he realized that he'd gone a little too far. "Aw, that was just a bunch of shit, I never even been *near* that ridge," he said, and he pointed to me. "I was just trying to get him uptight because this is his last operation, and he's already fucked up about it." He laughed, but he was looking at the ground.

Now, while we waited for him, a Marine came up to Lengle and me and asked if we'd like to look at some pictures he'd taken. Marines felt comfortable around Lengle, who looked like a college basketball star, six-seven and very young (actually, he was thirty), a Nevadan who'd parlayed a nice-kid image into a valuable professional asset. The pictures were in a little imitation-leather folder, and you could tell by the way the Marine stood over us, grinning in anticipation as we flipped over each plastic page, that it was among his favorite things. (He'd also taken some "number-one souvenirs," he said, leaving the details to our imaginations.) There were hundreds of these albums in Vietnam, thousands, and they all seemed to contain the same pictures: the obligatory Zippo-lighter shot ("All right, let's burn these hootches and move out"); the severed-head shot, the head often resting on the chest of the dead man or being held up by a smiling Marine, or a lot of heads, arranged in a row, with a burning cigarette in each of the mouths, the eyes open ("Like they're *lookin'* at you, man, it's scary"); the VC suspect being dragged over the dust by a half-track or being hung by his heels in some jungle clearing; the very young dead with AK-47's still in their hands ("How old would you say that kid was?" the grunts would ask. "Twelve, thirteen? You just can't tell with gooks"); a picture of a Marine holding an ear or maybe two ears or, as in the case of a guy I knew near Pleiku, a whole necklace made of ears, "love beads" as its owner called them; and the one we were looking at now, the dead Viet Cong girl with her pajamas stripped off and her legs raised stiffly in the air.

"No more boom-boom for that mamma-san," the Marine said, that same, tired remark you heard every time the dead turned out to be women. It was so routine that I don't think he even realized that he'd said it.

"You posed that one," Lengle said.

"Not me," the Marine said, laughing.

"Now come on, you rascal. You mean you found her just like that?"

"Well, some other guy fixed her that way, and it was funny, 'cause that guy got zapped later on the same day. But look, look at that bitch there, cut right in half!"

"Oh, that's a honey," John said, "really terrific."

"I was thinkin' about sending some in to the *Stars and Stripes*. You think the *Stripes* would run 'em?"

"Well . . ." We were laughing now, what could you do? Half the combat troops in Vietnam had these things in their packs, snapshots were the least of what they took after a fight, at least pictures didn't rot. I'd talked to a Marine who'd taken a lot of pictures after an operation on the Cua Viet River, and later, when he was getting short and nervous about things, he'd brought them to the chaplain. But the chaplain had only told him that it was forgivable and put the pictures in his drawer and kept them.

A couple of Marines were talking to Flynn and Wheeler about their cameras, the best place to buy this lens, the right speed to use for that shot, I couldn't follow any of it. The grunts were hip enough to the media to take photographers more seriously than reporters, and I'd met officers who refused to believe that I was really a correspondent because I never carried cameras. (During a recent operation, this had almost gotten me bumped from the Command chopper because the colonel, for reasons of his own, was partial to photographers. On that one, a company of his battalion had made contact with a company of Viet Cong and forced them out on a promontory, holding them there between their fire and the sea for the gunships to kill. This particular colonel loved to order the chopper in very low so that he could fire his .45 into the Cong, and he'd always wanted pictures of it. He was doubly disappointed that day; I'd not only turned up without a camera, but by the time we got there all the VC were dead, about 150 of them littered across the beach and bobbing in and out with the waves. But he fired off a few clips anyway, just to keep his piece working.)

Marines were all around us now, about fifteen of them, and one, a short, heavy kid with a flat, dark face and the bearing of an overdeveloped troll, came up and looked hard at us.

"You guys're reporters, huh? Boy, you really get it all fucked up," he said. "My old man sends me stuff from the papers, and he thinks you're all full of shit."

A couple of Marines booed him, most of them laughed. Lengle laughed too. "Well, podner, what can I tell you? I mean, we try, we really take a shot at it."

"Then why can't you guys just tell it right?"

"Fuckin' Krynski," someone said, hitting the kid hard on the back of the head. According to his helmet, it was the Avenger himself, and he'd come to work for us now, just in time. He looked like a freshman in divinity school—clear blue eyes, smooth snub nose, cornsilk hair and a look of such trust and innocence that you hoped there would always be someone around to take care of him. He seemed terribly embarrassed about what had just been said to us.

"Don't you listen to that asshole," he said. "God *damn*, Krynski, you don't know any fuckin' thing about it. These guys are number-one dudes, and that's no shit."

"Thank you, friend," Lengle said.

"I didn't mean nothin'," Krynski said. "Don't go gettin' your balls in an uproar."

But the Avenger wasn't letting it go. "Man, these guys take plenty of chances, they eat C's just like us, and sleep in the mud, and all that good shit. They don't have to stand around here and listen to you bitch. They don't even have to be here at all!"

"Now what's *that* supposed to mean?" Krynski said, looking really puzzled. "You mean you guys *volunteer* to come over here?"

"Well, dumb shit, what'd you think?" the Avenger said. "You think they're just some dumb grunt like you?"

"Oh man, you *got* to be kidding me. You guys *asked* to come here?"

"Sure."

"How long do you have to stay?" he asked.

"As long as we want."

"Wish *I* could stay as long as *I* want," the Marine called Love Child said. "*I'd* been home las' March."

"When did you get here?" I asked.

"Las' March."

The lieutenant who had been supervising the blasting looked down from the lz and yelled for someone named Collins.

"Yes Sir?" the Avenger said.

"Collins, get your bod up here."

"Yes Sir."

There was some movement on the lz now, the platoon had reached the clearing. Stone came out first, backing out very fast with his camera up, referring quickly to the ground just behind him between shots. Four Marines came out next, carrying a fifth on an improvised litter. They brought him to the center of the clearing and set him down carefully on the grass. We thought at first that he was dead, taken off by a booby trap on the trail, but his color was much too awful for that. Even the dead held some horrible light that seemed to recede, vanishing through one layer of skin at a time and taking a long time to go completely, but this kid had no color about him anywhere. It was incredible that anything so motionless and white could still be alive.

"Collins," the lieutenant said, "you go find the Old Man. Tell him we've got a real serious heat casualty here. Remember, tell him serious."

"Yes Sir," the Avenger said, starting at a slow run along the ridge toward the CP.

Dana took a few more pictures and then sat down to change film. His fatigues were completely darkened with sweat, but except for that he showed no signs of exertion. The rest of the column was coming off of the trail now, dropping in the clearing like sniper victims, the packs going first, staggering a few feet and falling. A few were smiling up at the sun like happy dreamers, more went face down and stopped moving except for some twitching in their legs, and the radio man made it all the way across the clearing to the commo section, where he eased the equipment from his back slowly, set his helmet very carefully on the ground for a pillow after picking his spot, and immediately fell asleep.

Stone ran over and photographed him. "You guys know something?" he said.

"What's that?"

"It's hotter than a bastard."

"Thanks."

We could see the colonel approaching, a short, balding man with flinty eyes and a brief black mustache. He was trussed up tightly in his flak jacket, and as he came toward us small groups of Marines broke and ran to get their flak jackets on too, before the colonel could have the chance to tell them about it. The colonel leaned over and looked hard at the unconscious Marine, who was lying now in the shade of a poncho being held over him by two corpsmen, while a third brushed his chest and face with water from a canteen.

Well hell, the colonel was saying, there's nothing the matter with that man, feed some salt into him, get him up, get him walking, this is the Marines, not the goddamned Girl Scouts, there won't be any damned chopper coming in *here* today. (The four of us must have looked a little stricken at this, and Dana took our picture. We were really pulling for the kid; if he stayed, we stayed, and that meant all night.) The corpsmen were trying to tell the colonel that this was no ordinary case of heat exhaustion, excusing themselves but staying firm about it, refusing to let the colonel return to the CP. (The four of us smiled and Dana took a picture. "Go away, Stone," Flynn said. "Hold it just like that," Stone said, running in for a closeup so that his lens was an inch away from Flynn's nose. "One more.") The Marine looked awful lying there, trying to work his lips a little, and the colonel glared down at the fragile, still form as though it was blackmailing him. When the Marine refused to move anything except his lips for fifteen minutes, the colonel began to relent.

He asked the corpsmen if they'd ever heard of a man dying from something like this.

"Oh, yes Sir. Oh, wow, I mean he really needs more attention than what we can give him here."

"Mmmmmm . . ." the colonel said. Then he authorized the chopper request and strode with what I'm sure he considered great determination back to his CP.

"I think it would have made him feel better if he could have shot the kid," Flynn said.

"Or one of us," I said.

"You're just lucky he didn't get you last night," Flynn said. The evening before, when Flynn and I had arrived together at the base camp, the colonel had taken us into the Command bunker to show us some maps and explain the operation, and a captain had given us some coffee in Styrofoam cups. I'd carried mine outside and finished it while we talked to the colonel, who was being very hale and friendly in a way I'd seen before and didn't really trust. I was looking around for some place to toss the empty cup, and the colonel noticed it.

"Give it here," he offered.

"Oh, that's okay, Colonel, thanks."

"No, come on, I'll take it."

"No, really, I'll just find a—"

"Give it to me!" he said, and I did, but Flynn and I were afraid to look at each other until he'd returned underground, and then we broke up, exchanging the worst colonel stories we knew. I told him about the colonel who had threatened to court-martial a spec 4 for refusing to cut the heart out of a dead Viet Cong and feed it to a dog, and Flynn told me about a colonel in the Americal Division (which Flynn always said was sponsored by General Foods) who believed that every man under his command needed combat experi-

ence; he made the cooks and the clerks and the supply men and the drivers all take M-16's and go out on night patrol, and one time all of his cooks got wiped out in an ambush.

We could hear the sound of our Chinook coming in now, and we were checking to see if we had all of our gear, when I took a sudden terrible flash, some total dread, and I looked at everyone and everything in sight to see if there was some real source. Stone had been telling the truth about this being my last operation, I was as strung out as anybody on a last operation, there was nothing between here and Saigon that didn't scare me now, but this was different, it was something else.

"Fuckin' heat . . . ," someone said. "I . . . oh, man, I just . . . can't . . . fuckin' . . . *make it!*"

It was a Marine, and as soon as I saw him I realized that I'd seen him before, a minute or so ago, standing on the edge of the clearing staring at us as we got ourselves ready to leave. He'd been with a lot of other Marines there, but I'd seen him much more distinctly than the others without realizing or admitting it. The others had been looking at us too, with amusement or curiosity or envy (we were splitting, casualties and correspondents this way out, we were going to Danang), they were all more or less friendly, but this one was different, I'd seen it, known it and passed it over, but not really. He was walking by us now, and I saw that he had a deep, running blister that seemed to have opened and eaten away much of his lower lip. That wasn't the thing that had made him stand out before, though. If I'd noticed it at all, it might have made him seem a little more wretched than the others, but nothing more. He stopped for a second and looked at us, and he smiled some terrifying, evil smile, his look turned now to the purest hatred.

"You fucking guys," he said. "You guys are *crazy!*"

There was the most awful urgency to the way he said it. He was still glaring, I expected him to raise a finger and touch each of us with destruction and decay, and I realized that after all this time, the war still offered at least one thing that I had to turn my eyes from. I had seen it before and hoped never to see it again, I had misunderstood it and been hurt by it, I thought I had finally worked it out for good and I was looking at it now, knowing what it meant and feeling as helpless under it this last time as I had the first.

All right, yes, it had been a groove being a war correspondent, hanging out with the grunts and getting close to the war, touching it, losing yourself in it and trying yourself against it. I had always wanted that, never mind why, it had just been a thing of mine, the way this movie is a thing of mine, and I'd done it; I was in many ways brother to these poor, tired grunts, I knew what they knew now, I'd done it and it was really something. Everywhere I'd gone, there had always been Marines or soldiers who would tell me what the Avenger had told Krynski, *You're all right, man, you guys are cool, you got balls.* They didn't always know what to think about you or what to say to you, they'd sometimes call you "Sir" until you had to beg them to stop, they'd sense the insanity of your position as terrified volunteer-reporter and it would seize them with the giggles and even respect. If they dug you, they always saw that you knew that, and when you choppered out they'd say goodbye, wish you luck. They'd even thank you, some of them, and what could you say to that?

And always, they would ask you with an emotion whose intensity would shock you to please tell it, because they really did have the feeling that it wasn't being told for them, that they were going through all of this and that somehow no one back in the World knew about it. They may have been a bunch of dumb, brutal killer kids (a lot of correspondents privately felt that), but they were smart enough to know that much. There was a Marine in Hue who had come after me as I walked toward the truck that would take me to the airstrip, he'd been locked in that horror for nearly two weeks while I'd shuttled in and out for two or three days at a time. We knew each other by now, and when he caught up with me he grabbed my sleeve so violently that I thought he was going to accuse me or, worse, try to stop me from going. His face was all but blank with exhaustion, but he had enough feeling left to say, "Okay, man, you go on, you go on out of here you cocksucker, but I mean it, you tell it! You tell it, man. If you don't tell it . . ."

What a time they were having there, it had all broken down, one battalion had taken 60 percent casualties, all the original NCO's were gone, the grunts were telling their officers to go die, to go fuck themselves, to go find some other fools to run up those streets awhile, it was no place where I'd have to tell anyone not to call me "Sir." They understood that, they understood a lot more than I did, but nobody hated me there, not even when I was leaving. Three days later I came back and the fighting had dropped off, the casualties were down to nothing and the same Marine flashed me a victory sign that had nothing to do with the Marine Corps or the fading battle or the American flag that had gone up on the Citadel's south wall the day before, he slapped me on the back and poured me a drink from a bottle he'd found in one of the hootches somewhere. Even the ones who preferred not to be in your company, who despised what your work required or felt that you took your living from their deaths, who believed that all of us were traitors and liars and the creepiest kinds of parasites, even they would cut back at the last and make their one concession to what there was in us that we ourselves loved most: "I got to give it to you, you guys got balls." Maybe they meant just that and nothing more, we had our resources and we made enough out of that to keep us going, turning the most grudging admissions into decorations for valor, making it all all right again.

But there was often that bad, bad moment to recall, the look that made you look away, and in its hateful way it was the purest single thing I'd ever known. There was no wonder left in it anywhere, no amusement, it came out of nothing so messy as morality or prejudice, it had no motive, no conscious source. You would feel it coming out to you from under a poncho hood or see it in a wounded soldier staring up at you from a chopper floor, from men who were very scared or who had just lost a friend, from some suffering apparition of a grunt whose lip had been torn open by the sun, who just couldn't make it in that heat.

At first, I got it all mixed up, I didn't understand and I felt sorry for myself, misjudged. "Well fuck you too," I'd think. "It could have been me just as easily, I take chances too, can't you see that?" And then I realized that that was exactly what it was all about, it explained itself as easily as that, another of the war's dark revelations. They weren't judging me, they weren't reproaching me, they didn't even mind me, not in any personal way. They only hated me, hated me the way you'd hate any hopeless fool who would put himself through this thing when he had choices, any fool who had no more need of his life than to play with it in this way.

"You guys are *crazy!*" that Marine had said, and I know that when we flew off of Mutter's Ridge that afternoon he stood there for a long time and watched us out of sight with the same native loathing he'd shown us before, turning finally to whoever was around, saying it maybe to himself, getting out what I'd actually heard said once when a jeepload of correspondents had just driven away, leaving me there alone, one rifleman turning to another and giving us all his hard, cold wish:

"Those fucking guys," he'd said. "I hope they die."

II

Name me someone that's not a parasite,
And I'll go out and say a prayer for him.
　　　—BOB DYLAN, "Visions of Johanna"

I keep thinking about all the kids who got wiped out by seventeen years of war movies before coming to Vietnam to get wiped out for good. You don't know what a media freak is until you've seen the way a few of those grunts would run around during a fight when they knew that there was a television crew nearby; they were actually making war movies in their heads, doing little guts-and-glory Leatherneck tap dances under fire, getting their pimples shot off for the networks. They were insane, but the war hadn't done that to them. Most combat troops stopped thinking of the war as an adventure after their first few firefights, but there were always the ones who couldn't let that go, these few who were up there doing numbers for the cameras. A lot of correspondents weren't much better. We'd all seen too many movies, stayed too long in Television City, years of media glut had made certain connections difficult. The first few times that I got fired at or saw combat deaths, nothing really happened, all the responses got locked in my head. It was the same familiar violence, only moved over to another medium; some kind of jungle play with giant helicopters and fantastic special effects, actors lying out there in canvas body bags waiting for the scene to end so they could get up again and walk it off. But that was some scene (you found out), there was no cutting it.

A lot of things had to be unlearned before you could learn anything at all, and even after you knew better you couldn't avoid the ways in which things got mixed, the war itself with those parts of the war that were just like the movies, just like *The Quiet American* or *Catch-22* (a Nam standard because it said that in a war everybody thinks that everybody else is crazy), just like all that combat footage from television ("We're taking fire from the treeline!" "Where?" "There!" *"Where?"* "Over *there!"* "Over WHERE?" "Over THERE!!" Flynn heard that go on for fifteen minutes once; we made it an epiphany), your vision blurring, images jumping and falling as though they were being received by a dropped camera, hearing a hundred horrible sounds at once—screams, sobs, hysterical shouting, a throbbing inside your head that threatened to take over, quavering voices trying to get the orders out, the dulls and sharps of weapons going off (Lore: When they're near they whistle, when they're really near they crack), the thud of helicopter rotors, the tinny, clouded voice coming over the radio, "Uh, that's a Rog, we mark your position, over." And out. Far out.

That feedback stalked you all over Vietnam, it often threatened you with derangement, but somehow it always left you a little saner than you had any right to expect. Sometimes its intrusions could be subtle and ferocious. One afternoon during the battle for Hue, I was with David Greenway, a correspondent for *Time,* and we found it necessary to move from one Marine position to another. We were directly across from the south wall of the Citadel and airstrikes had dropped much of it down into the street, bringing with it torn, stinking portions of some North Vietnamese who had been dug in there. We had to make a run of something like 400 meters up that street, and we knew that the entire way was open to sniper fire, either from the standing sections of the wall on our right or from the rooftops on our left. When we'd run to our present position an hour earlier, David had gone first, and it was my turn now. We were crouching among some barren shrubbery with the Marines, and I turned to the guy next to me, a black Marine, and said, "Listen, we're going to cut out now. Will you cover us?" He gave me one of those amazed, penetrating looks. "You can go out there if you want to, baby, but shee-it . . ." and he began putting out fire. David and I ran all doubled over, taking cover every forty meters or so behind boulder-sized chunks of smashed wall, and halfway through it I started to laugh, looking at David and shaking my head. David was the most urbane of correspondents, a Bostonian of good family and impeccable education, something of a patrician even though he didn't care anything about it. We were pretty good friends, and he was willing to take my word for it that there was actually something funny, and he laughed too.

"What is it?" he said.

"Oh man, do you realize that I just asked that guy back there to *cover us?*"

He looked at me with one eyebrow faintly cocked. "Yes," he said. "Yes, you did. Oh, isn't that *marvelous!*"

And we would have laughed all the way up the street, except that toward the end of it we had to pass a terrible thing, a house that had been collapsed by the bombing, bringing with it a young girl who lay stretched out dead on top of some broken wood. The whole thing was burning, and the flames were moving closer and closer to her bare feet. In a few minutes they were going to reach her, and from our concealment we were going to have to watch it. We agreed that anything was better than that and we finished the run, but only after David spun around, dropped to one knee and took a picture of it.

A few days after that, David's file from Hue appeared in *Time,* worked over into that uni-prose which all news magazines and papers maintained, placed somewhere among five or six other Vietnam stories that had come in that week from the five or six other reporters *Time* kept in Vietnam. About five months after that, a piece I'd written about the battle appeared in *Esquire,* turning up like some lost dispatch from the Crimea. I saw it in print for the first time on the day that we returned from Mutter's Ridge, while the issue of *Time* which carried David's story was on sale in Saigon and Danang within a week of the events described. (I remember that issue in particular because General Giap was on the cover and the South Vietnamese would not allow it to be sold until a black X was scrawled over each copy, disfiguring but hardly concealing Giap's face. People were doing weird things that Tet.) What all of this means is that, no matter how much I love the sound of it, there's no way that I can think of myself as a war correspondent without stopping to acknowledge the degree to which it's pure affectation. I never had to run back to any bureau office to file (or, worse, call it in from Danang over the knotted clot of military wires, "Working, operator, I said working, hello, working. . . . Oh, you moron, *working!"*). I never had to race out to the Danang airfield to get my film on the eight-o'clock scatback to Saigon; there wasn't any bureau, there wasn't any film, my ties to New York were as slight as my assignment was vague. I wasn't really an oddity in the press corps, but I was a peculiarity, an extremely privileged one. (An oddity was someone like the photographer John Schneider, who fixed a white flag to his handlebars and took a bike from the top of

Hill 881 North over to Hill 881 South during a terrible battle, in what came to be known as Schneider's Ride; or the Korean cameraman who had spent four years in Spain as a matador, who spoke exquisite, limpid Castilian and whom we called El Taikwando; or the Portuguese novelist who arrived at Khe Sanh in sports clothes, carrying a plaid suitcase, under the impression that field gear could be bought there.)

I'd run into Bernie Weinraub in Saigon, on his way to *The New York Times* bureau carrying a bunch of papers in his hand. He'd be coming back from a meeting with some of "the beautiful people" of the Joint U.S. Public Affairs Office, and he'd say, "I'm having a low-grade nervous breakdown right now. You can't really see it, but it's there. After you've been here awhile, you'll start having them too," laughing at the little bit of it that was true as much as at the part of it that had become our running joke. Between the heat and the ugliness and the pressures of filing, the war out there and the JUSPAO flacks right here, Saigon could be overwhelmingly depressing, and Bernie often looked possessed by it, so gaunt and tired and underfed that he could have brought out the Jewish mother in a Palestinian guerrilla.

"Let's have a drink," I'd say.

"No, no, I can't. You know how it is, we on the *Times* . . ." He'd start to laugh. "I mean, *we* have to file every day. It's a terrible responsibility, there's so little time. . . . I hope you'll understand."

"Of course. I'm sorry, I just wasn't thinking."

"Thank you, thank you."

But it was fine for me to laugh; he was going back to work, to write a story that would be published in New York hours later, and I was going across the street to the terrace bar of the Continental Hotel for a drink, possibly to write a few leisurely notes, probably not. I was spared a great deal, and except for a small handful of men who took their professional responsibilities very solemnly, no one ever held that against me. Whatever they came to know about the war was one thing; I know how they tried to get it into their stories, how generous they were as teachers and how embittering it all could become.

Because they worked in the news media, for organizations that were ultimately reverential toward the institutions involved: the Office of the President, the Military, America at war and, most of all, the empty technology that characterized Vietnam. There is no way of remembering good friends without remembering the incredible demands put on them from offices thousands of miles away. (Whenever the news chiefs and network vice-presidents and foreign editors would dress up in their Abercrombie & Fitch combat gear and come by for a firsthand look, a real story would develop, Snow In The Tropics, and after three days of high-level briefings and helicopter rides, they'd go home convinced that the war was over, that their men in the field were damned good men but a little too close to the story.) Somewhere on the periphery of that total Vietnam issue whose daily reports made the morning papers too heavy to bear, lost in the surreal contexts of television, there was a story that was as simple as it had always been, men hunting men, a hideous war and all kinds of victims. But there was also a Command that didn't feel this, that rode us into attrition traps on the back of fictional kill ratios, and an Administration that believed the Command, a cross-fertilization of ignorance, and a press whose tradition of objectivity and fairness (not to mention self-interest) saw that all of it got space. It was inevitable that once the media took the diversions seriously enough to report them, they also legitimized them. The spokesmen spoke in words that had no currency left as words, sentences with no hope of meaning in the sane world, and if much of it was sharply queried by the press, all of it got quoted. The press got all the facts (more or less), it got too many of them. But it never found a way to report meaningfully about death, which of course was really what it was all about. The most repulsive, transparent gropes for sanctity in the midst of the killing received serious treatment in the papers and on the air. The jargon of Progress got blown into your head like bullets, and by the time you waded through all the Washington stories and all the Saigon stories, all the Other War stories and the corruption stories and the stories about brisk new gains in ARVN effectiveness, the suffering was somehow unimpressive. And after enough years of that, so many that it seemed to have been going on forever, you got to a point where you could sit there in the evening and listen to the man say that American casualties for the week had reached a six-week low, only eighty GI's had died in combat, and you'd feel like you'd just gotten a bargain.

If you ever saw stories written by Peter Kann, William Touhy, Tom Buckley, Bernie Weinraub, Peter Arnett, Lee Lescaze, Peter Braestrup, Charles Mohr, Ward Just or a few others, you'd know that most of what the Mission wanted to say to the American public was a psychotic vaudeville; that Pacification, for example, was hardly anything more than a swollen, computerized tit being forced upon an already violated population, a costly, valueless program that worked only in press conferences. Yet in the year leading up to the Tet Offensive ("1967—Year of Progress" was the name of an official year-end report) there were more stories about Pacification than there were about combat—front page, prime time, just as though it was really happening.

This was all part of a process which everyone I knew came grudgingly to think of as routine, and I was free of it. What an incredible hassle it would have been, having to run out to the airport to watch the Mayor of Los Angeles embrace Mayor Cua of Saigon. (L.A. had declared Saigon its Sister

City, dig it, and Yorty was in town to collect. If there had been no newspapers or television, Cua and Yorty never would have met.) I never had to cover luncheons given for members of the Philippine Civic Action Group or laugh woodenly while the Polish delegate to the International Control Commission lobbed a joke on me. I never had to follow the Command to the field for those interminable get-togethers with the troops. ("Where are you from, son?" "Macon, Georgia, Sir." "Real fine. Are you getting your mail okay, plenty of hot meals?" "Yes, Sir." "That's fine, where you from, son?" "Oh, I don't know, God, I don't know, I don't *know!*" "That's fine, real fine, where you from, son?") I never had to become familiar with that maze of government agencies and sub-agencies, I never had to deal with the Spooks. (They were from the real Agency, the CIA. There was an endless Vietnam game played between the grunts and the Spooks, and the grunts always lost.) Except to pick up my mail and get my accreditation renewed, I never had to frequent JUSPAO unless I wanted to. (That office had been created to handle press relations and psychological warfare, and I never met anyone there who seemed to realize that there was a difference.) I could skip the daily briefings, I never had to cultivate Sources. In fact, my concerns were so rarefied that I had to ask other correspondents what they ever found to ask Westmoreland, Bunker, Komer and Zorthian. (Barry Zorthian was the head of JUSPAO; for more than five years he *was* Information.) What did anybody ever expect those people to *say?* No matter how highly placed they were, they were still officials, their views were well established and well known, famous. It could have rained frogs over Tan Son Nhut and they wouldn't have been upset; Cam Ranh Bay could have dropped into the South China Sea and they would have found some way to make it sound good for you; the Bo Doi Division (Ho's Own) could have marched by the American embassy and they would have characterized it as "desperate"—what did even the reporters closest to the Mission Council ever find to write about when they'd finished their interviews? (My own interview with General Westmoreland had been hopelessly awkward. He'd noticed that I was accredited to *Esquire* and asked me if I planned to be doing "humoristical" pieces. Beyond that, very little was really said. I came away feeling as though I'd just had a conversation with a man who touches a chair and says, "This is a chair," points to a desk and says, "This is a desk." I couldn't think of anything to ask him, and the interview didn't happen.) I honestly wanted to know what the form was for those interviews, but some of the reporters I'd ask would get very officious, saying something about "Command postures," and look at me as though I was insane. It was probably the kind of look that I gave one of them when he asked me once what I found to talk about with the grunts all the time, expecting me to confide (I think) that I found them as boring as he did.

And just-like-in-the-movies, there were a lot of correspondents who did their work, met their deadlines, filled the most preposterous assignments the best they could and withdrew, watching the war and all its hideous secrets, earning their cynicism the hard way and turning their self-contempt back out again in laughter. If New York wanted to know how the troops felt about the assassination of Robert Kennedy, they'd go out and get it. ("Would you have voted for him?" "Yeah, he was a real good man, a real good man. He was, uh, young." "Who will you vote for now?" "Wallace, I guess.") They'd even gather troop reflections on the choice of Paris as the site of the peace talks. ("Paris? I dunno, sure, why not? I mean, they ain't gonna hold 'em in Hanoi, now are they?"), but they'd know how funny that was, how wasteful, how profane. They knew that, no matter how honestly they worked, their best work would somehow be lost in the wash of news, all the facts, all the Vietnam stories. Conventional journalism could no more reveal this war than conventional firepower could win it, all it could do was take the most profound event of the American decade and turn it into a communications pudding, taking its most obvious, undeniable history and making it into a secret history. And the very best correspondents knew even more than that.

There was a song by the Mothers of Invention called "Trouble Comin' Every Day" that became a kind of anthem among a group of around twenty young correspondents. We'd play it often during those long night gatherings in Saigon, the ashtrays heaped over, ice buckets full of warm water, bottles empty, the grass all gone, the words running, "You know I watch that rotten box until my head begin to hurt, From checkin' out the way the newsmen say they get the dirt" (bitter funny looks passing around the room), "And if another woman driver gets machine-gunned from her seat, They'll send some joker with a Brownie and you'll see it all complete" (lip-biting, flinching, nervous laughter), "And if the place blows up, we'll be the first to tell, 'Cause the boys we got downtown are workin' hard and doin' swell . . ." That wasn't really about *us*, no, we were *so* hip, and we'd laugh and wince every time we heard it, all of us, wire-service photographers and senior correspondents from the networks and special-assignment types like myself, all grinning together because of what we knew together, that in back of every column of print you read about Vietnam there was a dripping, laughing death-face; it hid there in the newspapers and magazines and held to your television screens for hours after the set was turned off for the night, an after-image that simply wanted to tell you at last what somehow had not been told.

On an afternoon shortly before the New Year, a few

weeks before Tet, a special briefing was held in Saigon to announce the latest revisions in the hamlet-rating system of the Pacification program, the A-B-C-D profiling of the country's security and, by heavy inference, of the government's popular support "in the countryside," which meant any place outside of Saigon, the boonies. A lot of correspondents went, many because they had to, and I spent the time with a couple of photographers in one of the bars on Tu Do, talking to some soldiers from the 1st Infantry Division who had come down from their headquarters at Lai Khe for the day. One of them was saying that Americans treated the Vietnamese like animals.

"How's that?" someone asked.

"Well, you know what we do to animals . . . kill 'em and hurt 'em and beat on 'em so's we can train 'em. Shit, we don't treat the Dinks no different than that."

And we knew that he was telling the truth. You only had to look at his face to see that he really knew what he was talking about. He wasn't judging it, I don't think that he was even particularly upset about it, it was just something he'd observed. We mentioned it later to some people who'd been at the Pacification briefing, someone from the *Times* and someone from the AP, and they both agreed that the kid from the Big Red One had said more about the Hearts-and-Minds program than they'd heard in over an hour of statistics, but their bureaus couldn't use his story, they wanted Ambassador Komer's. And they got it and you got it.

I could let you go on thinking that we were all brave, witty, attractive and vaguely tragic, that we were like some incomparable commando team, some hot-shit squadron, the Dreaded Chi, danger-loving, tender and wise. I could use it myself, it would certainly make for a prettier movie, but all of this talk about "we" and "us" has got to get straightened out.

At the height of the Tet Offensive alone, there were between 600 and 700 correspondents accredited to the Military Assistance Command, Vietnam. Who all of them were and where all of them went was as much a mystery to me and to most of the correspondents I knew as it was to the gentle-tempered bull-faced Marine gunnery sergeant assigned to the department of JUSPAO which issued those little plastic-coated MACV accreditation cards. He'd hand them out and add their number to a small blackboard on the wall and then stare at the total in amused wonder, telling you that he thought it was all a fucking circus. (He's the same man who told a television star, "Hold on to your ass awhile. You people from the electronic media don't scare me anymore.") There was nothing exclusive about that card or its operational match, the Bao Chi credential of the Republic of South Vietnam; thousands of them must have been issued over the years. All they did was admit you to the Vietnam press corps and tell you that you could go out and cover the war if you really wanted to. All kinds of people have held them at one time or another: feature writers for religious organs and gun magazines, summer vacationers from college newspapers (one paper sent two, a Hawk and a Dove, and we put it down because it hadn't sent a Moderate over as well), second-string literary figures who wrote about how they hated the war more than you or I ever could, syndicated eminences who houseguested with Westmoreland or Bunker and covered operations in the presence of Staff, privileges which permitted them to chronicle fully our great victory at Tet, and to publish evidence year after year after year that the back of the Cong had been broken, Hanoi's will dissolved. There was no nation too impoverished, no home-town paper so humble that it didn't get its man in for a quick feel at least once. The latter tended to be the sort of old reporter that most young reporters I knew were afraid of becoming someday. You'd run into them once in a while at the bar of the Danang press center, men in their late forties who hadn't had the chance to slip into uniform since V-J Day, exhausted and bewildered after all of those briefings and lightning visits, punchy from the sheer volume of facts that had been thrown on them, their tape recorders broken, their pens stolen by street kids, their time almost up. They'd been to see Cam Ranh Bay and quite a bit of the countryside (Mission diction, which meant that they'd been taken out to look at model or "New Life" hamlets), a crack ARVN division (where?), even some of our boys right there at the front (where?), and a lot of Military Information Office people. They seemed too awed by the importance of the whole thing to be very clear, they were too shy to make friends, they were all alone and speechless, except to say, "Well, when I came over here I thought it was pretty hopeless, but I have to admit, it looks like we've gotten things pretty much under control. I must say, I've been awfully impressed . . ." There were a lot of hacks who wrote down every word that the generals and officials told them to write, and a lot for whom Vietnam was nothing more than an important career station. There were some who couldn't make it and left after a few days, some who couldn't make it the other way, staying year after year, trying to piece together their very real hatred of the war with their great love for it, that rough reconciliation that many of us had to look at. A few came through with the grisliest hang-ups, letting it all go every chance they got, like the one who told me that he couldn't see what all the fuss had been about, *his* M-16 never jammed. There were Frenchmen who'd parachuted into Dien Bien Phu during what they loved to call "the First Indochina War," Englishmen sprung alive from *Scoop* (a press-corps standard because it said that if the papers didn't get it, it didn't happen), Italians whose only previous experience had been shooting fashion, Koreans who were running PX privileges into small fortunes, Japanese who trailed so many wires that transistor jokes were inevitable, Vietnamese who took up combat photography to avoid the draft, Americans who spent all their days in Saigon drinking at the bar of L'Amiral Restaurant with Air America pilots. Some filed nothing but hometowners, some took the social notes of the American community, some went in the field only because they couldn't afford hotels, some never left their hotels. Taken all together, they accounted for most of the total on Gunny's blackboard, which left a number of people, as many as fifty, who were gifted or honest or especially kind and who gave journalism a better name than it deserved, particularly in Vietnam. Finally, the press corps was as diffuse and faceless as any regiment in the war, the main difference being that many of us remained on our own orders.

It was a characteristic of a lot of Americans in Vietnam to have no idea of when they were being obscene, and some correspondents fell into that, writing their stories from the daily releases and battlegrams, tracking them through with the cheer-crazed language of the MACV Information Office, things like "discreet burst" (one of those tore an old grandfather and two children to bits as they ran along a paddy wall one day, at least according to the report made later by the gunship pilot), "friendly casualties" (not warm, not fun), "meeting engagement" (ambush), concluding usually with 17 or 117 or 317 enemy dead and American losses "described as light." There were correspondents who had the same sensibility concerning the dead as the Command had: Well, in a war you've got to expect a little mud to get tracked over the carpet, we took a real black eye but we sure gave Charlie a shitstorm, we consider this a real fine kill ratio, real fine. . . . There was a well-known correspondent of three wars who used to walk around the Danang press center with a green accountant's ledger. He'd sit down to talk and begin writing everything you'd say, entering it in, so to speak. The Marines arranged for a special helicopter (or "fragged a chopper," as we used to call it) to take him in and out of Khe Sanh one afternoon, weeks after it had become peaceful again. He came back very cheerful about our great victory there. I was sitting with Lengle, and we recalled that, at the very least, 200 grunts had been blown away there and around 1,000 more wounded. He looked up from his ledger and said, "Oh, two hundred isn't anything. We lost more than that in an hour on Guadalcanal." We weren't going to deal with that, so we sort of left the table, but you heard that kind of talk all the time, as though it could invalidate the deaths at Khe Sanh, render them somehow less dead than the dead from Guadalcanal, as though light losses didn't lie as still as moderate losses or heavy losses. And these were American dead they were talking about; you should have heard them when the dead were Vietnamese.

So there we all were, no real villains and only a few heroes, a lot of adventurers and a lot of drudges, a lot of beautiful lunatics and a lot of normals, come to report what was ultimately the normals' war; and somehow, out of all that, a great number of us managed to find and recognize each other. You could be hard about it and deny that there was a brotherhood working there, but then what else could you call it? It wasn't just some wartime clique of buddies, it was too large in number for that, including members of at least a dozen cliques, some of them overlapping until they became indistinguishable, others standing in contemptuous opposition to one another; and it was far too small to incorporate the whole bloated, amorphous body of the Vietnam press corps. Its requirements were unstated because, other than sensibility and style, it had none. Elsewhere, it would have been just another scene, another crowd, but the war gave it urgency and made it a deep thing, so deep that we didn't even have to like one another to belong. There was a lot that went unsaid at the time, but just because it was seldom spoken didn't mean that we weren't very much aware of it or that, in that terrible, shelterless place, we weren't grateful for each other.

It made room for correspondents who were themselves members of Saigon's American Establishment, it included young marrieds, all kinds of girl reporters, a lot of Europeans, the Ivy-League-in-Asia crowd, the Danang bunch, the Straights and the Heads, formals and funkies, old hands (many of whom were very young) and even some tourists, people who wanted to go somewhere to screw around for a while and happened to choose the war. There was no way of thinking about "who we were" because we were all so different, but where we were alike we were really alike. It helped if you went out on operations a lot or if you were good at your work, but neither was very necessary as long as you knew something of what the war was (as opposed to what the Mission and MACV told you it was), and as long as you weren't a snob about it. We were all doing terribly upsetting work, it could often be very dangerous, and we were the only ones who could tell, among ourselves, whether that work was any good. Applause from home meant nothing next to a nice word from a colleague. (One reporter loved to call his New York superiors "those leg motherfuckers," taking from Airborne the term for anyone who was not jump-qualified; if you can appreciate the 4th Division Lurp who called himself "The Baptist" even though he was an Episcopalian, you get the idea.) We were all studying the same thing, and if you got killed you couldn't graduate.

We were serious enough about what we were doing over

there, but we were also enchanted by it (not even the most uncomplicated farmboy pfc can go through a war without finding some use for it), and even when you got tired, felt you'd had too much, grown old in an afternoon, there were ways to take that and work it back into the style that we all tried to maintain. Things had to get really bad before you saw the war as clearly as most troops came to see it, but those times were rare enough and we (Those Crazy Guys . . .) were incorrigible. Most of us had times when we swore that we'd never go near any of it again if we could only be allowed out this once, everybody made those deals, but a few days in Danang or Saigon or even Hong Kong or Bangkok would get you over that, and the choice to go back was still there, still yours, priceless option, property of the press corps.

Friendships were made directly, with none of the clutter that had once seemed so necessary, and once they were made they outvalued all but your oldest, most special friendships. Your scene before Vietnam was unimportant, nobody wanted to hear about it, and we often seemed a little like those Green Berets out in their remote, harassed outposts, groups of eight or twelve Americans commanding hundreds of local mercenaries who could be as hostile as the Cong, who often *were* Cong; living together this way for months at a time without ever learning each other's first names or hometowns. You could make friends elsewhere, a Special Forces captain in the Delta, a grunt up in Phu Bai, some decent, witty (and usually suffering) member of the Embassy Political Section. But whether you hung out with them or with other correspondents, all you ever talked about anyway was the war, and they could come to seem like two very different wars after a while. Because who but another correspondent could talk the kind of mythical war that you wanted to hear described? (Just hearing the way Flynn pronounced the word "Vietnam," the tenderness and respect that he put in it, taught you more about the beauty and horror of the place than anything the apologists or explainers could ever teach you.) Who could you discuss politics with, except a colleague? (We all had roughly the same position on the war: we were in it, and that was a position.) Where else could you go for a real sense of the war's past? There were all kinds of people who knew the background, the facts, the most minute details, but only a correspondent could give you the exact mood that attended each of the major epochs: the animal terror of the Ia Drang or the ghastly breakdown of the first major Marine operation, code-named Starlight, where the Marines were dying so incredibly fast, so far beyond the Command's allowance, that one of them got zipped into a body bag and tossed to the top of a pile of KIA's while he was still alive. He regained consciousness up there and writhed and heaved until his bag rolled to the ground, where some corpsmen found him and saved him. The Triangle and Bong Son were as remote as the Reservoir or Chickamauga, you had to hear the history from somebody you could trust, and who else could you trust? And if you saw some piece of helmet graffiti that seemed to say everything, you weren't going to pass it along to some colonel or tell it to a Psyops official. "Born to Kill" placed in all innocence next to the peace symbol, or "A sucking chest wound is Nature's way of telling you that you've been in a firefight" was just too good to share with anyone but a real collector, and, with very few exceptions, those were all correspondents.

We shared a great many things: field gear, grass, whiskey, girls (that Men Without Women trip got old all the time), sources, information, hunches, tips, prestige (during my first days there bureau chiefs from *Life* and CBS took me around to introduce everyone they could think of, and somebody did as much for other new arrivals), we even shared each other's luck when our own seemed gone. I was no more superstitious than anyone else in Vietnam, I was very superstitious, and there were always a few who seemed so irrefutably charmed that nothing could make me picture them lying dead there; having someone like that with you on an operation could become more important than any actual considerations about what might be waiting on the ground for you. I doubt whether anything else could be as parasitic as that, or as intimate.

And by some equation that was so wonderful that I've never stopped to work it out, the best and the bravest correspondents were also usually the most compassionate, the ones who were most in touch with what they were doing. Greenway was like that, and so were Jack Laurence and Keith Kay, who worked together as a reporter-camera team for CBS for nearly two years. And there was Larry Burrows, who had been photographing the war for *Life* since 1962, a tall, deliberate Englishman of about forty with one of the most admirable reputations of all the Vietnam correspondents. We were together on one of the lz's that had been built for the operation that was supposedly relieving Khe Sanh, and Burrows had run down to take pictures of a Chinook that was coming in to land. The wind was strong enough to send tarmac strips flying fifty feet across the lz and he ran through it to work, photographing the crew, getting the soldiers coming down the incline to board the chopper, getting the kids throwing off the mailbags and cartons of rations and ammunition, getting the three wounded being lifted carefully on board, turning again to get the six dead in their closed body bags, then the rise of the chopper (the wind now was strong enough to tear papers out of your hand), photographing the grass blown flat all around him and the flying debris, taking one picture each of the chopper rearing, settling and departing. When it was gone he looked at me, and he seemed to be in the most open distress. "Sometimes one feels like such a bastard," he said.

And that was one more thing we shared. We had no secrets about it or the ways it could make you feel. We all talked about it at times, some talked about it too much, a few never seemed to talk about anything else. That was a drag, but it was all in the house; you only minded it when it came from outside. All kinds of thieves and killers managed to feel sanctimonious around us; battalion commanders, civilian businessmen, even the grunts, until they realized how few of us were making any real money in it. There's no way around it, if you photographed a dead Marine with a poncho over his face and got something for it, you were *some* kind of parasite. But what were you if you pulled the poncho back first to make a better shot, and did that in front of his friends? Some other kind of parasite, I suppose. Then what were you if you stood there watching it, making a note to remember it later in case you might want to use it? Those combinations were infinite, you worked them out, and they involved only a small part of what we were thought to be. We were called thrill freaks, death-wishers, wound-seekers, war-lovers, hero-worshipers, closet queens, dope addicts, low-grade alcoholics, ghouls, communists, seditionists, more nasty things than I can remember. There were people in the military who never forgave General Westmoreland for not imposing restrictions against us when he'd had the chance in the early days. There were officers and a lot of seemingly naïve troops who believed that if it were not for us, there would be no war now, and I was never able to argue with any of them on that point. A lot of the grunts had some of that sly, small-town suspicion of the press, but at least nobody under the rank of captain ever asked me whose side I was on, told me to get with the program, jump on the team, come in for the Big Win. Sometimes they were just stupid, sometimes it came about because they had such love for their men, but sooner or later all of us heard one version or another of "My Marines are winning this war, and you people are losing it for us in your papers," often spoken in an almost friendly way, but with the teeth shut tight behind the smiles. It was creepy, being despised in such casual, offhanded ways. And there were plenty of people who believed, finally, that we were nothing more than glorified war profiteers. And perhaps we were, those of us who didn't get killed or wounded or otherwise fucked up.

Just in the regular course of things, a lot of correspondents took close calls. Getting scratched was one thing, it didn't mean that you'd come as close as you could have, it could have been closer without your even knowing it, like an early-morning walk I took once from the hilltop position of a Special Forces camp where I'd spent the night, down to the teamhouse at the foot of the hill, where I was going to have some coffee. I walked off the main trail onto a smaller trail and followed it until I saw the house and a group of eight giggling, wide-eyed Vietnamese mercenaries, Mikes, pointing at me and talking very excitedly. They all grabbed for me at once when I reached the bottom, and as it was explained to me a moment later, I'd just come down a trail which the Special Forces had rigged out with more than twenty booby traps, any one of which could have taken me off. (Any One Of Which ran through my head for days afterward.) If you went out often, just as surely as you'd eventually find yourself in a position where survival etiquette insisted that you take a weapon ("You know how this thang works 'n' airthang?" a young sergeant had to ask me once, and I'd had to nod as he threw it to me and said, "Then git some!", the American banzai), it was unavoidable that you'd find yourself almost getting killed. You expected something like that to happen, but not exactly that, not until events made things obvious for you. A close call was like a loss of noncombatant status: you weren't especially proud of it, you merely reported it to a friend and then stopped talking about it, knowing in the first place that the story would go around from there, and that there wasn't really anything to be said about it anyway. But that didn't stop you from thinking about it a lot, doing a lot of hideous projecting from it, forming a system of pocket metaphysics around it, getting it down to where you found yourself thinking about which *kind* of thing was closer: that walk down the hill, the plane you missed by minutes which blew apart on the Khe Sanh airstrip an hour later and fifty miles away, or the sniper round that kissed the back of your flak jacket as you grunted and heaved yourself over a low garden wall in Hue. And then your *Dawn Patrol* fantasy would turn very ugly, events again and again not quite what you had expected, and you'd realize that nothing ever came closer to death than the death of a good friend.

In the first week of May 1968, the Viet Cong staged a brief, vicious offensive against Saigon, taking and holding small positions on the fringes of Cholon and defending parts of the outlying areas that could be retaken only from the Y Bridge, from the racetrack grounds, from Plantation Road and the large French graveyard that ran for several hundred yards into a grove and a complex of Viet Cong bunkers. The offensive's value as pure revolutionary terror aside (those results were always incalculable, our good gear notwithstanding), it was more or less what MACV said it was, costly to the VC and largely a failure. It cost the Friendlies too (between Saigon and the A Shau, it was the week that saw more Americans killed than any other in the war), a lot more damage was done to the city's outskirts, more homes were bombed out. The papers called it either the May Offen-

sive, .he Mini-Offensive (you know I'm not making that up),
or the Second Wave; it was the long-awaited Battle of
Algiers-in-Saigon that had been manically predicted by the
Americans for practically every weekend since the Tet
Offensive had ended. In its early hours, five correspondents
took a jeep into Cholon, past the first files of refugees (many
of whom warned them to turn back), and into a Viet Cong
ambush. One of them escaped (according to his own story)
by playing dead and then running like an animal into the
crowds of Cholon. He said that they had all yelled, "Bao
Chi!" a number of times, but that they had been machine-
gunned anyway.

It was more like death by misadventure than anything
else, as if that mattered, and of the four dead correspondents,
only one had been a stranger. Two of the others were good
acquaintances, and the fourth was a friend. His name was
John Cantwell, an Australian who worked for *Time,* and he
had been one of the first friends I'd made in Vietnam. He was
a kind, congenial mock-goat whose talk was usually about
the most complex, unimaginable lecheries, architectural con-
structions of monumental erotic fantasies. He had a Chinese
wife and two children in Hong Kong (he spoke fluent Chinese, he'd take it through the Cholon bars for us sometimes),
and he was one of the few I knew who really hated Vietnam
and the war, every bit of it. He was staying only long enough
to earn the money to settle some debts, and then he was
going to leave for good. He was a good, gentle, hilarious
man, and to this day I can't help thinking that he wasn't
supposed to get killed in Vietnam, getting killed in a war was
not John's scene, he'd made no room for that the way some
others had. A lot of people I had liked a lot, GI's and even
some correspondents, had already died, but when Cantwell
got murdered it did more than sadden and shock me. Because he was a friend, his death changed all the odds.

In that one brief period of less than two weeks it became a war of our convenience, a horrible convenience, but ours. We could jump into jeeps and minimokes at nine or ten and drive a few kilometers to where the fighting was, run around in it for a few hours and come back early. We'd sit on the Continental terrace and wave each other in, get stoned early and stay up late, since there was no question of 5:30 wake-ups. We'd been scattered all over Vietnam for months now, friends running into friends now and again, and this put everyone together. There was no other time when that was needed so badly. A day after John and the others died, a strange, death-charged kid named Charlie Eggleston, a UPI photographer, got killed at the Cemetery, reportedly while returning fire at a Viet Cong position. (He willed everything he had to Vietnamese charities.) A Japanese photographer was killed later that same day, a Brazilian lost a leg the day after that and somewhere in there another correspondent was killed; by then everyone had stopped counting and worked at keeping it away. Again in the Cemetery, a bullet tore through Co Rentmeister's hand and lodged under the eye of another photographer, Art Greenspahn. A Frenchman named Christien Simon-Pietrie (known as "Frenchy" to his movie-warped friends) was hit above the eye by some shrapnel from the same round which crippled General Loan; not a serious wound but one more out of too many, more than correspondents had ever received at one time. By the fifth day, eight had died and more than a dozen others had been wounded. We were driving toward the racetrack when an MP stepped in front of our car to ask for identification.

"Listen," he said, "I saw those four other guys and I never want to see any more like that. You know those guys? Then what the fuck do you want to go in there for? Don't you people ever learn? I mean, I *saw* those guys, believe me, it ain't worth it."

He was firm about not letting us through, but we insisted and he finally gave up.

"Well, I can't really stop you. You *know* I can't stop you. But if I could, I would. You wouldn't be driving up to no shit like those four guys."

In the early evenings we'd do exactly what correspondents did in those terrible stories that would circulate in 1964 and 1965, we'd stand on the roof of the Caravelle Hotel having drinks and watch the airstrikes across the river, so close that a good telephoto lens would pick up the markings on the planes. There were dozens of us up there, like aristocrats viewing Borodino from the heights, at least as detached about it as that even though many of us had been caught under those things from time to time. There'd be a lot of women up there, a few of them correspondents (like Cathy Leroy, the French photographer, and Jurati Kazikas, a correspondent of great, fashion-model beauty), most of them the wives and girls of reporters. Some people had tried hard to believe that Saigon was just another city they'd come to live in; they'd formed civilized social routines, tested restaurants, made and kept appointments, given parties, had love affairs. Many had even brought their wives with them, and more often than not it worked out badly. Very few of the women really liked Saigon, and the rest became like most Western women in Asia: bored, distracted, frightened, unhappy and, if left there too long, fiercely frantic. And now, for the second time in three months, Saigon had become unsafe. Rockets were dropping a block from the best hotels, the White Mice (the Saigon police) were having brief, hysterical firefights with shadows, you could hear it going on as you dropped off to sleep; it was no longer simply a stinking, corrupt, exhausting foreign city.

At night, the rooms of the Continental would fill with correspondents drifting in and out for a drink or a smoke before bed, some talk and some music, the Rolling Stones singing, "It's so very lonely, You're two thousand light years from home," or "Please come see me in your Citadel," that word putting a chill in the room. Whenever one of us came back from an R&R we'd bring records, sounds were as precious as water: Hendrix, the Airplane, Frank Zappa and the Mothers, all the things that hadn't even started when we'd left the States. Wilson Pickett, Junior Walker, *John Wesley Harding*, one recording worn thin and replaced within a month, the Grateful Dead (the name was enough), the Doors, with their distant, icy sound. It seemed like such wintry music; you could rest your forehead against the window where the air-conditioner had cooled the glass, close your eyes and feel the heat pressing against you from outside. Flares dropped over possible targets three blocks away, and all night long, armed jeeps and massive convoys moved down Tu Do Street toward the river.

When we were down to a hard core of six or seven, we'd talk tired, stoned talk about the war, imitating commanders who were always saying things like, "Well, Charlie's dug in there pretty good, but when we can get him out where we can see him we find we're getting some real decent kills, we got Charlie outgunned for sure, only thing is we can't kill him if we can't see 'cause Charlie's always running. Come on, we'll take you up and get you shot at." We talked about a discotheque we were going to open in Saigon, the Third Wave, with a stainless-steel dance floor, blow-ups of the best war photographs on the walls, a rock group called Westy and the KIA's. (Our talk had about as much taste as the war did.) And we'd talk about LZ Loon, the mythical place where it got dark so fast that by the time you realized that there wouldn't be another chopper in until morning, you'd already picked a place to sleep for the night. Loon was the ultimate Vietnam movie location, where all of the mad colonels and death-spaced grunts we'd ever known showed up all at once, saying all the terrible, heartbreaking things they always said, so nonchalant about the horror and fear that you knew you'd never really be one of them no matter how long you stayed. You honestly didn't know whether to laugh or cry. Few people ever cried more than once there, and if you'd used that up, you laughed; the young ones were so innocent and violent, so sweet and so brutal, beautiful killers.

One morning, about twenty-five correspondents were out by the Y Bridge working when a dying ARVN was driven by on the back of a half-ton pick-up. The truck stopped at some barbed wire, and we all gathered around to look at him. He was nineteen or twenty and he'd been shot three times in the chest. All of the photographers leaned in for pictures, there was a television camera above him, we looked at him and then at each other and then at the wounded Vietnamese again. He opened his eyes briefly a few times and looked back at us. The first time, he tried to smile (the Vietnamese did that when they were embarrassed by the nearness of foreigners), then it left him. I'm sure that he didn't even see us the last time he looked, but we all knew what it was that he'd seen just before that.

That was also the week that Page came back to Vietnam. *A Scrambler to the Front* by Tim Page, *Tim Page* by Charles Dickens. He came a few days before it started, and people who knew about his luck were making jokes blaming the whole thing on his return. There were more young, apolitically radical, wigged-out crazies running around Vietnam than anybody ever realized; between all of the grunts turning on and tripping out on the war and the substantial number of correspondents who were doing the same thing, it was an authentic subculture. There were more than enough within the press corps to withstand a little pressure from the upright, and if Flynn was the most sophisticated example of this, Page was the most extravagant. I'd heard about him even before I came to Vietnam ("Look him up. If he's still alive"), and between the time I got there and the time he came back in May, I'd heard so much about him that I might have felt that I knew him if so many people hadn't warned me, "There's just no way to describe him for you. Really, no way."

"Page? That's easy. Page is a child."

"No, man, Page is just crazy."

"Page is a crazy child."

They'd tell all kinds of stories about him, sometimes working up a passing anger over things he'd done years before, times when he'd freaked a little and become violent, but it always got softened, they'd pull back and say his name with great affection. "Page. Fucking Page."

He was an orphan boy from London, married at seventeen and divorced a year later. He worked his way across Europe as a cook in the hotels, drifting east through India, through Laos (where he claims to have dealt with the Spooks, a little teen-age espionage), into Vietnam at the age of twenty. One of the things that everybody said about him was that he had not been much of a photographer then (he'd picked up a camera the way you or I would pick up a ticket), but that he would go places for pictures that very few other photographers were going. People made him sound crazy and ambitious, like the Sixties Kid, a stone-cold freak in a country where the madness raced up the hills and into the jungles, where everything essential to learning Asia, war, drugs, the whole adventure, was close at hand.

The first time he got hit it was shrapnel in the legs and stomach. That was at Chu Lai, in '65. The next time was during the Buddhist riots of the 1966 Struggle Movement in

Danang: head, back, arms, more shrapnel. (A *Paris-Match* photograph showed Flynn and a French photographer carrying him on a door, his face half covered by bandages, *"Tim Page, blessé à la tête."*) His friends began trying to talk him into leaving Vietnam, saying, "Hey, Page, there's an airstrike looking for you." And there was; it caught him drifting around off course in a Swift boat in the South China Sea, blowing it out of the water under the mistaken impression that it was a Viet Cong vessel. All but three of the crew were killed, Page took over 200 individual wounds, and he floated in the water for hours before he was finally rescued.

They were getting worse each time, and Page gave in to it. He left Vietnam, allegedly for good, and joined Flynn in Paris for a while. He went to the States from there, took some pictures for Time-Life, got busted with the Doors in New Haven, traveled across the country on his own (he still had some money left), doing a picture story which he planned to call "Winter in America." Shortly after the Tet Offensive, Flynn returned to Vietnam, and once Page heard that, it was only a matter of time. When he got back in May, his entrance requirements weren't in order, and the Vietnamese kept him at Tan Son Nhut for a couple of days, where his friends visited him and brought him things. The first time I met him he was giggling and doing an insane imitation of two Vietnamese immigration authorities fighting over the amount of money they were going to hold him up for, "Minh phung, auk nyong bgnyang gluke poo phuc fuck fart, I mean you should have *heard* those beastly people. Where am I going to sleep, who's got a rack for Page? The Dinks have been mucking about with Page, Page is a *very* tired boy."

He was twenty-three when I first met him, and I can remember wishing that I'd known him when he was still young. He was bent, beaten, scarred, he was everything by way of being crazy that everyone had said he was, except that you could tell that he'd never get really nasty again when he flipped. He was broke, so friends got him a place to sleep, gave him piastres, cigarettes, liquor, grass. Then he made a couple of thousand dollars on some fine pictures of the Offensive, and all of those things came back on us, twice over. That was the way the world was for Page; when he was broke you took care of him, when he was not he took care of you. It was above economics.

"Now, would Ellsworth Bunker like the Mothers of Invention?" he'd say. (He wanted to rig loudspeakers around the Lower House and along the park facing it and play the freakiest music he could find as loud as the equipment would permit.)

"On your head, Page," Flynn would say.

"No. I ask you, would William C. Westmoreland dig the Mothers or wouldn't he?"

His talk was endlessly referential, he mixed in images from the war, history, rock, Eastern religion, his travels, literature (he was very widely read and proud of it), but you came to see that he was really only talking about one thing, Page. He spoke of himself in the third person more than anyone I ever knew, but it was so totally ingenuous that it was never offensive. He could get very waspish and silly, he could be an outrageous snob (he was a great believer in the New Aristocracy), he could talk about people and things in ways that were nearly monstrous, stopping short of that and turning funny and often deeply tender. He carried all kinds of clippings around with him, pictures of himself, newspaper stories about the times he'd been wounded, a copy of a short story that Tom Mayer had written about him in which he got killed on an operation with the Korean Marines. He was especially vain about that story, very proud and completely spooked by it. That first week back, he'd had things brought around to where he could remember them again, remembering that you could get killed here, the way he almost had those other times, the way he had in the story.

"*Look* at you," he'd say, coming into the room at night. "Every one of you is *stoned*. Look at you, what are you doing there if it isn't rolling a joint? Grinning, Flynn, grinning is sinning. Dope is hope. Help! Give us a bit of that, will you? I ain't doin' no evil, give us just a toke. Ahhhhh, yesh! It *can't* be my turn to change the record because I've only just come in. Are any birds coming by? Where are Mimsy and Poopsy? [His names for two Australian girls who dropped over some evenings.] Women is good, women is necessary, women is definitely good for business. Yesh."

"Don't smoke that, Page. Your brain is already about the consistency of a soggy quiche lorraine."

"Nonsense, utter nonsense. Why don't you roll a five-handed joint while I prepare a steamboat for this ugly, filthy roach?" He'd jab his misshapen left index finger at you to underline key words, taking the conversation wherever his old child's whimsey took his thoughts, planning projects which ranged from full-scale guerrilla ops in New York City to painting the front of the hotel in Day-Glo colors in the belief that the Vietnamese would love it. "They're all stoned all the time anyway," he'd say. If any girls showed up, he'd tell them lurid stories about the war, about the Middle East (both he and Flynn had caught a couple of days of the June War, flying down from Paris for it), about venereal diseases he'd had, talking to them the way he'd talk to anybody. He only had one way of speaking, it could have been to me or the Queen, it didn't matter. ("What do you mean, of *course* I love the Queen. The Queen's a very lovable bird.") If he was too absorbed to talk, he'd stand in front of a full-length mirror and dance to the Doors for an hour at a time, completely lost in it.

When Saigon became quiet again during the third week of May, it seemed as though the war had ended. Nothing was happening anywhere, and I realized that after seven months straight of this I needed some time out. Saigon was the place where you always noticed how tired your friends looked anyway; a place needs a lot of character for that, and in Saigon you could look perfectly marvelous one day and then perfectly terrible the next, and friends were telling me about it. So while Flynn went up for a month with the 4th Division Lurps, walking point on unearthly four-man night patrols through the Highlands (he came back from that one with three rolls of exposed film), I left for a month in Hong Kong, followed by practically everyone I knew. It was like moving my scene intact to more pleasant surroundings, a recess session. Page came over to buy expensive toys: more cameras, a fish-eye lens, a Halliburton. He stayed for a week and talked of nothing but how awful Hong Kong was, how Singapore was much, much groovier. When I got back to Vietnam in early July, he and I spent ten days in the Delta with the Special Forces, and then we went to Danang to meet Flynn. (Page called Danang "Dangers," with a hard g. In a war where people quite seriously referred to Hong Kong as "Hongers" and spoke of running over to Pnompers to interview Sukie, a British correspondent named Don Wise made up a Vietnam itinerary: Canters, Saigers, Nharters, Quinners, Pleikers, Quangers, Dangers and Hyoo-beside-the-Sea.)

Page's helmet decor now consisted of the words HELP, I'M A ROCK! (taken from another Zappa song) and a small Mao button, but he didn't have much chance to wear it. Things were still quiet everywhere, fini la guerre, I wanted to leave in September and it was already August. We went out on operations, but all of them were without contact. That was fine with me, I didn't want contact (what the hell for?), that month in Hong Kong had been good in a lot of ways, one of them being the leisure it offered me to recall with some precision just how awful Vietnam could be. Away from it, it was a very different place. We spent most of August on China Beach sailing and goofing, talking to Marines who'd come down for in-country R&R, coming back in the late afternoons to the press center by the Danang River. It was perfectly peaceful, better than any vacation could be, but I knew that I was going home, I was short, and a kind of retrospective fear followed me everywhere.

In the bar of the press center, Marines and members of the Naval Support Activity, all information specialists, would gather after a long day in the IO Shop to juice a little until it got dark enough for the movie to start outside. They were mostly officers (no one under E-6 was allowed in the bar, including a lot of combat grunts whom many of us had tried to bring in for drinks over the past year), and there was a constant state of mistrust between us. The Marines from the Combat Information Bureau seemed to like most civilian reporters about as well as they liked the Viet Cong, maybe a little less, and we grew sick of their constant attempts to impose Marine order on our lives there. That winter, you'd return to the press center from places that were too terrible to believe, and a lot of our tack would become impaired in transit, causing stupid quarrels over things like tee shirts and shower clogs in the dining room and helmets worn in the bar. We'd walk in now from China Beach and they'd all look at us, wave, laugh harshly and ask us how it was going.

"We're winning," Flynn would say cryptically, smiling pleasantly, and they'd smile back uncertainly.

"Look how nervous Page makes them," Flynn said. "He really makes the Marines nervous."

"Freak," Page said.

"No, honest to God, I mean it. Look, the minute he walks

in they sort of shy like ponies, they move just a little closer together. They don't like your hair, Page, and you're a foreigner, and you're insane, you really spook the shit out of them. They might not be sure of how they feel about this war, some of them may even think it's wrong, some of them may dig Ho a little bit, they're not sure about a lot of things, but they're sure about you, Page. You're the enemy. 'Kill Page!' You wait, man. Wait, Page."

Just before I went back to Saigon to begin arrangements for flying home, the three of us met at a place called Tam Ky, near the mouth of the Perfume River, where Page was trying out his fish-eye lens on the airboats that had just come back to Vietnam after an earlier failure in the war. We rode around on those for a day and then took a boat downriver to Hue, where we met Perry Dean Young, a reporter for UPI who came from North Carolina. (Flynn called him "the fullest flowering of southern degeneracy," but the closest to degeneracy any of us ever came was in our jokes about it, about what bad, dope-smoking cats we all were. We were probably less stoned than the drinkers in our presence, and our livers were holding up.) Perry had a brother named Dave who ran the small Naval detachment that had been set up during the battle, directly across from the south wall of the Citadel. For months now, Flynn and I had been living vicariously off of each other's war stories, his Ia Drang stories and my Hue stories, and Perry's brother got a Navy truck and drove us around the city while I gave a running commentary which would have been authoritative if only I'd been able to recognize any of it now. We were sitting on the back of the truck on folding chairs, bouncing around in the heat and dust. Along the park that fronted the river we passed dozens of lovely young girls riding their bicycles, and Page leaned over and leered at them, saying, "Good mornin', little schoolgirl, I'm a li'l schoolboy too."

When I'd been here before, you couldn't let yourself be seen on the riverbank without machine guns opening upon you from the opposite bank, you couldn't breathe anywhere in Hue without rushing somebody's death into your bloodstream, the main bridge across the river had been dropped in the middle, the days had been cold and wet, the city had been composed seemingly of destruction and debris. Now it was clear and very warm, you could stop by the Cercle Sportif for a drink, the bridge was up and the wall was down, all the rubble had been carted away.

"It *couldn't* have been *that* bad," Page said, and Flynn and I laughed.

"You're just pissed because you missed it," Flynn said.

"That's you you're talking about boy, not Page."

And I was realizing for the first time how insanely dangerous it had been, seeing it in a way I hadn't in February.

"No," Page said. "It got awfully exaggerated, Hue. I know it couldn't have been that bad, I mean look around. I've seen worse. Much, much worse."

I meant to ask him where, but I was already in New York when I thought of it.

III

Back in the World now, and a lot of us aren't making it. The story got old or we got old, a great deal more than the story had taken us there anyway, and many things had been satisfied. Or so it seemed when, after a year or two or five, we realized that we were simply tired. We came to fear something more complicated than death, an annihilation less final but more complete, and we got out. Because (more lore) we all knew that if you stayed too long you became one of those poor bastards who had to have a war on all the time, and where was that? We got out and became like everyone else who has been through a war: changed, enlarged and (some things are expensive to say) incomplete. We came back or moved on, keeping in touch from New York or San Francisco, Paris or London, Africa or the Middle East; some fell into bureaus in Chicago or Hong Kong or Bangkok, coming to miss the life so acutely (some of us) that we understood what amputees went through when they sensed movement in the fingers or toes of limbs lost months before. A few extreme cases felt that the experience there had been a glorious one, while most of us felt that it had been merely wonderful. I think that Vietnam was what we had instead of happy childhoods.

During my first month back I woke up one night and knew that my living room was full of dead Marines. It actually happened three or four times, after a dream I was having those nights (the kind of dream one never had in Vietnam), and that first time it wasn't just some holding dread left by the dream, I knew they were there, so that after I'd turned on the light by my bed and smoked a cigarette I lay there for a moment thinking that I'd have to go out soon and cover them. I don't want to make anything out of this and I certainly don't want sympathy; going to that place was my idea to begin with, I could have left anytime, and as those things go I paid little enough, almost nothing. Some guys come back and see their nightmares break in the streets in daylight, some become inhabited and stay that way, all kinds of things can trail after you, and besides, after a while my thing went away almost completely, the dream, too. I know a guy who had been a combat medic in the Central Highlands, and two years later he was still sleeping with all the lights on. We were walking across 57th Street one afternoon and passed a blind man carrying a sign that read, MY DAYS ARE DARKER

THAN YOUR NIGHTS. "Don't bet on it, man," the ex-medic said.

Of course coming back was a down. After something like that, what could you find to thrill you, what compared, what did you do for a finish? Everything seemed a little dull, heaviness threatened everywhere, you left little relics lying around to keep you in touch, to keep it real, you played the music that had been with you through Hue and Khe Sanh and the May Offensive, tried to believe that the freedom and simplicity of those days could be maintained in what you laughingly referred to as "normal circumstances." You read the papers and watched television, but you knew what those stories were really all about beforehand, and they just got you angry. You missed the scene, missed the grunts and the excitement, the feelings you'd had in a place where no drama had to be invented, ever. You tried to get the same highs here that you'd had there, but none of that really worked very well. You wondered whether, in time, it would all slip away and become like everything else distant, but you doubted it, and for good reason. The friendships lasted, some even deepened, but our gatherings were always stalked by longing and emptiness, more than a touch of Legion Post Night. Smoking dope, listening to the Mothers and Jimi Hendrix, remembering compulsively, telling war stories. But then, there's nothing wrong with that. War stories aren't really anything more than stories about people anyway.

In April I got a call telling me that Page had been hit again and was not expected to live. He had been up goofing somewhere around Cu Chi, digging the big toys, and a helicopter he was riding in was ordered to land and pick up some wounded. Page and a sergeant ran out to help, the sergeant stepped on a mine which blew his legs off and sent a two-inch piece of shrapnel through Page's forehead above the right eye and deep into the base of his brain. He retained consciousness all the way to the hospital at Long Binh. Flynn and Perry Young were on R&R in Vientiane when they were notified, and they flew immediately to Saigon. For nearly two weeks, friends at Time-Life kept me informed by telephone from their daily cables; Page was transferred to a hospital in Japan and they said that he would probably live. He was moved to Walter Reed Army Hospital (a civilian and a British subject, it took some doing), and they said that he would live but that he'd always be paralyzed on his left side. I called him there, and he sounded all right, telling me that his roommate was this very religious colonel who kept apologizing to Page because he was only in for a check-up, he hadn't been wounded or anything fantastic like that. Page was afraid that he was freaking the colonel out a little bit. Then they moved him to the Institute for Physical Rehabilitation in New York, and while none of them could really explain it medically, it seemed that he was regaining the use of his left arm and leg. The first time I went to see him I walked right past his bed without recognizing him out of the four patients in the room, even though he'd been the first one I'd seen, even though the other three were men in their forties and fifties. He lay there grinning his deranged, uneven grin, his eyes were wet, and he raised his right hand for a second to jab at me with his finger. His head was shaved and sort of lidded now across the forehead where they'd opened it up ("What did they find in there, Page?" I asked him. "Did they find that quiche lorraine?") and caved in on the right side where they'd removed some bone. He was emaciated and he looked really old, but he was still grinning very proudly as I approached the bed, as if to say, "Well, didn't Page step into it this time?" as though two inches of shrapnel in your brain was the wiggiest goof of them all, that wonderful moment of the Tim Page Story where our boy comes leering, lurching back from death, twin brother to his own ghost.

That was that, he said, *fini Vietnam,* there could be no more odds left, he'd been warned. Sure he was crazy, but he wasn't *that* crazy. He had a bird now, a wonderful English girl named Linda Webb whom he'd met in Saigon. She'd stayed with him in the Long Binh hospital even though the shock and fear of seeing him like that had made her pass out fifteen times on the first evening. "I'd really be the fool, now, to just give that one up, now, wouldn't I?" he said, and we all said, Yes, man, you would be.

On his twenty-fifth birthday there was a big party in the apartment near the hospital that he and Linda had found. Page wanted all of the people to be there who, he said, had bet him years ago in Saigon that he'd never make it past twenty-three. He wore a blue sweat suit with a Mike patch, black skull and bones, on his sleeve. You could have gotten stoned just by walking into the room that day, and Page was so happy to be here and alive and among friends that even the strangers who turned up then were touched by it. "There's Evil afoot," he kept saying, laughing and chasing after people in his wheelchair. "Do no Evil, think ye no Evil, smoke no Evil. . . . Yesh."

A month went by and he made fantastic progress, giving up the chair for a cane and wearing a brace to support his left arm.

"I've a splendid new trick for the doctors," he said one day, flinging his left arm out of the brace and up over his head with great effort, waving his hand a little. Sometimes he'd stand in front of a full-length mirror in the apartment and survey the wreckage, laughing until tears came, shaking his head and saying, "Ohhhhh, fuck! I mean, just *look* at that, will you? Page is a fucking hemi-plegic," raising his cane and stumbling back to his chair, collapsing in laughter again.

He fixed up an altar with all of his Buddhas, arranging prayer candles in a belt of empty .50-caliber cartridges. He put in a stereo, played endlessly at organizing his slides into trays, spoke of setting out Claymores at night to keep "undesirables" away, built model airplanes ("Very good therapy, that"), hung toy choppers from the ceiling, put up posters of Frank Zappa and Cream and some Day-Glo posters which Linda had made of monks and tanks and solid soul brothers smoking joints in the fields of Vietnam. He began talking more and more about the war, often coming close to tears when he remembered how happy he and all of us had been there.

One day a letter came from a British publisher, asking him to do a book whose working title would be "Through with War" and whose purpose would be to once and for all "take the glamour out of war." Page couldn't get over it.

"Take the glamour out of war! I mean, how the bloody hell can you do *that?* Go and take the glamour out of a Huey, go take the glamour out of a Sheridan. . . . Can *you* take the glamour out of a Cobra or getting stoned at China Beach? It's like taking the glamour out of an M-79, taking the glamour out of Flynn." He pointed to a picture he'd taken, Flynn laughing maniacally ("We're winning," he'd said), triumphantly. "Nothing the matter with *that* boy, is there? Would you let your daughter marry that man? Ohhhh, war is *good* for you, you can't take the glamour out of that. It's like trying to take the glamour out of sex, trying to take the glamour out of the Rolling Stones." He was really speechless, working his hands up and down to emphasize the sheer insanity of it.

"I mean, you *know* that, it just *can't be done!*" We both shrugged and laughed, and Page looked very thoughtful for a moment. "The very *idea!*" he said. "Ohhh, what a laugh! Take the bloody *glamour* out of bloody *war!*"

Breathing Out

I am going home. I have seen a lot of Vietnam in 18 months.
May Lord help this place. DEROS 10 Sept 68.

Mendoza was here. 12 Sept 68. Texas.

Color me gone. (Mendoza is my buddy.)

Release graffiti on the walls at Tan Son Nhut airport, where
Flynn, almost overtly serious for a second, gave me a kind of
blessing ("Don't piss it all away at cocktail parties") and
Page gave me a small ball of opium to eat on the flight back;
stoned dreaming through Wake, Honolulu, San Francisco,
New York and the hallucination of home. Opium space, a
big round O, and time outside of time, a trip that happened
in seconds and over years; Asian time, American space, not
clear whether Vietnam was east or west of center, behind me
or somehow still ahead. "Far's I'm concerned, this one's over
the day I get home," a grunt had told us a few weeks before,
August 1968, we'd been sitting around after an operation
talking about the end of the war. "Don't hold your breath,"
Dana said.

Home: twenty-eight years old, feeling like Rip Van
Winkle, with a heart like one of those little paper pills they
make in China, you drop them into water and they open out
to form a tiger or a flower or a pagoda. Mine opened out into
war and loss. There'd been nothing happening there that
hadn't already existed here, coiled up and waiting, back in

the World. I hadn't been anywhere, I'd performed half an act; the war only had one way of coming to take your pain away quickly.

It seemed now that everybody knew someone who had been in Vietnam and didn't want to talk about it. Maybe they just didn't know how. People I'd meet would take it for granted that I was articulate, ask me if I minded, but usually the questions were political, square, innocent, they already knew what they wanted to hear, I'd practically forgotten the language. Some people found it distasteful or confusing if I told them that, whatever else, I'd loved it there too. And if they just asked, "What was your scene there?" I wouldn't know what to say either, so I'd say I was trying to write about it and didn't want to dissipate it. But before you could dissipate it you had to locate it, Plant you now, dig you later: information printed on the eye, stored in the brain, coded over skin and transmitted by blood, maybe what they meant by "blood consciousness." And transmitted over and over without letup on increasingly powerful frequencies until you either received it or blocked it out one last time, informational Death of a Thousand Cuts, each cut so precise and subtle you don't even feel them accumulating, you just get up one morning and your ass falls off.

There was a black grunt with the 9th Division who called himself the Entertainer. When I asked him why he said, " 'Cause I rock and I roll," and flipped the selector switch on his 16 back and forth between semi and full. He walked away, moving almost in two sections like his ass was stalking his chest, so that his dog tags flopped hard against him. He spun on his heel and did it backward for a few yards. Then he stopped and reached over his head. When he pulled his arm down a heavy rain came pouring in. "I been here so long I can call these motherfuckers in on the *dime.*" He put a lot of energy and care into his jive, it had made him a star in his unit, but he wasn't just some feets-do-yo-stuff spade. So when he told me that he saw ghosts whenever they went on night patrol I didn't laugh, and when he said that he'd started seeing his own out there I think I freaked a little. "Naw, that's cool, that's cool, motherfucker was be*hind* me," he said. "It's when he goes and moves up in front that you're livin' in a world of hurt." I tried to say that what he probably had seen was the phosphorescence that gathered around rotting tree trunks and sent pulsing light over the ground from one damp spot to another. "Crazy," he said, and, "Later."

They were bulldozing a junction into Route 22 near Tay Ninh and the old Iron Triangle when the plows ran into some kind of VC cemetery. The bones started flying up out of the ground and forming piles beside the furrows, like one of those films from the concentration camps running backward. Instamatic City, guys racing like crazy with their cameras, taking snaps, grabbing bones for souvenirs. Maybe I should have taken one too; three hours later back in Saigon I wasn't that sure whether I'd really seen it or not. While we were there and the war seemed separate from what we thought of as real life and normal circumstance, an aberration, we all took a bad flash sooner or later and usually more than once, like old acid backing up, residual psychotic reaction. Certain rock and roll would come in mixed with rapid fire and men screaming. Sitting over a steak in Saigon once I made nasty meat connections, rot and burning from the winter before in Hue. Worst of all, you'd see people walking around whom you'd watched die in aid stations and helicopters. The boy with the huge Adam's apple and the wire-rimmed glasses sitting by himself at a table on the Continental terrace had seemed much more nonchalant as a dead Marine two weeks before at the Rockpile than he did now, wearing the red 1st Division patch, trying to order a Coke from the waiter while a couple of margouilla lizards chased each other up and down the white column behind his head. I thought for a second that I was going to faint when I saw him. After a fast second look I knew that he wasn't a ghost or even a double, there actually wasn't much resemblance at all, but by then my breath was gummed up in my throat and my face was cold and white, shake shake shake. "Nothing to worry about boy," Page said. "Just your nineteenth nervous breakdown."

They were always telling you that you mustn't forget the dead, and they were always telling you that you shouldn't let yourself think about them too much. You couldn't remain effective as a soldier or a reporter if you got all hung up on the dead, fell into patterns of morbid sensitivity, entered perpetual mourning. "You'll get used to it," people would say, but I never did, actually it got personal and went the other way.

Dana used to do a far-out thing, he'd take pictures of us under fire and give them to us as presents. There's one of me on the ramp of a Chinook at Cam Lo, only the blur of my right foot to show that I'm not totally paralyzed, twenty-seven pushing fifty, reaching back for my helmet and the delusion of cover. Behind me inside the chopper there's a door gunner in a huge dark helmet, a corpse is laid out on the seat, and in front of me there's a black Marine, leaning in and staring with raw raving fear toward the incoming rounds; all four of us caught there together while Dana crouched down behind the camera, laughing. "You fuck," I said to him when he gave me the print, and he said, "I thought you ought to know what you look like."

I don't have any pictures of Dana, but there's not much chance I'll forget what he looked like, that front-line face, he never got anything on film that he didn't get on himself, after three years he'd turned into the thing he came to photograph. I have pictures of Flynn but none by him, he was in so deep he hardly bothered to take them after a while. Definitely off of media, Flynn; a war behind him already where he'd confronted and cleaned the wasting movie-star karma that had burned down his father. In so far as Sean had been acting out, he was a great actor. He said that the movies just swallowed you up, so he did it on the ground, and the ground swallowed him up (no one I ever knew could have dug it like you, Sean), he and Dana had gone off somewhere together since April 1970, biking into Cambodia, "presumed captured," rumors and long silence, MIA to say the least.

There it is, the grunts said, like this: sitting by a road with some infantry when a deuce-and-a-half rattled past with four dead in the back. The tailgate was half lowered as a platform to hold their legs and the boots that seemed to weigh a hundred pounds apiece now. Everyone was completely quiet as the truck hit a bad bump and the legs jerked up high and landed hard on the gate. "How about that shit," someone said, and "Just like the motherfucker," and "There it is." Pure essence of Vietnam, not even stepped on once, you could spin it out into visions of laughing lucent skulls or call it just another body in a bag, say that it cut you in half for the harvest or came and took you under like a lover, nothing ever made the taste less strong; the moment of initiation where you get down and bite off the tongue of a corpse. "Good for your work," Flynn would say.

Those who remember the past are condemned to repeat it too, that's a little history joke. Shove it along, dissolve your souvenirs: a pair of fatigues that started to fit about a week before I left, an ashtray from the Continental, a pile of snaps, like one of me on the top of a hill called Nui Kto, one of the Seven Sisters in the Delta, standing around with some Cambodian mercenaries (bandits actually, every squad carried pliers for pulling gold teeth), all looking like we're having a great time waiting for the choppers to come and take us off, only way out; we had the entire base and the top, but everything in between was all full up with Viet Cong. A *National Geographic* map of Indochina with about a hundred pencil marks, every place I ever went there, dots and crosses and big crosses even, wherever I'd been in or near combat and my vanity had told me I'd pulled through, not "scathed"; attached to every mark and the complex of faces, voices and movements that gathered around each one. Real places, then real only in the distance behind me, faces and places sustaining serious dislocation, mind slip and memory play. When the map fell apart along the fold lines its spirit held together, it landed in safe but shaky hands and one mark was enough, the one at LZ Loon.

At dark they finished the perimeter, doubled the guard and sent half the company out on patrols; a brand-new no-name Marine lz in the heart of Indian country. I slept like a morphine sleeper that night, not knowing which was awake or asleep, clocking the black triangle of the raised tent flap as it turned dark blue, fog white, sun yellow, and it felt okay to get up. Just before I flew back to Danang they named it LZ Loon, and Flynn said, "That's what they ought to call the whole country," a more particular name than Vietnam to describe the death space and the life you found inside it. When we rebuilt Loon on China Beach that day we laughed so hard we couldn't sit up.

I loved the door, loved it when the ship would turn a little and tilt me toward the earth, flying at a hundred feet. A lot of people thought it opened you to some kind of extra danger, like ground fire spilling in on you instead of just severing the hydraulic system or cutting off the Jesus nut that held the rotor on. A friend of mine said he couldn't do it, it put him close to rapture of the deep, he was afraid he'd flip the latch on his seat belt and just float out there. But I was afraid anyway, more afraid closed in, better to see, I didn't go through all of that not to see.

At midnight over Vinh Long, the gunship made seven or eight low runs above a company of Viet Cong on the eastern edge of the city. At first the tracers just snapped away into the dark, spending themselves out in sparks or skipping once or twice on the ground. Then flares showed a lot of men running out in the open, and our tracer lights began disappearing abruptly. The smoke from white phosphorus was so bright against the darkness that you had to squint a little to look at it. By four, half the city was on fire. Reporters weren't allowed on gunships, but this was the second night of the Tet Offensive, total hysteria and no rules. I never got to ride in one again.

A gunship flew on either side of us going into Hue, escorting a Chinook that carried a slingload of ammunition. We followed the river and headed into the Citadel through a narrow slot with heavy trees on the right and a cemetery on the left. At a hundred feet we began drawing fire. Ground-fire reflex, clench your ass and rise up in your seat a few inches. Pucker, motherfucker; you used muscles you didn't even know you had.

Once I was in a chopper that took a hit and dropped about 300 feet until the pilot pumped his pedals into auto-rotate, restoring us to the air and the living. Dragging back to base camp, we passed over three ships shot down close together, two of them completely smashed and the third almost intact, surrounded by the bodies of the crew and the brigade commander, all killed after they'd reached the ground.

Later that day I went out on a joypop in a Loach with the
Cav's star flier. We flew fast and close to the ground, contour
flying, a couple of feet between the treads and the ground,
treetops, hootch roofs. Then we came to the river where it
ran through a twisting ravine, the sides very steep, almost a
canyon, and he flew the river, taking us through blind turns
like a master. When we cleared the ravine he sped straight
toward the jungle, dipping where I'd been sure he would rise,
and I felt the sharp freezing moment of certain death. Right
in there under the canopy, a wild ship-shaking U turn in the
jungle, I couldn't even smile when we broke clear, I couldn't
move, everything looked like images caught in a flash with all
the hard shadows left in. "That dude can fly 'em right up his
own ass," someone said back at the lz, and the pilot came
over and said, "Too bad we didn't get shot at. I'd like to've
shown you my evade."

In the Special Forces A Camp at Me Phuc Tay there was a
sign that read, "If you kill for money you're a mercenary. If
you kill for pleasure you're a sadist. If you kill for both
you're a Green Beret." Great sounds at Me Phuc Tay, the
commander dug the Stones. At An Hoa we heard "Hungry for
those good things baby, Hungry through and through," on
the radio while we tried to talk to an actual hero, a Marine
who'd just pulled his whole squad back in from deep serious,
but he was sobbing so hard he couldn't get anything out. "Galveston oh Galveston I'm so afraid of dying," at LZ Stud, two
kids from Graves having a quarrel. "He's all haired off 'cause
they won't let him sew Cav patches on the bags," one said,
and the other, pouting heavily, said, "Fuck you. I mean it
man, fuck you. I think it looks real sharp." Only one song
from Hue, "We gotta get out of this place if it's the last thing
we ever do"; a reporter friend looking totally mind-blown, he
woke up that morning and heard two Marines lying near him
making love. "Black is black I want my baby back," at China

Beach with IGOR FROM THE NORTH, every card in his deck
an ace of spades. He wore a sombrero and a serape and his
face went through about as many changes as a rock when a
cloud passes over it. He almost lived on the beach, every time
he added to the count they'd send him down as reward. He
spoke twice in an hour in a spooky clipped language of his
own like slow rounds, finally he got up and said, "Got to go
Dong Ha kill more," and went. "I said shot-gun, shoot 'em
'fore they run now," at Nha Trang, talking to a man just
starting his second tour. "When I come home I seen how
scared you all was. I mean it wasn't no damn combat situation or nothing like that, but believe you me, you was scared.
I seen it here and I seen it there, so what the fuck? I come
back." No sounds at all on the road out of Can Tho, twenty
of us in a straight line that suddenly ballooned out into a
curve, wide berth around a Vietnamese man who stood without a word and held his dead baby out to us. We made tracks
and we made dust in our tracks, I swore to God I'd get out
soonest, all it took was eight more months.

Out on the street I couldn't tell the Vietnam veterans from
the rock and roll veterans. The Sixties had made so many
casualties, its war and its music had run power off the same
circuit for so long they didn't even have to fuse. The war
primed you for lame years while rock and roll turned more
lurid and dangerous than bullfighting, rock stars started falling like second lieutenants; ecstasy and death and (of course
and for sure) life, but it didn't seem so then. What I'd
thought of as two obsessions were really only one, I don't
know how to tell you how complicated that made my life.
Freezing and burning and going down again into the sucking
mud of the culture, hold on tight and move real slow.

That December I got a Christmas card from a Marine I'd

known in Hue. It showed a psychotic-art Snoopy in battered jungle fatigues, a cigarette clenched in his teeth, blasting away with an M-16. "Peace on Earth, Good Will Toward Men," it read, "and Best Wishes for a Happy One-Niner-Six-Niner."

Maybe it was classic, maybe it was my twenties I was missing and not the Sixties, but I began missing them both before either had really been played out. The year had been so hot that I think it shorted out the whole decade, what followed was mutation, some kind of awful 1969-X. It wasn't just that I was growing older, I was leaking time, like I'd taken a frag from one of those anti-personnel weapons we had that were so small they could kill a man and never show up on X-rays. Hemingway once described the glimpse he'd had of his soul after being wounded, it looked like a fine white handkerchief drawing out of his body, floating away and then returning. What floated out of me was more like a huge gray 'chute, I hung there for a long time waiting for it to open. Or not. My life and my death got mixed up with their lives and deaths, doing the Survivor Shuffle between the two, testing the pull of each and not wanting either very much. I was once in such a bad head about it that I thought the dead had only been spared a great deal of pain.

Debriefed by dreams, friends coming in from the other side to see that I was still alive. Sometimes they looked 500 years old and sometimes they looked exactly as I'd known them, but standing in a strange light; the light told the story, and it didn't end like any war story I'd ever imagined. If you can't find your courage in a war, you have to keep looking for it anyway, and not in another war either; in where it's old and jammed until the rocks start moving around, a little light and air, long time no see. Another frequency, another information, and death no deterrent to receiving it. The war ended, and then it really ended, the cities "fell," I watched the choppers I'd loved dropping into the South China Sea as their Vietnamese pilots jumped clear, and one last chopper revved it up, lifted off and flew out of my chest.

I saw a picture of a North Vietnamese soldier sitting in the same spot on the Danang River where the press center had been, where we'd sat smoking and joking and going, "Too much!" and "Far out!" and "Oh my God it gets so freaky out there!" He looked so unbelievably peaceful, I knew that somewhere that night and every night there'd be people sitting together over there talking about the bad old days of jubilee and that one of them would remember and say, Yes, never mind, there were some nice ones, too. And no moves left for me at all but to write down some few last words and make the dispersion, Vietnam Vietnam Vietnam, we've all been there.

FIRE IN THE LAKE
*The Vietnamese
and the Americans in Vietnam*
by Frances FitzGerald

This landmark book by one of our most acclaimed journalists was the first to portray the war not only from the American point of view but also through the eyes of the Vietnamese themselves. Meshing historical, political, and cultural analysis with a sure command of narrative, *Fire in the Lake* gives life to the most important and elusive figures in the conflict.

*Winner of the Pulitzer Prize,
the National Book Award, and the Bancroft Prize*
History/Political Science/0-679-72394-3

DISPATCHES
by Michael Herr

These pieces portray the frightening, grotesque, and absurd aspects of a senseless war as seen from the trenches.

"What a passionate, compassionate, brilliant book this is. With uncanny precision it summons up the very essence of that war— its space diction, its surreal psychology, its bitter humor—the dope, the dexedrine, the body bags, the rot, all of it. . . . I believe it may be the best personal journal about war, any war, that any writer has ever accomplished."

—Robert Stone, *Chicago Tribune*

Vintage International
Military History/Vietnam/0-679-73525-9

ONCE UPON A DISTANT WAR
David Halberstam, Neil Sheehan,
Peter Arnett—Young War Correspondents
and Their Early Vietnam Battles
by William Prochnau

The American reporters who came to Vietnam in 1961 expected to write about an exotic little war in a country of tigers and elephants. What they found instead was a debacle in the making, in which American pilots flew missions illegally while their Vietnamese counterparts strafed the presidential palace. When they reported what they saw, they were pilloried for it at home. But they ended up making history simply by telling the truth.

"Riveting . . . a mythic creation."—*Washington Post Book World*

History/Vietnam/0-679-77265-0

A BRIGHT SHINING LIE
John Paul Vann and America in Vietnam
by Neil Sheehan

When he came to Vietnam in 1962, Lieutenant Colonel John Paul Vann was the one clear-sighted participant in an enterprise riddled with arrogance and self-deception, a charismatic soldier who put his life and career on the line in an attempt to convince his superiors the war should be fought another way. By the time he died, Vann had embraced the follies he once decried. Sheehan's tragic biography of John Paul Vann is also a sweeping history of America's seduction, entrapment, and disillusionment in Vietnam.

Winner of the Pulitzer Prize and
the National Book Award

History/Biography/0-679-72414-1

Available at your local bookstore, or call toll-free to order:
1-800-793-2665 (credit cards only).